PHILOPONUS

Against Proclus
On the Eternity of
the World 6-8

PHILOPONUS

Against Proclus
On the Eternity of
the World 6-8

Translated by
Michael Share

Duckworth

First published in 2005 by
Gerald Duckworth & Co. Ltd.
90-93 Cowcross Street, London EC1M 6BF
Tel: 020 7490 7300
Fax: 020 7490 0080
inquiries@duckworth-publishers.co.uk
www.ducknet.co.uk

A catalogue record for this book is available
from the British Library

ISBN 0 7156 3234 5

Acknowledgements

The present translations have been made possible by generous and
imaginative funding from the following sources: the National En-
dowment for the Humanities, Division of Research Programs, an
independent federal agency of the USA; the Leverhulme Trust; the
British Academy; the Jowett Copyright Trustees; the Royal Society
(UK); Centro Internazionale A. Beltrame di Storia dello Spazio e del
Tempo (Padua); Mario Mignucci; Liverpool University; the Leventis
Foundation; the Arts and Humanities Research Board of the British
Academy; the Esmée Fairbairn Charitable Trust; the Henry Brown
Trust; Mr and Mrs N. Egon; the Netherlands Organisation for
Scientific Research (NWO/GW); the Cultural Attaché of the Greek
Embassy in London. The editor wishes to thank David Furley,
Donald Russell, Alan Lacey, Edward Watts, and Teun Tieleman for
their comments and John Bowin, Devin Henry and Inna Kupreeva
for preparing the volume for press.
    A special grant for the preparation of this volume for press was
provided by the Council of Gresham College, to which the series
editor is very grateful.

Typeset by Ray Davies
Printed and bound in Great Britain by
Biddles Ltd, King's Lynn, Norfolk

Contents

Preface

Richard Sorabji

This volume continues the translation of Philoponus' work in 18 chapters, which is one of the most interesting of all post-Aristotelian Greek philosophical texts. It was written at a crucial moment in the defeat of paganism by Christianity. In 529 AD, the Emperor Justinian put an end to teaching in the pagan Neoplatonist school in Athens, where Proclus had in the fifth century AD been the most devout pagan teacher, St Benedict is thought to have founded the monastery in Monte Cassino, and, again on behalf of Christianity, Philoponus in Alexandria attacked Proclus' arguments that the universe had no beginning in his *Against Proclus On the Eternity of the World*. Philoponus was one of the cleverest of the Neoplatonist philosophers, a pupil of Ammonius in Alexandria, but he was a Christian, and he used his profound knowledge of the Neoplatonist and Aristotelian traditions to turn the pagans' own views against themselves.

Our text records, and replies to, the 18 arguments of Proclus' *Against the Christians on the Eternity of the World*, as well as quoting a little of Proclus' *Examination of Aristotle's Objections to Plato's Timaeus*. It will suffice to indicate just a few of the original arguments and ideas in chapters 6 to 8, and I shall select two issues from the longest chapter, 6.

In VI.29, 238,3-240,9; and VIII.1, 297, 21-300,2, Philoponus reports that Proclus had adapted an argument from Aristotle's *Physics* 8.10. Since bodies are finite in size, the largest body, the universe, cannot house the infinite power needed to maintain it in existence (Aristotle had only said 'in motion') for ever. That power must therefore be housed in something incorporeal and external to it, God. Proclus in Athens laments Aristotle's failure to apply the argument to existence as well as to motion. But Proclus' pupil Ammonius in Alexandria claimed that this was what Aristotle had intended (so Simplicius *in Phys.* 1363,4-12), and this interpretation of Aristotle was to prevail.

Philoponus now infers from Proclus' view that the world is perishable so far as its own nature is concerned and that hence God has to override its nature. The imperishability it acquires from God is therefore above its nature or super-natural (*huper phusin*), 237,10-15; 240,22. Consequently, Philoponus infers, 242,15-22, since it is perishable so far as its own nature is concerned, it is also subject to being generated with a beginning. As Lindsay Judson has pointed out, there is a tacit assumption here that God could not override its natural generability in the way he overrides its natural perishability.[1] The argument is set out more clearly in the Arabic summary of a lost longer exposition by Philoponus.[2]

At VI.7-8, Philoponus makes much of Plato himself having described the universe in *Timaeus* 27C, 28B-C, 37D-38C as 'generated'. His discussion reveals the techniques of interpretation applied to Plato's text by others. In VI.8, 145,13-147,25, we learn that the Middle Platonist Taurus had tried to evade the most obvious implication of 'generated' by distinguishing 4 alternative senses of 'generated', and the Neoplatonist Porphyry had tried to add others. Two of Taurus' meanings had been exploited by Proclus. Taurus had also, as we learn in VI.22, 191,15ff., interpreted Plato's question at *Timaeus* 27C whether the universe has come to be, *or* is ungenerated, as if the 'or' meant 'if'. Others had emended Plato's text. Alexander is said at VI.27, 214,10-20, to have reported others as emending 'or' to 'even though', while others again, according to Philoponus at VI.22, 193,9-11, had emended 'ungenerated' (*agenês*) to 'ever in process of generation' (*aeigenês*). Aristotle had already recorded that some people took Plato's talk of the universe having been generated to be a fiction like that used by geometers drawing diagrams, to clarify the structure of something by showing it being built up in sequences, when it was never really so built, *On the Heavens* 279b32 - 280a10. Here we have a window onto ancient techniques of textual criticism.

*

A new introduction to the Commentators will appear in R.R.K. Sorabji, *The Philosophy of the Commentators, 200-600 AD: A Sourcebook*, London, Duckworth, 2004.

Notes

1. Lindsay Judson, 'God or nature? Philoponus on generability and perishability', in Richard Sorabji (ed.), *Philoponus and the Rejection of Aristotelian Science*, London & Ithaca, NY 1987. See also Richard Sorabji, *Matter, Space and Motion*, London & Ithaca, NY 1988, ch. 15.

2. Translated by S. Pines, 'An Arabic summary of a lost work of John Philoponus', *Israel Oriental Studies* 2, 1972, 320-52, at 323-4, and reproduced in Sorabji *Matter, Space and Motion*, London & Ithaca, NY 1988, ch. 15.

Introduction

This translation is made from Rabe's 1899 Teubner edition,[1] the only modern critical edition of the Greek text. Departures from Rabe's text, many of which are based on Rabe's own suggestions in the critical apparatus, are mentioned in the notes as they occur and listed separately in front of the translation. Words in square brackets in the translation do not occur in the Greek but have been inserted to clarify the sense. Greek words are occasionally given in transliteration when it is thought their presence may help the reader.

The single manuscript on which our knowledge of the Greek text of Philoponus' work is based is incomplete at either end, and the original title of the work is quite uncertain. I discussed the ancient references to the work and the status of Rabe's Latin title, on which the English title on the title-page of this volume is based, in the introduction to my translation of its first five chapters in this series, to which I refer the reader. In this introduction and in the notes I shall refer to Philoponus' work as *Aet.*, an abbreviation based on the Latin title.

Proclus' proofs have recently been re-edited and translated into English by Helen S. Lang and A.D. Macro and there is an earlier English translation of them by the English Neoplatonist Thomas Taylor and a German one by Matthias Baltes.[2] In contrast, only small portions of Philoponus' refutations of them have ever been translated into any modern language.

Since they also apply here, it is probably worth repeating the remarks I made in the introduction to my translation of chapters 1-5 of *Aet.* on some of my translation decisions.[3]

In Plato's *Timaeus*, from which much of the terminology used in *Aet.* and in the creation debate in general derives, the world, or universe, is variously referred to as *ho kosmos, ho ouranos* or *to pan*.

kosmos originally meant 'order' and, secondarily, 'adornment', and it never lost these connotations, but by Plato's day the meaning 'world-order' or simply 'world' was well-established. Common English equivalents are 'cosmos' and 'world' and I have opted for the latter.[4]

ouranos literally means 'heaven' but in the *Timaeus* Plato uses it interchangeably with kosmos (cf. *Tim.* 28B) and Aristotle at *Cael.* 278b ff. says that it may be used of (a) the outermost circumference of the universe, (b) the heavens as a whole, including the stars, the sun, the moon and the planets (c) the universe as a whole. In *Aet.* it normally seems to be used in the second of Aristotle's three senses, but it is not always easy to see what is intended. I translate 'heaven'.

My rendering of *to pan*, which literally means 'the all', is 'the universe'.

I have thought it important to distinguish clearly between *aiônios* ('eternal'), *aïdios* ('everlasting') and *aei* ('always', 'for ever', etc.) in the translation. Proclus always reserves *aiônios* for entities which are outside of time, such as God or transcendental form, but uses *aïdios* or *aei* either of these same entities or of things which endure for ever in time, which, for him, include the world, matter, imminent form, generation and time itself. For Philoponus in *Aet.* things are a little more complicated. In reporting and refuting Proclus' arguments he observes the same distinctions; for example, he nowhere claims that Proclus is saying that the kosmos is *aiônios*. However, for him only eternal things are in fact *aïdios* and in one fairly lengthy passage (114,19-116,1) he can use *aiônios* and *aïdios* interchangeably to distinguish eternal things from those which exist in time. (In his earlier commentaries, where he acts primarily as a reporter of Ammonius, he was, of course, quite prepared to use *aïdios* of things which exist in time; at *in GC* 1,9-16, for example, he used it of the heavenly bodies and the four elements. Surprisingly, however, apart from two occasions in *Opif.*, he uses *aiônios* only in *Aet.*).[5]

Using 'everlasting' for *aïdios* entails using 'everlastingness' for *aïdiotês* (although I retain the by now traditional 'eternity' in the volume title) and I have even thought it best to use the unlovely coinage 'co-everlasting' rather than 'co-eternal' to translate *sunaïdios*.

Like Plato in the *Timaeus*, Proclus and Philoponus most commonly refer to the maker of the kosmos as *ho theos* or *ho dêmiourgos*. (Although Proclus does not use the former before Argument 8, and only once there).

Common translations of *dêmiourgos* are 'demiurge', 'craftsman' (a more or less literal rendering of one of the senses of the Greek word) and 'creator'. In translating the *Timaeus* I would use either 'demiurge' or 'craftsman', but in Proclus and Philoponus the term has, I think, lost much of its original force and I have opted for 'creator', partly because doing so makes it easier to find English equivalents for the related words *dêmiourgein* ('to create'), *dêmiourgêma* ('a creation'), *dêmiourgia*, ('creation') and *dêmiourgikos* ('creative').

It is still common to translate *theos* 'God' rather than 'god' when it occurs in a Christian author, whereas one is often torn between 'God', 'god' and 'the god' when it occurs in Plato or one of the Neoplatonists. Because Philoponus is clearly writing as a Christian,[6] I have thought it best to translate it 'God' when Philoponus uses it in one of his own arguments, and I have, for ease of application as much as anything, but also because I think he often reads *theos* as 'God' in such cases (indeed, he often writes as if he were debating a fellow monotheist),[7] extended this to passages that he quotes from Plato, Aristotle, Proclus and other authors and to the single instance in which Proclus uses it in this volume. I have not, on the other hand, as a rule capitalised pronouns or other words which refer to God.

Both creationists and anti-creationists were eager to enrol Plato on their side and Philoponus' debate with Proclus and other creationists is in part over the correct interpretation of the *Timaeus*. In this debate one of the key issues was the correct interpretation of the verb *ginesthai* and related words when applied to the *kosmos*.

The LSJ article on *ginesthai* (which is there listed under its earlier spelling *gignesthai*) is organised into two main sections. The first is headed 'abs. [sc. without a predicate], come into being', and includes, amongst others, subsections headed 'to be born', and 'to be produced'. The second is headed 'foll. by a Predicate, come into a certain state, become, and (in past tenses) to be'. There is no doubt that Plato often uses *ginesthai* of the physical world to express the idea that it is in perpetual flux, always changing and 'becoming' different (a usage which, although he commonly uses the verb without a predicate, would fall under LSJ II), and this is not a matter of dispute between Proclus and Philoponus (see especially VI.15-16). The question at issue between them is whether he also applies the verb to the *kosmos* as a whole in a sense that would fall under LSJ I. Philoponus claims that he does, at *Tim.* 28B for example, where he understands *gegonen* in the sense 'it has come into being' (or perhaps even 'it has been generated', or 'it has been created'), while Proclus argues that he does not, unless perhaps in a very attenuated sense. This, of course, means that the same words will often mean something different to Proclus and Philoponus, which makes life difficult for the translator. One popular solution, which I shall adopt, is to translate *ginesthai* 'to come to be', which can, with charity, be understood as embracing both 'to come into being' and 'to become', and as therefore adequately covering most relevant senses of *ginesthai*. (This only applies to contexts where the creation of the *kosmos* is at issue. *ginesthai* is something of a portmanteau word and I translate it in many different ways in other contexts).

The choice of 'come to be' for *ginesthai* raises the possibility of something like 'coming-to-be' and 'admitting of coming-to-be' (or, on a different view of the word, 'having-come to-be') for the related words *genesis* and *genêtos*, as used by Hussey in his translation of the third and fourth books of Aristotle's *Physics*.[8] However, the two words are both very common in *Aet.* and in some passages, especially in the case of *genêtos*, this would become intolerably cumbersome, so I have, rather illogically, opted for 'generation' for *genesis* and 'generated' *for genêtos*.

The choice of 'generated' for *genêtos* raises another issue. Verbal adjectives in *-tos* (of which *genêtos* is one) may express possibility or have the force of a perfect passive participle. Some display only one of

these possibilities, others, including *genêtos*, as the entries in LSJ and
Lampe when taken together show, both. Of course, when an adjective is
capable of either signification, it is not always clear which is intended.
In fact, one suspects that the writer would often not have found it easy
to say. This being so, it is not surprising that *genêtos* in *Aet.* has been
read either way. To take only two examples, Dillon,[9] when translating
the excerpts from Taurus in *Aet.* VI, renders it 'created', while Judson,
in his article on generability and perishability in Philoponus,[10] prefers
'generable'. My own view is that the 'perfect passive' sense of the word
is usually uppermost in the minds of both Proclus and Philoponus and
it is for that reason that I have preferred 'generated' to 'generable'. (In
fact, it seems to me that in VI.9, in the course of dismissing the first of
the various meanings that Taurus had proposed for *genêtos*, Philoponus
comes close to rejecting the meaning 'generable' altogether).

In philosophical texts, including *Aet.*, *ginesthai*, *genesis* and *genêtos*
are often opposed to *phtheiresthai*, *phthora* and *phthartos*. *phtheiresthai*
is the passive of *phtheirein* ('to destroy') and so can be rendered 'to be
destroyed', but 'to perish', 'to pass away' and 'to cease to be' are all
commoner. I usually (but not, as the Greek-English Index shows, always) use 'perish' for *phtheiresthai* and 'perishable' for *phthartos*. For
phthora, because 'perishing' does not always work well, I usually use
'passing out of existence'.[11]

I discuss the translation of a number of other words in the notes,
usually at their first occurrence.

My translation of chapters 1-8 of *Aet.* was originally to have been
published in one volume, but at a late stage it became apparent that it
could not be kept within the volume-size limit for the series. In dividing
the material between the two volumes we have decided to repeat some
of the notes from the earlier volume in this volume and an attentive
reader may detect other effects of splitting of the original volume,
particularly in the indexes.

The early stages of the preparation of this translation were supported
by a grant from the Australian Research Council. I would like to thank
David Furley, Donald Russell, Alan Lacey, Edward Watts, and Teun
Tieleman who each read part of a draft of the translation and made
many valuable suggestions, the Ancient Commentators on Aristotle
Project editorial team for assistance, patience and support, and Richard
Sorabji for his advice and encouragement.

Notes

1. H. Rabe (ed.), *Ioannes Philoponus de Aeternitate Mundi contra Proclum*
(Leipzig, 1899) (reprinted Hildesheim, etc., 1984).

2. H. Lang and L. Macro (eds.), *On the Eternity of the World* (De Aeternitate
Mundi), *Proclus* (Berkeley, etc., 2001). Thomas Taylor, *The Fragments That
Remain of the Lost Writings of Proclus, Surnamed the Platonic Successor* (San
Diego, 1988) [originally published 1825], 35-92. M. Baltes, *Die Weltentstehung*

des platonischen Timaios nach den antiken Interpreten (Leiden, 1976), vol. 2, 134-64. Lang and Macro's edition includes a Greek text based on Rabe's, with their translation of it, a text and translation of Isḥâq ibn Ḥunayn's Arabic version of Proclus' first proof by Jon McGinnis, the Latin version of Proclus' proofs from the earlier of the two surviving sixteenth-century Latin translations of *Aet.*, a substantial introduction and useful notes.

3. Lang and Macro have a useful section describing some of the difficulties of translating Proclus and documenting some of their translation decisions. (op. cit., 28-33).

4. For more on the history and meaning of *kosmos*, see W.K.C. Guthrie, *A History of Greek Philosophy*, vol. 1 (Cambridge, 1967) 110-11 and 208 n. 1.

5. For an overview of the use of *aïdios, aei* and other time words in antiquity see R. Sorabji, *Time, Creation and the Continuum*, 112-17. Proclus elsewhere explicitly distinguishes temporal and non-temporal uses of *aïdios* and *aei* and Philoponus too finds room for a non-temporal use of *aei* both in *Aet.* (104-7) and in other works; references ibid., 115, nn. 66, 67 and 74.

6. I demonstrated this in the introduction to *Philoponus: Against Proclus On the Eternity of the World* 1-5 (London, 2004) in this series.

7. cf. my remarks at ibid., p. 12 n. 40.

8. Hussey, E. (tr.), *Aristotle's* Physics *Books III and IV* (Oxford, 1983).

9. J. Dillon, *The Middle Platonists: a Study of Platonism, 80 BC to AD 220* (London, 1977), 242-3.

10. L. Judson, 'God or nature? Philoponus on generability and perishability', in R.R.K. Sorabji (ed.), *Philoponus and the Rejection of Aristotelian Science* (London & Ithaca, NY, 1987).

11. There is a good discussion of possible translations of *ginesthai* and *phtheiresthai* in the introduction to C. Williams, *Aristotle's* de Generatione et Corruptione (Oxford, 1982).

Departures from Rabe's Text

Emendations other than my own are credited. Those attributed to Rabe and the two attributed to Brinkmann and Kroll are based on suggestions printed in Rabe's apparatus. All departures from Rabe's text are also recorded in the footnotes, in the case of my own emendations often with a brief justification. I do not indicate Rabe's own departures from the manuscript tradition either in the translation or in the notes.

119,21-22	Punctuating with a comma instead of a full stop in 21 and a full stop instead of the first colon in 22.
119,22	Adding *ara* after *adunaton* (Rabe).
120,6	Adding *epei* before *panti*.
120,7	Deleting *eipen*.
120,20	Adding *kai* before *hoti* (Rabe).
124,23	Adding *tôi* before *ouk*.
124,24	Deleting *tôi* (Rabe).
125,21	Changing *diandikh'* to *tandikh'*.
127,1	Changing *ekhei* to *eikhen* (Rabe).
131,9	Adding *dialusai* after *boulêtheiê* (Rabe).
136,2	Changing *teleutaion* to *teleutan*.
142,23	Changing *hote* to *tote* (Rabe).
147,5	Changing *legoito* to *legetai* and omitting *de*.
150,1	Changing *tou genêtou* to *tôn genêtôn* (Rabe).
150,11-12	Changing *ginomenon* to *genomenon* (Rabe).
155,2	Adding *on* after *diastaton* (Rabe).
156,13	Changing the second *kai* to *ei* (Rabe).
157,1	Changing *gar* to *kai* (Rabe).
159,1	Changing *onta* to *onti*.
161,16	Changing *elaben* to *estin labein*.
167,7	Changing *eipômen* to *eipomen*.
170,14	Changing *ta* to *to* (Rabe).
170,28	Adding *ei* before *en* and changing *ekhein* to *ekhei* (Rabe).
180,16	Changing *monôi* to *monon*.
180,23	Adding *ou* before *ta men*.
182,10	Changing *genomenôi* to *ginomenôi* (Rabe).
182,19	Changing *genomenon ... genomenon* to *ginomenon ... ginomenon* (Rabe).

187,18	Punctuating with a full stop rather than a comma after *ginomena*.
189,3	Changing *autôi* to *tôi*.
189,25	Adding *khreia* after *ên* (Brinkmann).
193,11	Changing *metalambanontes* to *metalambanousin* (Rabe).
196,1	Changing *autêi* to *autê*.
196,3	Changing *en têi* to *en hêi*.
204,21	Deleting *ou*.
204,22	Changing *all'* to *kai ouk*.
206,10	Adding *to* before *khronikês* (Rabe).
207,15	Changing *pros* to *pôs* (Rabe).
207,27	Adding *aei* before *ontôn*.
208,14	Adding *de* after *lêthês* (Rabe).
208,15	Changing *autôi* to *autêi*.
208,23	Changing *horasthai* to *orthais einai* (Rabe).
210,19-20	Deleting *to khrômasin einai*.
212,24	Changing *tinôn* to *sunistamenôn*.
213,3-4	Deleting *tautês de phêsin tês doxês kai tous Stôïkous gegonenai*.
214,19	Adding *tois eis* after *dôsei* (Rabe).
215,3	Changing *gignesthai* to *einai* (Rabe).
215,7	Changing *ginesthai* to *ginetai*.
215,12	Changing *toioutos* to *toioutôs*.
215,14	Changing *ekeinos* to *ekeinôs*.
215,24	Adding *hôste* before *dêlonoti* (Rabe).
215,25	Changing *auton* to *autou* or *autôi*.
216,6	Changing *antitithêsin* to *anatithêsin*.
217,9	Punctuating with a comma rather than a full stop after *tauton*.
218,1	Adding *ho ton kubon* before *pher'* (Rabe).
218,22	Adding *ti* before *ex*.
222,13	Changing *gar* to *de* (Rabe).
222,19	Changing *ex aiônos* to *exô henos*.
226,19	Adding *hoti* before the first *to*.
226,25	Deleting *phêsin*.
239,14	Changing *apolabonta* to *apolabon*.
243,10	Adding *arkhê ouk an eiê* after *kinêseôs*.
244,17	Changing *kinei* to *ekhei*.
245,17	Changing *huph' heautês* to *hup' autês* (Rabe).
245,25	Changing *to* to *tôi* (Rabe).
245,26	Changing *kinêton* to *akinêton*.
246,12	Adding *einai* after *thaterois* (the reader).
264,28	Changing *legein* to *legei* (Rabe).
265,12	Deleting *zôiôn* (Rabe).
267,9	Adding *einai* after *sôma*.
274,17	Adding *ê* before *kinoumenon* (Rabe).

275,11	Punctuating with a full stop rather than a semicolon after *dunamei*.
276,19	Removing the semicolon and enclosing *legô de tropon kinêseôs* in parentheses.
279,26	Changing *ei oun allo ê palin* to *ê oun allo palin* (Rabe).
281,4	Changing *ê* to *hêmas*.
283,3-5	Deleting *endekhetai ... megethos*.
289,22	Changing *henoutai* to *henountai* (Rabe).
290,24	Changing *epikheirountes hôs phasin helikoeidôs auto* to *epikheirountes helikoeidôs phasin auto* (Rabe).
294,7	Deleting *ê* (Rabe).
294,23-295,1	Changing *dioti sterêsis estin, hai de sterêseis eis hexin* to *dioti sterêseis eisin tines eis hexeis*.
295,24	Changing *to* to *te* and *hômologêmenon* to *hômologêmenôn* (Rabe).
300,20	Changing *astheneian* to *athanasian*.
302,19	Adding *ôn* after *ara* (Kroll).
302,20	Changing *aiônôn* to *autou ontôn* (Rabe).
302,25	Changing *phtheiresthai* to *phtheiretai* (Rabe).
304,15	Adding *to* before *pan* and changing *genesthai* to *ginesthai* (Rabe).
304,18	Adding *ou* before *têi Platônos*.
308,12	Deleting *kai* before *hêi* (Rabe).
309,21-22	Changing *ek tou psukhrou to thermon* to *ek tou thermou to psukhron*.
310,3	Punctuating with a full stop rather than a comma after *kosmon*.
311,17	Adding a question mark after *oun*.

PHILOPONUS
Against Proclus
On the Eternity of
the World 6-8

Translation

<John Philoponus the Alexandrian's Against the Arguments of Proclus Concerning the Everlastingness of the World>

The Sixth Argument[1] of Proclus the Successor[2]

The sixth [argument]: if the creator alone bound the world together,[3] he alone may unbind it. For, he[4] says, it is in every way indissoluble except for the one who bound it together; for it belongs everywhere to the one who knows a bond to know also the unbinding of what he has bound together; and it belongs to the one who knows how to unbind [something] to unbind [it].

    119,15

    20

But the creator would not unbind the world. It is he himself who says[5] 'it is the act of an evil being to wish to unbind what has been well put together and is in a good state', and it is inconceivable that a truly good being should become evil. Therefore[6] it is not possible for the world to be unbound; for it will not be [unbound] by anyone else because only its creator can unbind it, nor by him who created it because 'it is the act of an evil being to wish to unbind what has been well put together'.[7] So either he did not put it together well and is not an excellent creator,[8] or he did put it together well and will not unbind it unless he becomes evil, which is impossible. And so the universe is indissoluble. And so it is imperishable.

    120,1

    5

And if it is imperishable, it is ungenerated; 'since[9] for everything that has come to be there is a passing out of existence', says[10] Socrates on the eve of Timaeus' discourse, not speaking for himself but claiming that it is the Muses that are speaking; and Timaeus did not, we can be confident, immediately assume that this doctrine of the Muses was irrelevant and make something that had come to be imperishable. So if this[11] is true, anything for which there is no passing out of existence is ungenerated. But there is no passing out of existence for the world. And so it is ungenerated. And so the world, if uncreated and imperishable, is everlasting.[12]

    10

The Sections of the Refutation of the Sixth Argument

    15

1. That they argue unfairly, forcing Plato's clear statements in regard to the generation of the world into conformity with their own view.

2. A description of the approach[13] [taken] in the sixth proof. And[14]

20   that even were it valid it would not harm the truth[15] since it sets out
      not from the nature of things but from Platonic hypotheses.

      3. A preliminary statement of the order and arrangement of the
      argument.

121,1 **4.** That Plato's statement[16] that 'it is the act of an evil being to
      wish to unbind what has been well put together and is in a good state'
      is false and absurd. And that just as God's goodness is the cause of
      the formation of the world, so is this same [quality] the cause of its
5   unbinding.

      5. That if, as they too believe, God has the power of unbinding the
      world, he will certainly also unbind it; but if he does not unbind it,
      either he does not even have the power of unbinding the world, and
      therefore not the power of binding it together either, or else, on their
10   reasoning, he will be imperfect, having only the power of unbinding
      without the actuality.

      6. That if it really is the act of an evil being to wish to unbind what
      has been well put together, and if God has the power to unbind the
      world, he will have the power to perform evil acts and to cause harm.

15   **7.** A selection[17] of Platonic passages [which show] that he means
      that the world is generated with respect to time[18] and a brief review
      of their sense.

      8. The number of senses in which the Platonic commentators
20   Taurus, Porphyry and Proclus claim 'generated' is used, and the
      sense in which each of them supposes that the world is so described
      by Plato.

      9. A refutation of the first of the [above] senses of 'generated',
      [namely,] that the world can be said to be generated as being in the
25   genus of things which are generated even though it has not come to
      be.

      10. That Porphyry states that the world is described as generated
      by Plato on the ground that it is notionally composite even though it
122,1 was not put together with respect to time, and the arguments he
      advances for this view.

      11. That this sense of 'generated' is unusual both among the
      Hellenes[19] and in common usage. And that they are bringing[20] a very
      serious charge against Plato, that of having used ambiguous terms.
5   And that even if he describes the world as generated in this sense, he
      still assigns a beginning to its existence.

10   **12.** That it is not possible to understand Plato's statement that
      the world began from a beginning of some kind in relation to one of
      the six beginnings,[21] I mean matter, form, instrument, efficient cause,
      paradigmatic [cause], final [cause].

      13. That in these [passages] Plato meant a temporal beginning.

15   **14.** That it would not be in keeping with Plato's sagacity to ask
      whether the world is composed of matter and form or simple. And

that Porphyry himself, constrained by Plato's statements, has invalidated his own supposition as to [the meaning of] 'generated'.

15. That Proclus claims that the world is said by Plato to be   20
generated in the sense that it has its being in coming to be and in the
sense that it is generated with respect to causation.

16. That Plato does hold that the world has its being in coming to
be but assigns a beginning to this generation. And that he is again   25
referring to a beginning with respect to time and not some other kind.

17. That even Porphyry says that the world is described as gener-   123,1
ated by Plato not just as being composite but also as having come to
be through the agency of God. And that [their] shifting between the
various senses of 'generated' is an indication that they are doing
violence to Plato's meaning.

18. That it is not possible that Plato was asking whether the   5
world is generated with respect to causation when he wrote[22] the
words 'whether it has always been, having no beginning [to its]
generation'[23] and other similar things.

19. That it is not possible to understand Plato to mean by 'gener-   10
ated' 'generated with respect to causation' but by 'ungenerated'
'ungenerated with respect to time' and not 'ungenerated with respect
to causation'.

20. That Plato himself clearly distinguished between his teaching
about the generation of the world with respect to time and his
teaching about its generation with respect to causation.

21. That it is not, as they claim, the case that Plato is hypotheti-   15
cally representing the world as coming to be by reason of piety or as
an aid to exposition; and that, by claiming that it is, they are under-
mining the previous senses of 'generated'.[24]

22. That Taurus is wrong to alter the disjunctive or interrogative
conjunction 'or' in the [passage] 'we who are about to discuss with
regard to the universe whether it has come to be *or* is ungenerated   20
(*agenês*)'[25] to 'if' and to write 'even if it is ungenerated'; and that
neither is it possible to read[26] 'is always coming to be' [instead of 'is
ungenerated'].[27]

23. That nor is it because the heavenly bodies are in continuous   25
movement that Plato describes the world as generated.[28]

24. That in the *Timaeus* Plato is not predicating generation of the   124,1
substance of soul but explaining by means of [an account of] the   5
generation of soul the relation in which the heavenly bodies stand
towards one another and the kind of movement that they exhibit as
a result of the soul that is within them. Including a brief recounting
of the generation of the soul in Plato.

25. That Plato cogently infers from the fact that the world is
visible and tangible, or, in a word, perceptible, that it is also generated with respect to time. Including [a demonstration] that the
elements themselves, both in their particular manifestations (*kata*   10

merê) and taken as a whole, and the world, which is composed of them, are generated and perishable.

26. That when Plato states that the things which always are have no generation, the one and only kind of generation he is denying of them is generation with respect to time.

27. Testimonies of philosophers that Plato means that the world is generated with respect to time and that he is stating that it has come to be neither [purely] hypothetically nor on the ground that it has its being in generation.

28. That given that Plato says that the world is by nature dissoluble and mortal it was consistent of him to declare that it has also come to be. And that ungenerability as Plato conceives of it is something which is associated with a thing that is immortal according to the definition of its own nature and not a thing which has an immortality which is acquired from another and [constantly] restored.[29]

29. That by the very words he uses when describing[30] the world as free of disease and ageless Plato shows that he does not believe that it is so by nature. And that even though there is nothing outside the world that could destroy it, it is none the less perishable because of the finite [nature] of its own power. And that Proclus has elsewhere explicitly accepted this very point.

The Refutation of the Sixth Argument

1. Although Plato nowhere declares[31] that the world is in any way ungenerated, but on the contrary everywhere loudly and clearly proclaims that it has come to be and is generated, not representing it as having come to be in one respect and not in another but simply and without any qualification representing it as having come to be, those who always prefer speciousness to the truth and are overmuch in love with the everlastingness of the world do not produce a refutation [of these positions] from their own perspective[32] but muddy the waters, twisting Plato's words to make them conform to their own position. But the very cleverness and subtlety of their arguments at once makes obvious to anyone with any wit the violence that they are doing to Plato's words;

For the language of truth is simple, and just [claims][33] do not need subtle explanations. They have the proper measure all by themselves. But the unjust argument is sick to its bones and needs ingenious remedies.[34]

If Plato really did believe that the world is ungenerated with respect to time, that is, that it had no beginning to its existence, they would have to be able to adduce at least one piece of evidence from his writings that clearly spells this out. But they cannot in fact do this

but, revelling in their extreme verbal ingenuity, try to convince us
that although we have heard Plato say that the world has 'come to   5
be', we should understand [him to mean] 'not come to be', and that,
although the man says that the heaven had a beginning [to its]
generation and did not exist before it came to be, we should not
understand him to mean that it had a beginning [to its] generation or
that it once did not exist but that it has co-everlasting existence with
him who created it.

   2. It is with this intention, then, that Proclus has composed the   10
sixth of his proofs, or rather in it too has once more transcribed the
words of Porphyry for our benefit; for in his commentary on the
Timaeus the latter quite clearly uses this same proof with a view to
establishing that Plato too holds that the world is everlasting. For,   15
assuming that the world is in Plato's view imperishable, he concludes
that it must also be ungenerated; for if, as Plato himself says in the
Phaedrus,[35] for anything that has come to be there is of necessity a
subsequent passing out of existence, it no doubt in every case follows   20
by conversion by negation[36] that if a thing does not perish it has not
come to be. So if Plato clearly states that the world is imperishable,
it is no doubt absolutely clear that it is also ungenerated.[37]

   So since the present argument seeks in this way to establish an   25
original situation from a later one,[38] concluding from the fact that the
world is in Plato's view imperishable that it is also in his view
ungenerated, perhaps we need not have gone to the trouble of expos-   127,1
ing the sophistical nature of the reasoning. For even if all of this
were[39] true, and Plato, as they claim, believed that the world is
ungenerated, the true account[40] would not in any way be harmed
by it. For the [supposed] refutation is not based on the facts, and
the facts are not necessarily in accord with Plato's notions. But   5
since it is good to come to the aid of the truth whenever it is
harmed, it is, I believe, right [for us], as far as is possible, to
vindicate Plato, who is being misrepresented.

   3. It makes sense, I think, to begin by examining the arguments   10
by which Plato sought to establish that the world will not perish [to
determine] whether they have any cogency or not. For in the present
[context] there is only one proof that is germane, I mean [the one to
the effect] that the creator, being good, will not unbind the world,
which has been well put together, if to wish to unbind what has been
well put together and is in a good state is the act of an evil being and   15
if it is impossible for the creator to become evil.[41] And second would
follow the investigation of Plato's intention, [with a view to determin-
ing] whether he means that the existence of the world has no
beginning or whether he concedes that it had a beginning to its
existence and did not exist before it came to be. And third, and after
these, [would come] showing that when Plato hypothesised that   20
the world has come to be and is imperishable, he was advancing

hypotheses that are in no way in conflict with one another, and that, in the form in which Plato advanced it, [the hypothesis that] the world
25   will not perish does not, as Proclus here concludes, indicate that Plato believed that it is also ungenerated.[42]

As a preliminary to the examination of the first of these questions we must quote the following passage from Plato.
    4.

128,1   Gods, offspring of gods, works of which I am the creator and father, which came to be through me and are indissoluble if I so will.[43] All that has been bound is dissoluble, but it is the act of an evil being to wish to unbind what has been well put together and is in a good state.[44]

5   Thus Plato.
'So if', says Proclus,[45]

it is inconceivable that a truly good being should become evil, it is not possible for the world to be unbound; for it will not be [unbound] by anyone else because only its creator can unbind it, nor by him who created it because 'it is the act of an evil being to wish to unbind what has been well put together'. So either he did not put it together well and is not an excellent creator, or he did put it together well and will not unbind it unless he becomes evil, which is impossible. And so the universe is indissoluble. And so it is imperishable.

That the universe *has* been well put together mere observation of
15   the things mentioned above[46] will attest, not to mention Holy Scripture, which says 'And God looked at all that he had made and behold it was all[47] very beautiful'.[48] And that the creator of what has been well put together is an excellent [creator] and that it is inconceivable that a truly good being should become evil the conceptions of God that are innate to all of us loudly proclaim.
20   But even though these things are so, I do not see the logical necessity whereby it is the act of an evil being to wish to unbind what has been well put together and is in a good state. No doubt everyone would agree that our bodies and those of all the animals and plants
129,1   have been well put together and that the varied structures of animals and plants neither lack anything nor have anything that is superfluous but each part independently fulfils its own need and all of them [together] cooperate to achieve the survival of the whole. But it has already been shown by us in the fourth chapter[49] that the creator
5   nevertheless wishes that each individual should be unbound and not have everlasting existence. For if he wanted each individual to be everlasting, it certainly would be everlasting. For it is absolutely

necessary that the creator should either want or not want individual   10
creatures to be perishable. If, therefore, it is false that he does not
want it (for if he did not want them to be perishable, they would
certainly have remained indissoluble), then it is true that the creator
wants them to be perishable. And if God wants individuals to be
perishable, and they have been well put together, then he wants   15
things that have been well put together to be unbound again. Therefore, in the opinion of these learned men, either these things were not
well put together, which is absurd, or, if they were well put together,
their creator, since he wishes to unbind what has been well put
together, must have become evil, if, as they maintain,[50] it is the act of
an evil being to wish to unbind what has been well put together and   20
is in a good state.

And the same absurdity would be revealed in no lesser measure if
one were to deploy this argument not, as they do, in relation to the
first creator but in relation to the heavenly gods whom the first
creator instructed to turn to the creation of mortal creatures.[51] There   25
is every necessity that they too, in carrying out their task of generation and destruction, will either not put [their handiwork] together
well or will become evil by unbinding what has been well put to-   130,1
gether. For a thing which is good in inferior measure is not evil. If this
were so, the sensible world would not be good either since it is greatly
inferior to the intelligible. (I make this point so that nobody will say
that, because the goodness found in particular creatures is inferior as   5
compared to that of the whole world, they are not well put together.)

And we have already shown in the thirteenth section of the fourth
chapter that even though the generation and destruction of mortal
creatures comes about through intermediary causes, whether heavenly or otherwise, the first creator is nevertheless more their cause
than are their proximate efficient causes; for it is he who also fur-   10
nishes causes later in the chain with the power to be causes.
Therefore the first creator would have the chief responsibility for the
generation and destruction of perishable things, and will either be the   15
creator of things that have not been well put together, or, if particular
creatures too have been well put together, as the very structure of a
living creature shows it has, God must become evil since he is
primarily and chiefly responsible for their destruction.

So since it is the case both that all particular [creatures] have been
put together well, and that God wishes them to be unbound, and it is   20
inconceivable that a good being should become evil, by the same
reasoning, one supposes, even though God should wish to unbind the
whole well-constructed world, there is no necessity that a good being
should on that account become evil. For it will assuredly, one supposes, be on account of that same goodness through which he   25
originally put the universe together that he will, if he wishes, unbind
it. When the person who tuned[52] a well-tuned lyre has put it out of

tune again once it has served the purpose for which he, its tuner, tuned it, no one with any sense will say that to wish to untune a well-tuned lyre is characteristic of an evil person and that it is only because he has first become evil that the musician has undone this
5   perfectly good tuning; on the contrary, it is, I think, clear to everyone that, just as he previously did well to tune it, so too did he do well to untune what he had tuned. Much more, then, is it the case that he who is truly good both originally put the world together because of his goodness, and will, if he wishes to unbind[53] it again, again have his
10   goodness as the cause of the unbinding, even if the reason for the unbinding is unknown to us. For we should not invariably assume that those things whose causes we do not know (and the reasons for many things, perhaps all, elude us) take place at random or for an evil purpose.

In my opinion, it is characteristic of young men and of those who are all agape for sensual [experience] that they suppose that when
15   visible beauty is undone, its undoer is on that account automatically evil. That is what might have been said by a man who, out of desire for her, was overwhelmed by the beauty of Helen and smitten by the peerless regularity and bloom of her [physical] features but had no
20   philosophical training in the science of the soul or any grasp of the laws of providence that relate to it. This, in my opinion, is the condition in which those who attend only to the visible beauty of the universe and have not been able to catch a glimpse of the most
25   excellent laws of providence, which God has devised for the salvation and perfection of rational beings in the universe, likewise find themselves.

5. We should also look at the question under discussion from another point of view.

'For [the world] is indissoluble', says[54] [Plato], 'by others than him
132,1 who bound it together'. And Proclus agrees with this, for he says:[55] 'It belongs everywhere to the one who knows a bond to know also the unbinding of what he has bound together; and it belongs to the one who knows how to unbind [a thing] to unbind it'.

5   If these are the views of Plato and Proclus, and only the creator is able to unbind the world but he will not unbind [it], then he will always have the ability to unbind [the world] as a mere ability and not in actuality. And therefore, at any rate if all potentiality is, as these learned men believe, imperfect, he is imperfect. And I would
10   add that he will have the power of unbinding [the world] to no good purpose if, as they claim, he has it for an infinite time but will never bring it to actuality.

But, as Aristotle says,[56] nothing numbered among everlasting things is merely potential; for it will exist to no purpose if it is never
15   brought to actuality. So either [1] not even the creator is able to unbind the world, and thus the world will not be dissoluble even for

the creator and not even the creator would know its unbinding (for it
is not possible to know [its] unbinding and be unable to unbind [it];
and if he does not know its unbinding and is unable to unbind it,
neither will he know its bond nor have the power of binding the 20
universe together; for it is true that knowledge of a bond and of its
unbinding belong to the same person and that he who is able to bind
is also without doubt the more easily able to unbind); or, [2] if,
because he bound it together, he is able to unbind the world but will
never unbind it, he will always for that reason be imperfect and 25
pointlessly possess the mere power of unbinding without the actuality; or, [3] if these alternatives are, on their own principles, absurd,
and God is able to unbind the world, he will assuredly unbind it.[57]

6. Come now, if you will bear with me, to the height of absurdity 133,1
to which this fine-sounding statement that 'it is the act of an evil
being to wish to unbind what has been well put together'[58] leads us.
For if the creator can unbind the world but would not unbind it unless
he became evil, then to unbind the world is evil; for if to unbind it is 5
not evil, he would not become evil by unbinding it. And if to unbind it
is evil, and if God has the power to unbind the world, then God, since
he has the power to do evil, also has the power to become evil. So if to
unbind is evil, and God has the power to unbind, then God also has 10
the power both to do evil and to become evil. If then to unbind it is
evil and he has the power to unbind it, then God has the power both
to do evil and to become evil. And what could be worse than this
unholy conception? So if it is impossible for goodness to become evil,
if, on the one hand,[59] unbinding the world is an evil thing, God will 15
not even have the power to unbind the world, and if he does not have
the power of unbinding it, nor will he have the power of binding it
together or have [actually] bound the world together; for they too
rightly believe that it is everywhere he who knows the bond who
knows how to unbind what he has bound together. So if he who knows
the bond also knows how to unbind it, then he who does not know how 20
to unbind it will not know the bond either. So if God did bind the
universe together and knows the bond of that which he bound together, then he will also know the unbinding of it and will be able to
unbind the universe. And if God, because he has bound it together
and it is he who knows the unbinding of a thing who can unbind it, 25
can unbind the world, then the unbinding of the world is not an evil
thing. For there is no potential for evil in God, for he who has the
potential for evil would also become evil, but light would no sooner 134,1
become darkness than goodness become evil. But if, on the other
hand, the unbinding of the world is not an evil act, and the world has
been well put together, then to wish to unbind what has been well put
together and is in a good state so far as harmony is concerned is not 5
the act of an evil being,[60] and God would not become evil by unbinding
the world

So it is worth considering who has produced theories of the nature of the world that are more consistent with common [human] conceptions about God: we who hold that the universe is both put together
10   and unbound again because of God's goodness, or they who are constrained by [our] common conceptions to say that God is able to unbind the universe but add that he would not unbind it unless he became evil – [a view] which has been shown to be tantamount to saying that God can do evil and become evil, and everyone would
15   agree that this goes beyond all [other forms of] impiety.

I shall, God permitting, set out the most natural[61] causes of the unbinding of the world elsewhere[62] since at present we have only undertaken to solve Proclus' puzzles. As far as these [puzzles] are
20   concerned, we shall now bring [our presentation of] the main objections to Proclus' sixth proof[63] to an end.[64] From here on, switching to the second of the topics announced at the beginning of the present
25   chapter,[65] I shall, as I promised earlier,[66] try to show how those who foist upon Plato the view that the world is everlasting utterly misrepresent him, and, both because I myself am keen to present Plato's
135,1 thought in his own words and because I shall be attempting to refute those who misinterpret him, I shall be compelled to write at considerable length. So if any reader is interested in an exact knowledge of
5   these matters, let him follow the argument through, but if anyone is not greatly concerned with Plato's opinion in regard to the present question and is keen to rely only on proofs drawn from the facts,[67] let him skip straight to the chapters which follow.[68]

10   7. Both the majority of those who have adhered to the views of Plato[69] and those who have been admirers of the philosophy of Aristotle, beginning with Aristotle himself,[70] have joined in asserting that Plato states that the world is generated with respect to time, that is to say, that it has had a beginning to its existence and did not
15   previously exist. But before setting forth the testimony of others, (which clearly shows us what Plato's views were on the generation of the world), it is appropriate to set forth first the actual words that Plato uses to affirm that the world is generated and has a beginning
20   and then examine the arguments which attempt to force these so clearly-expressed statements of Plato into conformity with [our opponents'] own views.

Well then, Plato's whole objective in the *Timaeus* is to teach about the generation and nature of the world. Listen to how he defines the
25   objective he is setting himself in the passages which follow. This is what he says:

Here, then, for your consideration, Socrates, is the programme of entertainment we have prepared for you. We decided that Timaeus, since he's the best astronomer among us and has
136,1 taken particular pains to inform himself about the nature of the

universe, should speak first, starting with the generation of the
world, and ending[71] with the nature of man.[72]

And again a few sentences later he adds this:

> Yes, Socrates, everyone with any sense at all certainly always   5
> invokes the gods at the outset of any undertaking, however
> small it may be. So if we aren't completely out of our minds, we
> who are about to discuss with regard to the universe whether it
> has come to be or is ungenerated must invoke the gods and   10
> goddesses and pray that all that we say shall above all be
> pleasing to them, and secondly to ourselves.[73]

In these passages Plato himself has clearly stated what his objective
is, namely, to write about the generation of the universe. Then, so
that no one will think that he has taken it for granted that the world
has come to be too readily and without any proof, he repeats his   15
original statement, recasting it as a problem,[74] and says that what he
proposes is to teach [us] whether the universe, that is the world, has
come to be or is ungenerated, after first carrying out a division of
existing things; for of these he says that some always exist and are   20
ungenerated, while others are generated and come to be. Dealing
with this first will help him come to grips with the [matter] under
investigation.

The passage immediately after the one we quoted above goes as
follows:

> As far as the gods are concerned, let that be our invocation. But
> we must also invoke our own abilities too, so that you may   137,1
> understand with as little difficulty as possible and I expound my
> thoughts on the matters before us as accurately as possible. We
> must in my opinion begin by making a distinction between that
> which always is and has no generation and that which comes to   5
> be but never is. The former, being always in the same state, may
> be grasped by thought with the aid of reason, the latter, which
> comes to be and perishes but never truly is, may be conjectured
> by belief along with irrational sensation. Further, everything
> that comes to be necessarily comes to be through the agency of   10
> some cause; for it is impossible for anything to have a generation
> without a cause.[75]

Here one should observe how Plato says that everything that may be
grasped by thought is ungenerated and always remains the same and
unchanging but states that everything that may [only] be conjectured
by belief and perceived [by the senses] – of this kind are all bodies and   15
the things that exist in bodies, for these alone are the subject of

sensation – comes to be and perishes but never really is; for everything of a bodily nature is observed to be in a state of change and
alteration, never remaining in the same condition but being continu-
20   ally restored, so to speak, by the replacement of what has been lost.
So it is immediately clear just from this division of existing things,
and before he has said anything about the world, that Plato believes
that the world is [in the class] of things which are generated; for he
has divided these existing things into two, into those that are ungen-
25   erated and those that are generated, stating that those that are
ungenerated are apprehended by thought and those that come to be
138,1 are conjectured [by belief] and perceived [by the senses]. If, then,
everything corporeal in the world is perceived [by the senses], it is
clear that Plato does not intend [the world] to be [in the class] of
things which are ungenerated but [in the class] of things which come
5   to be and perish and never really are. For just as each particular
thing, for instance this animal or this plant, is, on account of the
continuity, so to speak, of its alteration, restored and repaired[76] by
the nature which has immediate governance of them, even so, says[77]
Plato (who believes that the heaven and the whole world are con-
10   structed from the same elements from which particulars have been
framed) is it (even though he supposes that it *is* immortal) a restored
immortality which accrues to [the world] since the power of the
creator continuously repairs it on account of all bodily nature invariably being in a state of change and alteration. This will be demon-
15   strated a little later.[78]

But perhaps it has not yet been made clear to us from what has
been said so far whether Plato gives the world a beginning to its
20   existence or not. For Proclus himself, in the work he has entitled *An
Examination of Aristotle's Criticisms of Plato's Timaeus*,[79] says, when
commenting on the passage of Plato that has just been quoted, that
while being has a single sense in Plato (it refers to the eternal and
supertemporal), that which comes to be has two. It can refer either to
25   that which is always coming to be or to that which [comes to be] at a
[particular] moment. Separate, or particular, things come to be at a
[particular] moment, everything that is universal[80] and the world as
a whole are always coming to be. For whilst, [he holds], intelligibles
139,1 always *are*, the world is always coming to be. So it is appropriate that,
setting out Plato's own statements about the world, we consider
whether it is Plato's belief, as Proclus claims, that the world is in an
everlasting [process of] generation, never having had a beginning to
its coming to be or its existence, or whether he assigns a beginning to
5   its being and its generation. For having stated that he is going to
discuss whether the universe has come to be or is ungenerated, and
having judged it appropriate to first teach us which things always are
10   and have no share in generation and which come to be but are
deprived of being, on the ground that this will help us grasp to which

of these types the world itself belongs, once he has given us this information, he next, in due order, moves to the question of whether the world has come to be or is ungenerated, the question that he had originally undertaken to examine. This is what he says:[81] 15

> As for the whole heaven – or let us call it the world or whatever else is most acceptable to it – about it we must first ask the question which one should begin by asking about anything: 20
> whether it has always been, having no beginning [to its] genera-
> tion, or has come to be, having started from some beginning. It
> has come to be; for it is visible and tangible and has body, and,
> [as we have seen], all such perceptible things, since they may be
> grasped by belief along with sensation, clearly come to be and
> are generated. And, once more, we say that what has come to be
> must come to be by the agency of some cause. Now, to find the 25
> maker and father of this universe is a [hard] task, and having
> found him it would be impossible to declare him to all. 140,1

So Plato here, having loudly and clearly stated that one should first ask about the world the question that one should begin by asking about anything, [that is,] whether it always is, having no beginning [to its] generation, or whether it has come to be and has some 5 beginning to its being, has decided that it has come to be and has started from some beginning; for if, he says, it is visible and tangible and has body, and all such things have been seen to come to be and be generated, it too, since it is generated, must have come to be, having started from some beginning. And so, when he spoke[82] of 'that 10 which has come to be[83] but never is', he was not then either attributing *beginningless* generation to perceptible things. So if the world has come to be and had a beginning to its being, it is clear that it would not be, contrary to this, either ungenerated or beginningless for Plato.

> And, indeed, a little further on, Plato himself says:[84] 15

> For there were no days or nights or months or years before the
> heaven came to be, but he contrived their generation at the same
> time as it was put together. All these are parts of time, and 'was'
> and 'will be' are forms of time that have come to be, which we 20
> incorrectly apply without thinking to everlasting being. For we
> say that it was or is or shall be, although on a true reckoning
> only 'is' belongs to it and both 'was' and 'shall be' should properly
> be said of generation which takes place in time; for this is
> movement, but it is not a characteristic of that which is always
> in the same state without any movement to become older or 25
> younger.

And a few words later:[85]

> But perhaps this is not the right time to go into these matters
> in detail. Time, then, came to be along with the heaven, in order
> that, having been generated together, they may also be dis-
> solved together, should a dissolution ever come to pass; and [it
> was made] after the pattern of the eternal nature, so that [the
> heaven] might be as similar as possible to [the pattern]. For the
> pattern will be for all eternity, while [the heaven] has been and
> is and shall be throughout the whole of time. As a result of this
> plan and purpose of God for the generation of time, in order that
> time might come to be, the sun and the moon and the five other
> stars which go under the name of planets came to be to define
> and preserve the numbers of time.

Thus Plato. And I at least believe that no commentary could
present Plato's meaning as clearly as he has made himself. He says
that days and nights and months and years, which are parts of time,
did not exist before the heaven came to be – [and] plausibly, for time
is the measure of the movement of the heaven. But if a 'before'[86]
pre-exists the framing of the heaven, how could the heaven and time
be without beginning? Moreover, to say that God contrived the generation of time and its parts along with the framing of the heaven is
indicative of their having had a beginning of some kind and an initial
coming into existence. For how could something that has existed from
eternity and always exists be said to have been contrived by the
creator at the same time as the heaven was being put together and
not to have existed before it came to be? For something that did not
exist before it came to be was in a state of non-existence prior to its
existence. And Plato certainly shows an exact knowledge of what
things 'before' and 'then' and similar time words should be used of
when he immediately goes on to rebuke those who apply these time
words – I mean 'was' and 'shall be' and the like, to which 'before' and
'then' are related – to the divine nature. Only 'is', he says, should be
said of God, stating this Mosaic [rule] quite explicitly. (For, appearing
to the prophet, God declared 'I am He who is'.[87]) If Plato thought that
it is brought[88] into existence by God from everlasting, without a
beginning to its being, how is it that, in the same breath as he rebukes
others for applying 'was' and 'shall be' to God, he falls foul of his own
charge? For if God *brings* the heaven and time into existence from
everlasting, the heaven and time are, I presume, *brought* into existence from everlasting; and, if this is so, there was not a time when
they were not being brought into existence. How is it, then, that he
says that there was no time before the heaven came to be?
      And if it is appropriate to talk of a time before it came to be in the
case of the heaven, it will also be appropriate to talk of a time before

he made [it] in the case of God. As Proclus himself says,[89] it is when
the maker makes that what comes to be comes to be. And the same
applies in the case of 'then'.[90]

If, then, time had always existed, and if Plato understands the   25
correct usage of time words and has just explained their correct
usage, he would never have ventured to use the words 'before the
heaven came to be', nor indeed the words 'but he now contrived their   143,1
generation at the same time as the heaven was put together' if he
believed that the existence of the world is without a beginning. For
what was then bringing the heaven into existence for the first time,
was not, I presume, bringing it into existence earlier. And if the   5
heaven and time did not exist before they came to be, and the maker
of these things was not making them before they came to be, then, as
I said,[91] Plato would not, if he really believed that God brings them
into existence from everlasting, have spoken in this way. For just as
God's being, which is always the same and unchanging, is not accept-   10
ing of the words 'was' or 'shall be' but only of the word 'is', so is an
everlasting production of the world not accepting of the words 'before'
or 'then'. But Plato has in fact used just these words of the generation
of the world; therefore he did not believe that it is brought into   15
existence from everlasting.

And if anyone should claim that just to say that God at first did not
bring [things] into existence but later brought [them] into existence
is to predicate change and movement of God (which is neither true
nor the opinion of Plato), let him return to what we said in the fourth
chapter;[92] for this kind of puzzle received a fitting solution there.   20

And surely all but the hopelessly contentious will be convinced by
the words 'time came to be along with the heaven, in order that,
having been generated together, they may also be dissolved together,
should their dissolution ever come to pass'.[93] For in order to show   144,1
[that this was] the very beginning (*prôtên arkhên*) of their formation,
he did not say 'time comes to be together with the heaven' but '[time]
came to be along with the heaven'. And he has shown that this is his
meaning by adding the words 'having been generated together, they
may also be dissolved together'. For, as far as its own nature is
concerned, for anything that has come to be and had a beginning to
its existence there is in every case a subsequent perishing; for Plato
himself says in the *Phaedrus* that 'a passing out of existence of
necessity comes to everything that has come to be'.[94] So, just as, in his 5
view, endlessness always attends upon anything that has had no
beginning to its existence (for anything that has not commenced
being will not cease being), [so], according to Plato, has the world had
a beginning, and [so], as far as the law of its nature is concerned, will 10
[it] definitely cease being. Since, then, Plato assigns a beginning of its
being to the world, he also, with reason, accepts the consequences of
natural law, even though he supposes that it remains indissoluble   15

because of a bond that is stronger than its own nature, the will of God.[95]

8. But those who are concerned to force everything into agreement with their own views and have not schooled their minds to follow the truth, when they should, if it seemed to them that Plato

20   was here at least mistaken, have, begging his pardon, recited that much-used mantra of theirs that 'Plato is dear but the truth is dearer'[96] (as Plato's own pupil, Aristotle, amongst others, has done[97]), have instead, taking little thought for their own consciences or the truth, grasped, as the proverb has it, at every straw[98] in their eager-

145,1 ness to enroll the [great] man's reputation on behalf of their own fraud. For some of the earlier commentators on Plato, including the Platonist Taurus and Porphyry the Phoenician, whom Proclus too has

5   followed, agree that Plato says that the world is generated, but not generated in the sense that it had a beginning to its being but in accordance with another kind of generation; for they say that 'generated' has a number of meanings. To avoid making their case for them and so as not to omit any of the senses of 'generated', I shall quote the

10   Platonist Taurus' own words, for this fellow has thought up many senses for 'generated'. Here, then, to quote his exact words,[99] is what he says in his commentary on the *Timaeus*:

There being a question as to whether the world is in Plato's view
15   ungenerated, philosophers have had different opinions on the matter. Aristotle states[100] that the *Timaeus* describes the world as generated since Timaeus says[101] 'it has come to be'. And, indeed, there is a work of his [sc. of Timaeus] in circulation on the universe as [something that is] generated.[102] And perhaps Plato's Timaeus means much the same thing when he says that the world is generated.[103] Theophrastus, on the other hand, in
20   *On Physical Opinions*[104] says that the world is in Plato's opinion generated and criticises him on that basis, but adds that he may be hypothesizing it as generated for the sake of clarity [of
25   exposition].[105] And some others have likewise been of the opinion that it is in Plato's view generated, although others [have thought that he held that it is] ungenerated.

Since those who claim that it is generated have, amongst
146,1 many other passages, seized upon the one where he says[106] 'It has come to be; for it is visible and tangible', we must distinguish the various senses of 'generated'. And in this way we shall learn
5   that Plato is not using 'generated' in the sense in which we describe as 'generated' things that have come into existence from any temporal beginning. As a matter of fact, it is falling back on this sense whenever the word 'generated' is used that has led the majority of people astray.

[1] Amongst things that are said to be 'generated', then, are

things which have not come to be but which are in the same
genus as things which are generated.[107] In this same way we   10
describe as visible things which have not, are not, and will not
be seen, but which are in the same genus as visible things, as if
there were, for example, a body of some kind at the centre of the
earth.

[2] Also described as 'generated' are things that are notionally
composite, even if they have not [actually] been put together. In
this sense the middle note [of the scale] is composed of the
highest and the lowest;[108] even though it has not [actually] been   15
put together [from them], we detect in it the value that they
have relative to each other. And the same applies to flowers and
animals. In the case of the world, composition and blending can
be seen to the extent that we can reduce it to the first sub-   20
stratum [sc. prime matter] by removing and separating off its
qualities.

[3] The world is said to be 'generated' because it is always in
[the process of] coming to be, changing, like Proteus, into all
sorts of shapes. Accordingly, earth and the [other components]
of the world below the moon are continuously changing into each
other, while the [parts] above the moon, although they are more
or less unvarying in their matter and undergo very little change,   25
change in their outward appearance, just as a mime, while
remaining one and the same person, takes on many different   147,1
appearances[109] according to the nature of his gestures. Thus
even the heavenly [regions] change and form different patterns
with the movements of the planets relative to the fixed stars and
of these relative to the planets.   5

[4] And [the world] is said[110] to be 'generated' because its
being is [derived] from another source, namely from God,
through whom it is ordered. In this way, even for those for whom
the world is quite definitely everlasting, the light that the moon
gets from the sun is generated, even though there has never
been a time when it has not been illuminated by it.[111]

If anyone wishes to say that it is in [any of] these senses that   10
the world is generated according to Plato, let him, but not if a
time [of generation] is intended and [they mean] that it originally did not exist but later came to be. [Plato] himself shows
how he should be understood when he says[112] '[whether it has
always been,] without a beginning, or has come to be, having   15
started from some beginning'. The words 'without a' and 'some'
make it clear that he does not mean us to understand a beginning with respect to time in the way that we say that Ephorus[113]
began his *History* with the Return of the Heraclidae. (Some
claim that the beginning that is associated with creating (*kata
to dêmiourgoun*) is of a different kind; the creator, the pattern

20   and matter are, [they hold], beginnings.[114] But these cannot
        properly be called beginnings.[115]) Moreover, he does not say[116]
25   'and is body' but 'and has body', indicating that it can be de-
        scribed as generated because its nature is of a kind, [namely,]
        corporeal, whose being consists in coming to be.

        Thus the aforesaid gentleman.
148,1   Proclus subscribes to the third and fourth [of these] senses [of
        'generated']. He too claims that Plato says that the world is generated
        not on the ground that it has had a beginning to its existence but [1]
5   on the ground that it has its being in coming to be[117] and also [2] that
        it is generated in that it has come to be through the agency of God and
        is not the cause of its own being – that is, that it is generated with
        respect to causation.
            And Porphyry adds other senses of 'generated' to those enumer-
        ated by Taurus. He says that a thing which is described as [subject
10   to] generation[118] is said to be generated even though it has never
        [actually] come to be; examples are words and syllables, because they
        can be analysed into letters and are composed of letters, and dia-
        grams, [among which] rectilinear figures, for example, are notionally
15   divided into triangles and constructed from triangles. It is, I presume,
        clear that this comes to the same thing as being composed of matter
        and form, for things which are generated in the sense that they are
        not simple but composed of matter and form are said to be generated
        on the same basis as diagrams are [said to be]: because things simpler
20   than either,[119] out of which their composition and into which their
        dissolution notionally (*theôreitai*) take place, are conceived of as
        having prior existence, they are, in contrast to things that are simple
        from every point of view and carry with them no notion of composi-
        tion, referred to as generated. Therefore these two [senses] should be
25   regarded as one.[120] And perhaps this is why the other of [our two]
        commentators[121] [sc. Taurus] has not even mentioned this sense.
            In addition, Porphyry says that things which derive their existence
149,1   from a [process of] generation and coming to be, for example a house
        or a ship or a plant or an animal, are also said to be generated. For
        this reason we do not describe a flash of lightning or a snapping of the
        fingers or anything else that exists and ceases to exist in an instant
5   as generated; as Aristotle also says,[122] all such things come to be
        without [a process of] generation and switch to non-existence without
        [a process of] decay.[123] It is clear that nobody would hold that the
        world is generated in the sense of having come to be through a
        [process of] generation, for God brought all things into existence
        together with the thought. This being so, we shall have no need of this
10   sense [of 'generated'] in our investigation of Plato's meaning.[124]
            Finally, Porphyry says [that things which are called generated in
        the] familiar, everyday sense, things that have had a beginning from

a [point of] time[125] without previously having existed, a sense in which
he claims Plato did *not* describe the world as generated, are said to   15
be generated.[126]

And so this leaves the remaining four senses in the field, that is,
[1] things which are in the genus of things which are generated even
though they have not [themselves] come to be, [2] things which are
generated in the sense that they are composed of matter and form
(the sense which has Porphyry's vote), [3] things which have their   20
being in coming to be, and [4] things which are generated with respect
to causation. I think that we should take each of these [senses] in turn
and ask whether it can be shown to be in accord with Plato's intentions. For once they have all been invalidated, the only alternative
left, whether they like it or not, is that Plato described the world as   25
generated with respect to time.

9. The first hypothesis [as to the meaning] of 'generated' [in
relation to the world] (that is, that it belongs in the genus of things   150,1
which are generated[127] even though it has not [itself] come to be)
seems to me to be rather as though one were to say that a thing is in
the genus of corporeal things even though it is not a corporeal thing,
or in the genus substance even though it is not a substance. And what   5
could be more ridiculous than that? Genera are predicated synonymously of what falls under them. So just as man, since it belongs to
the genus of animals, is an animal, and stone, being in the genus of
corporeal things, is a corporeal thing, so must anything in the genus
of visible things be a visible thing and anything in the genus of things   10
which are generated be generated. And if it is by any means possible
for a thing which has not come to be[128] but actually exists to be in the
genus of things which are generated, as they say the world is, then by
conversion by negation[129] it is also possible for a thing to have come
to be although it is not in the genus of things which are generated.   15
But a thing which is not in the genus of things which are generated
must, one imagines, be ungenerated. So there will be an ungenerated
thing which has come to be. If these things are impossible (for one and
the same thing will be opposite things at the same time and in the
same respect), then it is also impossible for anything which has not
come to be to be in the genus of things which are generated; for the   20
one follows from the other.

And there is another way in which the argument can be brought to
the same absurd conclusion. If Plato when inquiring whether the
world belongs to the class of things which are generated or of things
which are ungenerated, opposed 'generated' and 'ungenerated', and if
when conceding that it is generated, he meant, as the philosophers   25
believe, that it is generated in such a way that it is in the genus of
things which are generated even though it has not come to be, then
for him 'ungenerated' likewise signifies something that is in the
genus of things which are ungenerated even though it is not [actually]   151,1

ungenerated. Therefore the same thing will both be ungenerated because it is in the genus of things which are ungenerated and also not ungenerated because it has come to be. [And] therefore [both sides of] a contradiction will be true of the same thing in the same way at the same time.

But in my opinion, these [arguments] are more deserving of ridicule than of rebuttal. Even body[130] below the centre [of the universe[131]], since it belongs to the genus of visible things, will certainly, I presume, be visible by nature. If it is never seen, it is not because it is not visible by nature that it is not seen but because there are solid bodies in the way [and] our sight cannot penetrate things which are not transparent. If the obstructing [bodies] were removed it would certainly be seen like anything else – and if there really had been anyone with eyes which, like those of Lynceus[132] in the myth, could 'easily see beneath the surface of the earth',[133] he would even have been able to see objects contained [in the regions] below the centre of the earth.[134] And so if the world too actually exists and is in the genus of things which are generated, it must also of necessity have come to be; [for] even though the origin of its generation has not come down to us, [this is] not because it is by nature ungenerated (in that case it would belong in the genus of things which are ungenerated rather than in that of things which are generated) but because our knowledge can only grasp things that currently exist.

And besides, a visible thing does not possess visibility by virtue of being seen[135] but by being of a nature to be seen; being seen is something that happens to it through a relation to seeing agents (*ta horônta*). For this reason, even if there is a visible thing that has never been seen because it is contained [in the regions] below the centre of the universe, it will none the less possess [the property of] being visible. It remains unseen because there are things in the way, not because it is not of a nature to be seen. Hence, if the obstacles were removed and something to see it were present, it would be seen straight away. And so a thing may be visible but never be seen, for to be seen is not the same as to be visible. But it is not possible for a thing that has never come to be and never will come to be to be generated; a thing that is generated does not possess the [characteristic of] being generated just by being of a nature to come to be but by the certainty that it has either come to be or is going to come to be; for generation is its path into existence. And it is impossible for something that has not yet come to be, is not now coming to be and is not of a nature to come to be at some time in the future either to be generated or to be described [as generated]. So, in whatever sense the world is said to be generated, there is every necessity that it have come to be in exactly that sense. It is not possible for it to be generated and not either have come to be, or be in the process of coming to be, or be going to come to be [in the sense] in which it is [described as]

generated; otherwise it would not be generated at all. So if the world
has not come to be [in the sense] in which it is generated, then it must 20
certainly be the case that it is neither coming to be now nor going to
come to be [in that sense], for the world would not be in one state now
and another at another time. And so, if it has not come to be [in the
sense] in which it is generated, it will not come to be at all. And if it
has neither come to be nor will come to be, it is not generated. And so
it is not possible for something that has not come to be [in the sense] 25
in which it is generated to be generated.

Finally, in addition to what has been said already, it is worth
noting that Plato does not simply say that the world is 'generated' but 153,1
everywhere uses 'has come to be' of it. In one place he says[136] 'we who
are about to discuss with regard to the universe whether it has come
to be or is ungenerated (*agenês*)', in another[137] 'whether it has always
been, having no beginning [to its] generation, or has come to be, 5
having started from some beginning. It has come to be; for it is visible
and tangible and has body', in yet another,[138] 'time, then, came to be
along with the heaven, in order that, having been produced together,
they may also be dissolved together', and [he uses] such [language]
throughout. And if Plato explicitly refers to it as 'having come to be' 10
and not just simply as 'generated', then surely those who say that it
is generated because it is in the genus of things which are generated
but that it has never yet come to be are, quite apart from the fact that
this hypothesis, as we have shown, issues in absurdity, in open 15
contradiction of him.

This, then, is our refutation of their first [supposed] sense of
'generated'.[139]

10. Second came things that are notionally composite even
though they have not [actually] been composed with respect to time.
For although all bodies are composed of matter and form, they have
not been composed with respect to time as a result of the coming
together of matter and form. Matter can never be observed free of 20
forms or be discovered [in that condition], nor indeed can enmattered
forms existing alone apart from matter; uncombined[140] (*ta hapla*)
they can be known only in thought. Only by it [sc. thought] are bodies
resolved into substratum and form and composed once more out of 25
these. They claim, then, that the world too is generated in the sense
that we can notionally resolve it into its components, that is, the first 154,1
substratum and the qualities stamped upon it. It is this sense of
'generated' that Porphyry above all subscribes to. Here, at any rate, 5
to quote his exact words, is what he says in the second book of his
commentary on the *Timaeus*:

Those who claim that [Plato believes that] the world is ungenerated with respect to time and that it is in some other sense
that he describes the world as generated must be ready, after

[first] enumerating the senses of 'generated', to determine which
10   of these senses the argument he advances for its having come to
be fits. For if it were not the case that he *demonstrated* that it
has come to be, it would be unclear in what sense he has
predicated 'having come to be' of the world, but if he does
advance a demonstration of this point, it is clear that he will be
describing the world as generated in whichever of the senses of
15   'generated' this demonstration fits and evident that any sense it
does not fit is eliminated. For Plato was by no means so witless
as to make assumptions that were invalid and in no way calcu-
lated to establish his conclusion.[141]

20   After these remarks, and after enumerating the senses of 'generated'
which were listed above,[142] Porphyry states that the world is described as generated by Plato in the sense that it is composed of
matter and form. The passage runs as follows:

I say, then, that [it is] in what we have shown to be the proper
25   sense of 'generated', that is, that which is composed of matter
155,1   and form; after first explaining that the demonstration fits this
meaning, we shall show that the demonstration is in accord with
it and that he has selected its axioms appropriately. For, if a
thing is 'visible and tangible and has body',[143] since [this means
that] it will be[144] three-dimensional and resistant [to touch] and
with bulk, it will not be simple but composed of matter and
form.[145]

Thus Porphyry.
5   **11.** In reply to all of these people, one can in the first place point
out that to use words that [normally] have one meaning in another,
rejecting customary terminology, is an act of great license and wilful-
10   ness. If what they say were true, they should be able to point to a place
in the dialogues where Plato clearly substitutes 'generated' for 'composed'. But neither has the common usage of mankind ever yet
substituted 'generated' for 'composed' when it has wanted to describe
something as composed, for usage knows that 'generated' means one
thing, 'composed' another, nor, if anyone [at all] has anywhere clearly
substituted 'generated' for 'composed', can [Porphyry], to my know-
15   ledge, provide us with evidence of this from any other early [philoso-
pher] or prose-writer. As we shall show when examining his views[146]
in another place,[147] when Aristotle enumerates the senses of 'gener-
20   ated' and 'ungenerated' in the first book of *On the Heaven*,[148] he
nowhere distinguishes being composed of matter and form as a sense
of 'generated' or being simple and incomposite as a sense of 'ungenerated'. How, then, could it be anything but absurd for Plato himself or
156,1   anyone else to so lightly replace normal word-usage by the novel and

unfamiliar? And, in particular, if he is really not employing the everyday sense but one that is unusual and unfamiliar, they are bringing a very serious charge against Plato, [namely], that of not first distinguishing the senses of 'generated' and then indicating which sense he is writing about. We have already shown[149] that this kind of practice is sophistical in the extreme.

But even if one were to overlook all of these considerations and concede to them that, in addition to its other senses, 'generated' may mean 'composed of matter and form', [problems would remain]. [For then] it would, I imagine, be perfectly obvious that if[150] in the [passage] at the outset where he defines the problem he is setting himself (when he says[151] that he is going to consider 'whether the universe has come to be or is ungenerated (*agenês*)') he is saying nothing other than that he is going to ask whether the world is simple or composed of matter and form (for if 'generated' means 'composed' in this passage for Plato, 'ungenerated' will clearly mean 'incomposite'), then when he subsequently states the actual problem [in the words] 'whether the world has always been, having no beginning [to its] generation, or has come to be, having started from some beginning',[152] he is without a doubt asking what he indicated at the outset, [that is], whether the world is simple or composed of matter and form. And so, thanks to this great license in the substitution of words, [the words] 'has always been' will also be employed as the equivalent of 'simple'; for when in the sequel he asks[153] 'whether [the world] has always been or has come to be', he is (substituting 'has always been' for '[is] ungenerated') posing the question that he said he intended to pose at the outset,[154] that is, whether the world has come to be or is ungenerated. So if 'generated' means 'composed' and, as a result of this, 'ungenerated' necessarily means 'incomposite and simple', and Plato has substituted 'always is' for 'ungenerated', then, according to him, 'always is' also means 'incomposite'.[155] And why did Plato have to resort to such extreme misuse of words when he should have conveyed his meaning concisely and in everyday language and said 'whether the world is simple or composed of matter and form'? For who ever substituted 'always is' for 'simple and incomposite'?

But let that too be conceded to them. If we substitute 'incomposite and simple' for 'always is' and 'is composed' for 'comes to be', as has been decreed by these latter-day linguistic lawgivers, the whole passage will read something like this: 'whether the world is simple, having no beginning to its composition, or whether it is composed, having started from some beginning'. But once again they are unable to conceal the truth. For if Plato is solely concerned with the question 'whether the universe is simple or composite', what does he mean by the addition 'having no beginning [to its] generation'? And, moreover, why does he add 'having started from some beginning' after 'has come to be'? It would have been enough just to say 'whether it has always

158,1   been or has come to be'. So by asking 'whether, always being (that is, "being simple"), it has no beginning to its generation (that is, according to them, to its composition), or whether it has come to be (that is, "has been composed"), having started from some beginning', and deciding that it has come to be (for he says: 'It has come to be'), he is
5   clearly stating that the world has been composed, having started from some beginning; for the whole of what he is asking is 'whether it has come to be, having started from some beginning', and he decides that it *has* come to be, having started from some beginning.

          And so Plato is acknowledging that the composition of the world
10   had a beginning, which is again to say that its being and existence did. For it was stated[156] that in the case of things that are composed of matter and form it is only in thought that the simple [elements] are conceived of as prior to the composites. The creator did not first bring matter and form into existence separately and combine them later,
15   but brought that which is composed of them into being at the same time as the simple [elements]. For matter and form are relatives and the one cannot exist without the other. So if he states that the composition of the world had a beginning and that God brought the simple [elements] and the composites formed from them into being at
20   the time of this composition, then, in assigning a beginning to the composition of the world, Plato also provides it with a beginning to its existence. For the existence of the world and its composition are not different things; it exists and is composite at the same time.

          12. If one does not understand 'beginning' and 'having started' in
25   this passage[157] temporally (by a temporal beginning I mean, as has been repeatedly stated,[158] not one that has taken place within a part of time, time already being in existence, but [for a thing] to begin
159,1   existing along with time, which had not previously existed[159]), one must, I imagine, understand 'beginning' causally.[160] If there is some other sense of 'beginning', it will not help us with the present inquiry,
5   so to go into it needlessly would be a waste of time.

          According to Plato, everything that comes to be has six causes: the material, the formal, the efficient, the paradigmatic, the instrumental, the final.[161] (In the case of a house, the builder is the efficient cause; the pattern is the plan in his head (*en autôi*) after which he
10   builds the house; the matter is the stones and timbers; the form, its shape; the instrument[s], the straight-edge, the plumbline, the chisel, and the rest; the end, the purpose for which it is made, [namely,] to shelter us from rain and heat). In my opinion, it is not possible to understand 'beginning' in the present context in any of these senses.
15   For [Plato] writes 'whether it has always been, having no beginning [to its] generation', adding 'having no beginning [to its] generation' after writing 'has always been' because if a thing always exists it follows that it has no beginning [to its] generation. So if 'generation'
20   is being substituted for 'composition' and 'always is' for 'is simple and

incomposite', and if 'beginning' is not to be understood temporally but
as referring to the efficient cause or the form or one of the other
[causes], it will follow that nothing simple and incomposite has any
of the beginnings of composite things. (The beginnings of composite
things are the six mentioned above.) Therefore nothing that is simple   25
will have a form or a pattern or a final or efficient cause. Therefore
God is the maker only of perceptible things, and forms can be seen
only in them. Therefore no rational soul, or any of the other intelligi-   160,1
bles, is a form or will have a pattern or an efficient or final cause.

And, further, if by 'beginning' he means one of [the six] mentioned   5
above, what does he mean when he writes 'or has it come to be, having
started from some beginning'? Why [, I mean,] does he write 'having
started from some beginning', in the singular? If he intends 'beginning' to refer to the causes of composite things, and if these are many,
(and in the case of the world according to Plato himself those enumer-   10
ated [above] with the exception of the instrumental; for God does not
need an instrument to bring anything at all into being), why ever,
after using the plural when denying a beginning to that which always
is (by writing that 'that which always exists has *no* beginning [to its]
generation'), does he use the singular when asserting that that which   15
comes to be has a beginning, and add the indefinite adjective 'some'
as well, when he writes 'or has it come to be, having started from some
beginning', when he should have used the plural, and written 'having
started from a number of beginnings', if, as Plato himself holds, the
causal beginnings of composite things (which we have listed above[162])
are indeed multiple? And even so it would be ridiculous to take   20
'having come to be' as equivalent to 'being composed' and ask whether
something that is composite is composed of a number of simple
[elements], since this would be like asking whether something composite is composite rather than simple.

And, moreover, what does 'having started' signify? If 'having
started' is not temporal in the present context, the only remaining   25
alternative is to take it too as equivalent to 'having been composed',
so that the whole of what Plato writes reads like this: 'or is composite,
being composed from some beginning'. (For, it seems to me, they will   161,1
prefer to spout any nonsense rather than accept Plato's plain and true
meaning.) But nothing composite is composed of some [one] thing but
rather of a number. So why does he write 'having started (i.e. having
been composed) from some beginning'?   5

And if anyone wants to take 'beginning' in this passage to mean
just the efficient [cause], clearly we shall also take it to mean the
efficient cause when he writes '[whether] it always was, having no
beginning [to its] generation'. [And], as before[163] (*palin*), taking it as
a consequence for things that always exist that they have no efficient   10
cause (*poiêtikên arkhên*), Plato is stating that only perceptible things
come to be through the agency of an efficient cause and that none of

the intelligibles does. And so God is the creator of perceptible things only and all intelligibles, of which our soul is one, are without a causal origin.

15   If this is absurd, then it is not possible to understand[164] 'having started from some beginning' in terms of any of the six causes. And so Plato means that the world started its existence from a [point of] time. For if, as Porphyry rightly holds,[165] no one is so devoid of wit as

20   to claim that Plato used invalid premisses, then anyone who believed that Plato makes hypotheses that lead to innumerable conclusions that are either worthy of ridicule or are absurdities of the grossest kind and who claimed that he employs incorrect words and uses

25   ambiguous terms without distinguishing their proper senses and that he is careless of the normal meanings of words and uses words in novel (*allôn*) senses unknown to the Hellenes,[166] would, I presume, be even more bereft of wits. But this is what these extraordinary

162,1   hypotheses[167] reduce Plato to. So neither, then, does 'generated' mean 'composed of form and matter' for Plato, nor in the present context can 'a beginning [to its] generation' mean anything other than one with respect to time.

5   **13.** That the word 'beginning' means a beginning with respect to time for Plato in the present context may also be gathered from what he says elsewhere in aporetic vein about the formation of the world. Here, to quote his exact words, is what he says in the sixth book of the *Laws:*[168]

10   Every man should be well aware of this much at least. Either the human race had no beginning at all and will never have an end but always was and ever is and will be, or else the passage of time since its beginning must have been immeasurably long.[169]

15   And in the *Epinomis*[170] the same [Plato] says this of all of the inhabitants of the heaven:

    And we must consider all the inhabitants of the heaven to be kinds of living creatures, which we must surely call the divine race of stars, which has been allotted the fairest of bodies and

20   the happiest and best of souls. And we are pretty much bound to assign to it conjecturally one of two lots. Either each of them is utterly and of absolute necessity imperishable and immortal and divine, or each has a lengthy and adequate term of life beyond which it would need nothing more.

25   So if, in aporetic mode, he says in these passages: 'We must hold one of two opinions about the lot of the human race and of all the

163,1   inhabitants of the heaven. Either they had no beginning [to their]

generation at all, and for this reason will have no end either, but always were and will be, or it is a great time since they first came to be and they have existed for an immeasurable age, the heavenly 5 bodies having a lengthy span of life',[171] and if he leaves the puzzles that he raises unresolved because it is not part of the task he had set himself in the *Laws*[172] to write about the generation of the world as a natural scientist would, but again raises the very same question for consideration in the *Timaeus*, [where he writes] 'whether the world has always been, having no beginning [to its] generation, or whether 10 it has come to be, having started from some beginning',[173] and [there] decides that the world has come to be and has a beginning [to its] generation, it is surely clear to everyone that, by puzzling once more in the *Timaeus* over the same beginning that he had puzzled over in the *Laws*, he is making it clear that this beginning is the generation 15 of the universe. And if in the *Laws* he is clearly puzzling over whether the heavenly bodies and the human race have a temporal beginning or not, then in the *Timaeus* too he is declaring that it is by having started from some temporal beginning that the world has come to be. And that Plato is not, as Porphyry believes,[174] arguing from invalid premises when he states that the world has a temporal beginning 20 will be demonstrated a little later.[175]

14. And how could it be in keeping with Plato's sagacity to agonise over a theory which is so obvious and which is familiar to everybody 25 who has as much as dabbled in natural science and which was, moreover, accepted by all natural scientists who preceded him, [namely, the theory] that every corporeal object is composed of sub- stratum and form (even though [these scientists] did differ over what 164,1 each of these is), as though he were about to solve some new problem for us, and to call upon the gods and goddesses to be his co-workers in discovering whether the world is a composite thing, being com- 5 posed of matter and form, or whether it is, on the contrary, simple, that is to say, incomposite?[176]

And why does he conduct his investigation as though it relates [only] to the universe as a whole? The problem as to whether it is constructed of matter and form is not one that is peculiar to the 10 universe (that is, the world) *qua* universe but one that arises in relation to any and every individual corporeal object that is generated and perishable, as for instance a particular volume of water or earth. Porphyry himself is a witness that this is true. Although he has previously stated that the world is said to be generated in that it is composed of matter and form, later, when commenting on the words 15 'the god, taking over all that was visible, not at rest but moving in a discordant and disorderly manner',[177] he, to quote his exact words, writes this:

The making of the world and the creation of body are not the

20   same thing, nor are the beginnings of body and of the world the
      same. For the world to come to be, both bodies and God must
      exist, for bodies to, there must be matter, God, and supervening
      [form][178] (one lot so that the matter may become body, and
      another to give order to the things that have become body). All
165,1 of these always come into existence at once and not separately
      over time, but instruction necessarily separates them so as to be
      able to explain that which comes to be accurately. The begin-
      nings of body are God, who is the begetter, matter, and the
      shapes that [Plato] will tell us about later, the things from which
5   bodies are composed being begotten of God; those of the world
      are bodies, which already exist through the agency of God, and
      God, who gives them order.[179]

And a bit later:

      It should be taken as evidence that the framing of body and that
      of the world are not in Plato's view the same thing and that at
      this point [the creator] takes over not matter but bodies that
10   have been produced from matter, that he says that what is taken
      over is visible – and what could visible things be other than
      bodies? Matter in his view is invisible and formless, being
      apprehended only with difficulty by [a kind of] spurious reason-
      ing[180] – and that he goes on to show the generation of bodies even
15   though he has [already] shown the framing of the world in this
      passage. After the generation of the world he *returns* to the
      generation of body.[181]

Now, if Porphyry can write this, which is both true and [an accurate
account of] Plato's position, why is it that earlier, when he was
claiming that the world is generated as being composed of matter and
20   form, he lost sight of the fact that the beginnings for the composition
of the world are not matter and form but bodies already composed of
matter and form, and that it is the composition and ordering of these
that have made the universe? And if matter and form are not the
166,1 beginnings for the world, then when Plato asks whether the world has
come to be and has a beginning to its existence, he is not asking
whether it is composite, being composed of matter and form. As
Porphyry himself says, this is the [mode of] generation of bodies, not
5   of the world, and Plato has undertaken to investigate the generation
of the world first with the intention of investigating the generation of
bodies afterwards. Porphyry himself, then, constrained by Plato's
express words, has handed us a concise refutation of the present
hypothesis [as to the meaning of] 'generated', but either he has not
10   seen that these matters are relevant to each other and that a contra-

diction is escaping his notice, or he has seen this but thought that he can keep quiet and so cheat the reader.

Nor, in my opinion, would anyone with any sense claim that even though it is not, for the reasons that have just been given, possible that the world was described as generated by Plato as being composed   15 of matter and form, it can nevertheless be so described as being composed of more than one body. No one with eyes and [any powers of] observation[182] would ask whether the world is a single, simple body or whether it is constituted of more than one. Nobody puzzles   20 over things that can be clearly grasped by our senses.

Those, then, who have foisted[183] these stupid hypotheses onto Plato are themselves completely stupid and truly devoid of wit. But this hypothesis too has now been adequately refuted and we shall move on to the examination of those that remain.   25

15. The third sense of 'generated' was that according to which the world has its being in coming to be. It is this sense above all that Proclus endorses in his comments on the passages under discussion.   167,1 At any rate, in the work that we mentioned earlier[184] entitled *An Examination of Aristotle's Criticisms of Plato's Timaeus*, when argu-   5 ing against Aristotle, who himself supposes that the world is everlasting but charges Plato with making it generated from a [point of] time (we have explained[185] in what sense 'from a [point of] time' is used in the case of the world), he endorses what Aristotle says about   10 the everlastingness of the world but claims that his accusations against Plato are unjust. In [Plato, he claims,] 'to have come to be' does not mean 'to have a beginning of being' but 'to be always coming to be'; supertemporal and eternal things have their being and their power and the perfection of their activity present to them all at once,   15 but nothing that exists in time has its own life present to it all at once. For if, he says,

> something is in time, even if it lasts for an infinite time, it exists at
> some [particular] time (for as much of it as there is [at a given time]
> is in a particular [part of] time, for time does not exist all at once),   20
> but it comes to be *ad infinitum*, not at some [particular] time.[186]

So he states that the universe is generated in the sense that it does not exist in the same way as things that always are but comes to be throughout the whole of time, always existing at each present mo- ment.[187] And he further states that the universe is generated in the   25 sense that it is not the cause of its own being but exists through the agency of another, which is the fourth sense of 'generated', namely, that which is generated with respect to causation. Thus Proclus too claims that Plato describes the world as generated in two senses – the   168,1 last two – of 'generated'.

16. I myself agree that Plato posits that all perceptible things   5

have their existence in coming to be; he does, after all, say,[188] with
reference to all perceptible things, that 'the latter, which comes to be
and perishes but never truly is, may be conjectured by belief along
with irrational sensation'. He holds, however, that this generation is
not beginningless but has had a beginning to its being,[189] [before
10   which] it did not previously exist – which is precisely what Aristotle
objects to;[190] for his saying that the world has its being in coming to
be is not automatic proof that Plato does not [also] say that this
generation originates from some beginning. Individual things, all of
15   which likewise have their being in coming to be, have one and all had
a beginning to their being. In fact Plato's own words will show that
he does not believe that the world is beginningless. 'Whether', he
says,[191] '[the world] has always been, having no beginning [to its]
generation, or has come to be, having started from some beginning'.
20   Observe that the question he puts to himself is whether [the world]
has no beginning [to its] generation or whether it has come to be,
having started from some beginning. It follows that he is seeking the
beginning of the generation of the world. If by 'has come to be' he had
simply meant that it has its being in coming to be, it would have been
25   enough to say 'whether it has always been, exempt from generation,
or has come to be'. (Although it would have been even more appropriate to say 'or *is* coming to be'). But he actually says 'having no
beginning [to its] generation' and, again, 'or has come to be, having
started from some beginning', always linking [the idea of] beginning
169,1   with [that of] generation. [And whereas] a thing that is everlastingly
coming to be 'has no beginning [to its] its generation', he actually says
that the world 'has come to be, having originated from some beginning'. For because [the words] 'has come to be' would perhaps have
seemed to some to indicate that the world [not only] exists through
5   the agency of the creator but has received its existence from everlasting (as Plato says is the case for eternal things, which have received
their being from God but exist eternally without [having originated]
from any beginning), he rules out this notion as far as the world is
10   concerned by adding 'having started from some beginning' after [the
words] 'has come to be'. Observe how he is clearly telling us two
things, namely, that the world has its being in generation and that
this generation has had a beginning to its being. On the one hand, by
means of [the words] 'it has come to be, having started from some
15   beginning' he indicates that its generation is not everlasting but has
had a beginning; on the other hand, by going on to say 'for it is visible
and tangible and has body, and, [as we have seen], all such perceptible things, since they may be grasped by belief along with sensation,
clearly come to be and are generated'[192] after [the words] 'it has come
to be', he indicates the continuity of the generation of perceptible
20   things given that they have their being in coming to be. For it is no
accident that in this passage, in writing '[as we have seen], [all such

perceptible things] clearly come to be and are generated', he adds 'generated' to 'come to be' again; [he does so] in order to show once more that the coming to be that he is referring to is not that of things that have existed from everlasting without any beginning but of things that have a beginning to their being. He is, then, as I have said, putting forward both of these positions. And he assigns the appropriate tense to each. To the beginning of being [he assigns the perfect tense] 'to have come to be', writing '[whether] it has come to be, having started from some beginning'; to the unbroken generation and change [which continues] unceasingly thereafter, [the present tense] 'to come to be', writing '[as we have seen, all such perceptible things] clearly come to be and are generated'. 'To come to be' is indicative of continuance in the present, which fits the continuous generation and alteration of the world; 'has come to be' signifies completed action in the past, which accords with the first beginning and origination of the generation of the world.

But seeing that Plato, if anyone, was well-versed in the correct use of words and used them correctly himself and would never have dashed anything off at random, why should I digress to argue what is obvious and well-known to everyone? But if anyone *does* hold Plato guilty of a lack of discrimination in his use of words and takes 'has come to be' as equivalent to 'comes to be',[193] what is there to prevent us from imitating their self-willed license and understanding 'is coming to be' as equivalent to 'having come to be'?

And how can 'having started from some beginning' be in accord with [their interpretation]? Something that is always coming to be cannot have started from some beginning of its coming to be. What can he mean by this beginning with which he says the generation of the world commenced other than a beginning to its existence and a temporal beginning? It is not possible to think of matter or form or any other kind of beginning in the present passage. What could it mean to say that the world has come to be (i.e. has its being in coming to be) by originating from matter or form or any of the other [causes]? For what does it mean to say that the world, although it comes to be for ever, began its generation from matter, unless they change the meaning of 'began' here as well? But then he would once more be asking whether the world is composite, not whether it has its being in coming to be.[194] But we have [already][195] refuted this.

That it is also impossible for 'beginning' in this passage to mean 'efficient cause' is clear from [a consideration] of things that always are and do not come to be. He states[196] that these 'have no beginning of generation'. And so it would follow that, as far as Plato is concerned, none of the intelligibles has an efficient cause, which is false, and absurd as well. If that *were* the case, it would be necessary to introduce many beginnings and not just one; as many in fact as there are intelligibles. But it is agreed that all things have a single origin.

10   And, moreover, if this was what he was asking (I mean whether the world has its being in coming to be), why did he answer 'it has come to be' and not 'it is coming to be'? And, again, why did he not write '*starting* from some beginning' rather than 'having started'?[197] To say 'always coming to be' is to encompass the origins of coming to

15   be in the present, and a thing of this kind is always beginning to come to be, and has not *begun* to come to be. And why does he write in the singular and without making distinctions when there are, as we have said,[198] a number of distinct beginnings of things that come to be?

It would seem, then, that in the present context 'beginning' can only mean a beginning of being and existence. This should suffice as

20   a refutation of the third [alleged] sense [of 'generated'].

17. It remains to consider in connection with the fourth category of the 'generated', which is the generated with respect to causation, whether when Plato says that the world has come to be, he means that it has come to be only with respect to causation; for, as I said,[199]

25   Proclus subscribes to this opinion as well, claiming that the universe is described as generated by Plato on the ground that it is not like

172,1 that which always is and is not the sole cause of its own being but exists through the agency of another. And so he takes it that 'generated' is also used by Plato on the ground that the world is not the

5   cause of its own being but has received the cause of its existence from God. And Porphyry too, even though he has stated that the world is described as generated by Plato because it is composite – and 'most truly'[200] [for that reason] at that – nevertheless goes on to say that it is described as generated with respect to causation. At any rate, commenting on the words 'this is in the truest sense[201] [its] cause

10   according to wise men, etc.',[202] he writes as follows:

If this is the beginning of the world in the truest sense[203] and it did not begin to come to be of itself and was not self-sufficient but arrived on the scene through the agency of God, coming to be through the agency of being,[204] and if the being of God is his

15   goodness, [then] God would in the true sense be its cause. And what is more, when he puzzles over 'whether [the world] has always been, having no beginning to its generation, or whether it has come to be, having started from some beginning',[205] we must understand him to be in doubt as to whether it exists as it is independently, without a maker, or came to be through the

20   agency of another and owes the beginning of its being to another.[206]

Well, in the first place I am at a loss as to how the same Plato asking in regard to the same world in the self-same [piece of] teaching 'whether it has always been, having no beginning to its generation,

25   or whether it has come to be, having started from some beginning'

could be asking at the same time whether it has come to be with respect to causation, whether it is composite, whether it has its being in coming to be, and [whether it has come to be] in any of the other senses of 'generated' that they add [to these]. In my opinion at least, the manner in which they pass so easily from one sense [of 'generated'] to another on different occasions is a very strong indication that they are giving a forced interpretation to Plato's words. Being unable to agree among themselves on a single sense of 'generated' [that holds good] for Plato throughout, they assume the one that suits them best in each passage.

[And], secondly, if [his use of the words] 'has come to be' does not indicate that the world has a beginning to its existence but that it has its existence from God and is not itself the cause of its own existence, Plato should have asked in so many words whether the world has its existence from God or not, and avoided the ambiguity of the word 'generated' so as not to leave his intention in any doubt. The greatest criticism that can be levelled at a dialectician is that he has used ambiguous terms [in framing] his questions or propositions without any qualification or distinction between the various senses of the terms.

18. And that it is not even possible to see a reference to coming to be with respect to causation alone in the words 'whether it has always been, having no beginning [to its] generation, or has come to be'[207] is clear from the following considerations.

If [the statement] that the world has come to be means for Plato that its existence has an efficient cause, and if he opposes 'having come to be' and 'not having come to be' (for he says[208] 'we who are about to discuss with regard to the universe whether it has come to be or is ungenerated (*agenês*)', and again,[209] 'whether it has always been, having no beginning [to its] generation, or has come to be'), it is clear that since [the words] 'it has not come to be' are being used as [they would be] in a [dialectical] problem,[210] they mean the opposite of 'it has come to be', that is, that its being has *no* efficient cause. So if we take 'it has not come to be' as equivalent to 'its being has no efficient cause' and 'it has come to be' to the opposite of that, we get something like this: 'We who are about to discuss with regard to the universe whether it exists through the agency of some efficient cause or not', and again, [in the other passage], 'whether the world has always been, having no creative cause of its existence, or whether it was brought into being through the agency of some efficient cause'. But I do not really imagine that Plato believed that [our] conception of the creator is so ambiguous as to think that we need to consider right at the outset, not just in regard to the world but in regard to everything – for he says[211] 'about it we must first ask the question which one should begin by asking about *anything*' – whether its existence depends on God or whether the contrary is the case and

173,1

5

10

15

20

174,1

5

10

15

each thing has independent existence (*automaton huparxin*). What is obvious is not made the subject of a [dialectical] problem. Aristotle says[212] that 'Whether the gods should be honoured' is not a dialectical
20   problem, for those who do propose such [topics as problems] are in need of chastisement rather than [dialectical] argument. I strongly reject the idea that [Plato] believes that one should ask in regard to anything and everything whether it exists thanks to the creator or independently and without an efficient cause. As Aristotle says[213] in his work *On the World*:

25   It is an ancient and ancestral tradition among all men that all
175,1   things come from God and that it is thanks to God that they exist
           for our benefit, and that there is nothing in nature that is
           independent and self-sufficient and entirely without the main-
           tenance he provides.

So how could anyone with any sense at all fail to respect even [our]
5   common conception of God and make the question whether each thing that exists owes its existence to God as its creator or is the cause of its own existence the subject of a dialectical problem?
     On the other hand, in the case of things of which it is not clear whether they have had a beginning to their existence or not, as with the human soul and the world and some other things, Plato does
10   think it makes sense that the first question of all asked about them should be whether they have had a beginning or not. It is because he was aware that this is a matter of doubt for most people as far as the human soul is concerned that he states[214] clearly in the *Timaeus*:

15   We are currently endeavouring to talk of the soul as later, but
           God did not make it junior to [the body]; having joined them
           together, he would not have allowed the elder to be ruled by the
           younger. It is, I suppose, because there is so much of the chance
           and random in our make up that we speak pretty much in that
           vein. Accordingly, since the soul was to be the mistress and to
20   rule [the body] as her subject, he constructed the soul prior and
           senior to the body in both birth and excellence from the following
           materials and employing the following method.

He is aware, then, that it is the common view that the human soul is later [in origin] than the framing of body. So in the case of things
25   of which it is doubtful whether there was a beginning to their being or not he holds that the first problem of all that should be investigated when considering them is whether they have always been, having no beginning to their generation and their existence, or whether they
176,1   have had a beginning to their being, not having existed previously. Therefore, since there are those who suppose that the world has

existed indefinitely and is without a beginning and those who suppose that it has had a beginning, not having existed previously, Plato
has with reason undertaken to look into this ahead of the other
questions that arise in connection with it.   5

And if one thinks that it is doubtful in the case of the entire world
whether it has its existence from God or not, and if the same applies
to each individual [part] as to the whole, then surely one would have
to suppose that it applied *a fortiori* to intelligibles. So Plato would be
inquiring in the passage under discussion (*en toutois*) whether any-   10
thing that exists at all has come to be through the agency of God
rather than each thing being the cause of its own existence. This is
equivalent to asking whether God is a creator at all or whether he is
entirely devoid of any such power. For anyone who thought it appropriate to ask in regard to everything there is whether it has its   15
existence from God would in effect be treating it as an open question
whether God has the power to create at all.

Unless, then, Plato, matching the godlessness of the Epicureans,   20
has decided that there is so much doubt in regard to God's creative
activity that he thinks it appropriate to ask about each thing that
exists whether it has God as the cause of its existence or not, and
whether God is a creator at all or not, [the words] 'whether it has come
to be or is ungenerated (*agenês*)'[215] (which are cast in the form of a
[dialectical] problem) are not asking whether the [world] has come to
be or not come to be with respect to causation.   25

Here is another argument. How could it be other than irrational to
invoke God as a co-worker in one's investigation of the world on the
ground that he is the cause of all good things, even the most insignifi-
cant, and then express doubt and puzzlement as to whether the
universe has received its existence from God? For at the outset of his   177,1
discourse on the world Plato's Timaeus speaks[216] as follows:

> Yes, Socrates, everyone with any sense at all certainly always
> invokes the gods at the outset of any undertaking, however   5
> small it may be. So, if we aren't completely out of our minds, we
> who are about to discuss with regard to the universe whether it
> has come to be or is ungenerated must invoke the gods and
> goddesses and pray that all that we say shall above all be
> pleasing to them, and secondly to ourselves.   10

So if it is usual for everyone, however little sense they may have, to
invoke God at the outset of every undertaking, however small, and if
this very act of supplicating God and seeking his assistance in all   15
things is that of one who accepts his mastery and dominion over all
things and that it is from him that being and well-being flow for all
things, how could it be other than irrational and a lapse into grossly
contradictory statements in regard to the same subject for Plato to

say that God should be invoked [to assist in] investigating whether
the universe has received its existence from God or whether, on the
20   contrary, the world is the cause of its own being? This would be
tantamount to saying that one should invoke him who is the cause of
the universe to assist in an investigation of the universe [which will
consider] whether he is the cause of the universe or not. Therefore
25   [the words] 'whether the world has come to be or is ungenerated'[217] do
not mean for Plato that it has either come to be or is ungenerated with
respect to causation.
178,1   And here is another consideration that shows the impossibility [of
their reading]. Plato writes:[218]

> We must in my opinion begin by making a distinction between
> that which always is and has no generation and that which
> 5   comes to be but never is. The former may be grasped by thought
> using reason, the latter may be conjectured by belief along with
> irrational sensation.

Now since the generated with respect to time and the ungenerated
with respect to time are opposed to each other, as too are the generated with respect to causation and the ungenerated with respect to
causation, and since Plato opposes the generated to the ungenerated
10   (he writes 'we must first make a distinction between that which
always is and has no generation and that which comes to be but never
is') and says that everything perceptible is generated and everything
intelligible is ungenerated, there is every necessity that if by that
which comes to be he means that which comes to be only with respect
15   to causation, then by that which does not come to be he likewise
means that which does not come to be with respect to causation. But
he says that everything intelligible is ungenerated. Therefore he
means that everything intelligible is ungenerated with respect to
causation. And therefore, according to them, Plato holds that God is
not the cause of any of the intelligibles. And therefore God will be the
20   creator only of perceptible things. And if this were so, there would no
longer be a single origin (*arkhê*) for all things but each intelligible will
itself be the cause of its own existence and there will be as many
origins (*arkhê*) as there are intelligibles. So, [as we have seen,] it is
25   worth looking [closely] at the absurdity they foist upon the philosopher as a result of this extraordinary hypothesis of theirs.
    Not that these are [really] the views of Plato. On the subject of the
cause of all things he writes[219] in his letter to Dionysius:

179,1   All things exist in relation to the king of all, and all things exist
on his account, and that is the cause of all beautiful things.

and again, in the fourth book of the *Laws*:[220]

God, as the ancient account has it, holding the beginning, the
end and the middle of all things that exist, completes his un-   5
swerving course, revolving according to nature['s laws],

the ancient account that he refers to being either that of Orpheus,
who writes:

Zeus was first, Zeus of the bright lightning is last, Zeus is the
head, Zeus is the middle, through Zeus all things are wrought,[221]

or the notion that all men hold in common of the god that presides   10
over all things, inasmuch as he is the cause of all things. At all events
Aristotle, as we mentioned a little earlier,[222] says[223] in the book that
he has written about the world that:

it is an ancient and ancestral tradition among all men that all   15
things come from God and that it is thanks to God that they
exist for our benefit, and that there is nothing in nature that is
independent and self-sufficient and entirely without the maintenance he provides.

And again the same [Aristotle], in book twelve of his *Metaphysics*,[224]
having demonstrated that the cause and beginning of all things is   20
one, repeats Homer's apophthegm that:

the rule of many is not a good thing; let there be one ruler.

But what need is there to adduce further evidence from these
[philosophers] when the matter is clear to all [and] when [Plato]
shows God as the creator of both the soul of the world, which is
intelligible, and of all rational souls in the *Timaeus*?[225]   25
So if Plato actually believes that God is the cause of all things, of
those that are first, of those in the middle, and of those that are last,
then when he says that intelligibles have not come to be, he does not   180,1
mean that they have not come to be with respect to causation, but
that they have not come to be with respect to time. And if he has
acknowledged that intelligibles do not come to be and that perceptible   5
things, which he has set in opposition to them, do come to be, and if
he has set the generated in opposition to the ungenerated in the same
way as he has the perceptible to the intelligible, then he is also saying
here that perceptible things have come to be with respect to time and
not [that they have come to be] with respect to causation; he will talk
about their efficient cause a little later.   10
19. If, in reply to the above, someone were to claim that by 'that
which comes to be' Plato means 'that which comes to be with respect
to causation' but by 'that which does not come to be' not 'that which

is ungenerated with respect to causation' but 'that which is ungenerated with respect to time', he would, through his own lack of
education, be accusing the philosopher of a profound ignorance of the
15   technique of division since that which is ungenerated with respect to
time is encompassed by that which is generated only with respect to
causation but not with respect to time. And indeed, according to
them, the world, being generated only[226] with respect to causation, is
20   ungenerated with respect to time; and rational souls likewise. But [in
carrying out a division] nobody opposes an including [class] to an
included. Rational [creature], for example, is not opposed to living
creature. One will not[227] say that of animate creatures with the
faculty of reason, some are living creatures, others rational [crea-
25   tures], for rational [creature] is included in living creature. And nor
[will one say] that of things there are, some are substances, others
bodies. In this case body is included in substance. What we actually
say is that of living creatures, some are terrestrial, others aquatic
181,1   (neither of these is included in the other), and, again, of things there
are, some are substances, others accidents. And no more, therefore,
will that which is ungenerated with respect to time be opposed to that
5   which is generated with respect to causation because, as I said,[228] that
which is ungenerated with respect to time is encompassed by that
which is generated only with respect to causation.

But why should I waste words attempting to prove what is obvious
[to everyone, namely,] that Plato was the first and almost the only
[philosopher] to observe the [full] rigour of the technique of division,
that he continually sings its praises and dubs it the coping-stone of
philosophy,[229] and that he finds fault with those who, like bad butchers,
10   divide things up without taking their joints into account?[230] Plato explicitly tells us in the text [of the *Timaeus*] that he opposes the intelligible
and the perceptible and being and non-being. His words are:

We must in my opinion begin by making a distinction between
15   that which always is and has no generation and that which is
always coming to be but never is. The former may be grasped by
thought with the aid of reason, the latter may be conjectured by
belief along with irrational sensation.[231]

And so Plato would not have botched the division into generated and
ungenerated by opposing that which is ungenerated with respect to
time but not ungenerated with respect to causation to that which is
20   generated only with respect to causation but not with respect to time.
Observe, at any rate, how in this passage too the antithesis that he
constructs is between things that are opposed in all respects, for he
sets not-being in opposition to being and 'never' to 'always'. And since
25   the being he is referring to is not the being which is opposed to
182,1   complete not-being (to that kind of not-being is opposed that which is

in existence in any way at all) but that which is in the sense that it is always completely the same and unchanging and is never observed to undergo change or alteration, in order to oppose its opposite to *that* kind of being, he sets in opposition to it not that which is not through non-existence but that which is never completely the same because it is observed to be in continuous alteration. So just as the opposition that he constructs in this passage is between things which are opposed in all respects and are unable to coexist, so, surely, when he sets that which comes to be in opposition to that which does not come to be,[232] is he [quite] consistently constructing a division into contradictories, for that which comes to be and that which does not come to be are unable to coexist with one another.

And so if 'not having a generation' does not mean 'not coming to be with respect to causation', but 'not having a temporal beginning to its being', it is certainly necessary that 'coming to be' should likewise mean the opposite of that, that is to say, 'having had a temporal beginning to its being'; and, conversely, if 'coming to be' means 'coming to be with respect to causation' and not with respect to time, then 'not coming to be' likewise means 'not coming to be with respect to causation'.[233]

But we have shown[234] that this verges on impiety and is false, for Plato everywhere states it as a philosophical principle (*pantakhou pephilosophêken*) that the cause of all things is one. So if this is false, 'always being and having no generation' must mean 'ungenerated with respect to time'. And therefore the 'generated' which is opposed to this means 'generated with respect to time'.

20. But what need is there to deal with these matters at length when it is possible to provide concise proof that Plato does not use 'comes to be' or 'has come to be' to describe generation with respect to causation anywhere in the passages we have been considering (*en toutois*)? For having talked of generation and beginning with respect to time in the passage where he says 'it has come to be; for it is visible and tangible and has body',[235] because he is aware that certain of the natural philosophers[236] who preceded him believed that the world has come to be from some beginning and is not everlasting, but almost all of them save one were ignorant of its efficient cause and only gave an account of its material causes, as though the production of form and [the advent of] order take place spontaneously, and only [this man,] Anaxagoras, as though awaking from a dream, as Plato himself says,[237] set mind over the universe and credited it with being the creative cause, Plato himself, after arguing that the world has come to be and has had a beginning to its being, immediately goes on without a break to tell of its efficient cause,[238] saying 'and, once more, we say that what has come to be must come to be by the agency of some cause; for it is impossible for anything to have a generation without a cause'.[239] [And] he does not put this forward in the form of

20   a problem but as one who draws a conclusion that follows from
previously accepted [premisses]; for once it is agreed that a thing is
generated it is immediately and self-evidently also implied that there
is an efficient cause of this generation. So without a doubt either
184,1   nature or art is the efficient cause of each thing that has come to be.
The natural philosophers who came before him, once they had agreed
that the world has come to be, should have drawn the same conclusion
and at once found their way back to[240] its efficient cause. Aristotle too
5   rebukes them for [failing to do] this in the second book of the *Physics*.[241] It is a matter for amazement, he says, that, although they said
that in the case of animals and plants nothing either exists or comes
to be by chance and held nature or mind responsible for everything
that comes to be in these spheres, they claimed that the heaven and
10   the most divine of visible things [i.e. the heavenly bodies] have arisen
spontaneously, and this although order is inescapable in the universe
and nothing has come about[242] by chance in the heaven. So for this
15   reason Plato too, having shown that the world is generated, deduced
from this its efficient cause.

But if, as [these] learned men believe, he has already told us about
the efficient cause in the passage where he says[243] that the world has
come to be, having started from some beginning, how is it that, as
though he has not previously mentioned it, he now adds 'and, once
20   more, we say that what has come to be must come to be by the agency
of some cause; for it is impossible for anything to have a generation
without a cause'?[244]

The matter can also be looked at in this way. If 'to have come to be,
having started from some beginning' meant to have come to be with
respect to causation, that is to say, to have an efficient cause of its
existence (and if, after saying 'It has come to be', he had continued
25   'and, once more, we say that what has come to be must come to be by
the agency of some cause'), he would have been saying something like
this: 'and, once more, we say that what has come to be from some
185,1   cause must come to be by the agency of some cause'. And this would
amount to saying that something that comes to be through the agency
of a cause comes to be through the agency of a cause, which is
ridiculous.

5   But even earlier, in the passage where he writes 'that which
always is and has no generation and that which is always coming to
be but never is',[245] Plato has once more made it clear that there too he
is not referring to generation with respect to causation but to generation with respect to time, all but saying 'of things there are, some
10   always are, while others have had a beginning to their being and to
their coming to be'. For after distinguishing between 'what always is
and has no generation and what is always coming to be but never is',
because he has been teaching [us] about things that either always are
or come to be with respect to time, he at once adds [a reference to] the

efficient cause of those that come to be when he writes[246] 'but every-   15
thing that comes to be necessarily comes to be through the agency of
some cause; for it is impossible for anything to have a generation
without a cause'. [And] he obviously talks throughout of generation
and of the efficient cause separately because, as far as he is concerned, [a thing's] coming to be does not indicate [the operation of] an   20
efficient cause; for [otherwise] the addition of 'but everything that
comes to be necessarily comes to be through the agency of some cause'
would be superfluous. For if when he says[247] 'it has come to be; for it
is visible and tangible and has body', he means by 'having come to be'
not 'having a beginning to its being' but 'having come to be through   25
the agency of some efficient cause', why does he also add 'but everything that comes to be necessarily comes to be through the agency of
some cause'? This would again be equivalent to saying 'everything   186,1
that comes to be through the agency of an efficient cause comes to be
through the agency of an efficient cause', which is ridiculous.

Therefore for [Plato] 'having come to be' means not 'having come to   5
be with respect to causation' but 'having a beginning to its being'.

21. It is a matter for amazement how these learned Platonic
commentators [first] muddy the waters by dreaming up a host of
meanings for 'generated' and then, so as not to seem to be contradicting the doyen of all philosophers when he puts forward the hypothesis
that the world is generated with respect to time, concede, as though   10
losing heart in the face of the refutation provided by the truth and
forgetting about their own arguments, that the world is indeed
described by Plato as generated in the sense that it has come to be
from some beginning without having previously existed but claim
that these things are being said [purely] hypothetically by the   15
philosopher for the sake of clarity of exposition and not because the
nature of things is really thus. For instance, the previously-
mentioned[248] Platonic commentator Taurus, commenting in his commentary on the *Timaeus* on the lemma 'we who are about to discuss
with regard to the universe whether it has come to be or is ungener-   20
ated',[249] writes, to quote his exact words, as follows:

Even though it is ungenerated. And the Poet[250] [likewise] 'even
though it were[251] later in birth'. And [this is] proof that the world
is ungenerated. At any rate he is saying that he will 'say[252] that
it has come to be, even though it is ungenerated'; for even in the   25
case of things that are ungenerated accounts (*logoi*) [which treat
them] as generated are produced as an aid to exposition.[253]   187,1

And again, a little later, the same man writes:

What then are the reasons for his hypothesising that the world
is generated when it is ungenerated? They are two, both philo-

5   sophical. The first exhorts to piety, the second is employed for
the sake of clarity.[254]

Because he is aware that most people only think of something
that is prior in time as a cause and believe that otherwise (*allôs*)
there is no cause, and there is a danger that they will as a result
start looking closely at the existence of providence, and because
10   he wishes to implant the belief that the world is governed by
providence, for the sake of those who are capable of understanding that this is so even otherwise (*allôs*)[255] he provides a
subtle hint that the world is ungenerated with respect to time,
but for the sake of those who cannot[256] [grasp this] he describes
it as generated and prays that they believe what he says in the
15   hope that they will at the same time be persuaded about providence.

And the second reason is that an account [of something] is
clearer when we encounter it as though it is actually taking
place. In this way people construct diagrams that have not
[really] been constructed as though they are [in the process of]
being generated.[257] Euclid, [for example,] because it was [a]
simpler [figure], defined the circle as 'a figure circumscribed by
20   a single line [such that] all of the straight lines meeting it from
[just] one of the points within it are equal to each other',[258] but
because he wanted to show the sphere as though [in the process
188,1   of] being generated, defined it as 'a semicircle rotating, while its
diameter remains stationary, until it returns to the same point',
although if he had wanted [to describe] one already in existence,
he would have defined it as 'a figure circumscribed by a single
surface [such that] all of the straight lines meeting it from [just]
5   one of the points within it are equal to each other'.[259] And it was
Plato's practice to present things in the process of development
for the sake of exposition. In this way in the *Republic*,[260] for
example, he shows the city as it develops so that the origins of
justice will become clearer during its establishment.

10   [It is true that] Theophrastus, after remarking that 'perhaps
he describes it as generated for the sake of clarity, in the way
that we follow diagrams as they develop', continues 'but perhaps
[its] generation is not of the same nature as that of diagrams'.[261]
And Aristotle says[262] the same thing. For he too asserts that in
15   the case of diagrams it is possible to postulate [the presence of]
contraries at the start but that it is not possible in the case of
the generation of the world, as though one were postulating [the
presence of] movement and rest, and order and disorder [at the
same time].[263] But rather than demanding that all of these
models be exactly alike, let them show that the world is *not* more
20   easily understood if it is assumed to be in the process of coming
to be than if he had described it as ungenerated. And how *can*

[the presence of] contraries be postulated even in diagrams? How could one postulate that a triangle is at rest and in movement at the same time?

So the world is in [Plato's] view ungenerated. And nobody should bother trying to show that it is generated from the *Atlantikos*[264] or the *Statesman*.[265] He will not find anything in his other writings able to serve as evidence that it is generated in the[266] *Timaeus*; the world is no less ungenerated in them.   189,1

How [the world] is [in fact] ungenerated and the reasons why [Plato nevertheless] describes it as generated has [now] been stated. So in so far as he hypothesises that it is generated it will be imperishable on account of God, but in so far as he [really] knows it to be ungenerated it will be imperishable on account of its own nature, just as all other ungenerated things are imperishable.   5

That is what the man says. And Porphyry,[267] and all who have come after him down to the present day, claim that the world is described by Plato as generated with respect to time [purely] hypothetically for the sake of clarity of exposition.   10

And let nobody accuse us of idle chatter because we are spending time on the refutation of views of this kind. If any of the arguments recorded above seem worthy of credence to anyone, then, I imagine, our refutation [of them] will certainly also seem in order (*akolouthos*). But should anyone have considered [their] hypothesis unconvincing, then it is assuredly not the person who reaps the corn but the one who has sown the seed who is responsible for the harvest. And what has seemed an unconvincing position to one person often strikes the mind of another as convincing. We must proclaim the truth free of all obstruction.[268]   15   20

Well then, if Plato (whatever his reasons may be for so hypothesising) hypothetically describes the world as having come to be with respect to time 'even though it is ungenerated',[269] what need[270] was there for them to waste words on the enumeration of the many senses of 'generated'? If Plato hypothesises a beginning to the generation of the world for the sake of piety or exposition, then it could no longer be true that the world is described by him as generated in one of the senses listed above.[271] In that case, both the 'objective of piety' and the 'method of exposition' will have gone by the board. For it is not possible at one and the same time to describe the world both as generated in [one or more of] those senses and, for the sake of either piety or didactic method, as having a beginning to its being. For if when he describes the world as generated he means that it is generated with respect to causation or in the sense that it is composite and not [that it is generated] with respect to time, how can they claim that it is being hypothesised to come to be and have a beginning to its   25   190,1   5   10 being for the sake of piety or exposition? The former position is destructive of the latter.

Besides, if Plato, as they claim, hypothesises that the world is
15   generated with respect to time for the sake of clarity of exposition, then he would certainly have said in so many words 'it is by nature ungenerated', but for the sake of clarity let us think of it as coming to be', so that nobody would take what was being put forward hypothetically for plain truth.
20   Moreover, to believe that Plato for piety's sake assigns a beginning of generation to the world even though it is ungenerated so that God's providence in regard to it will be believed is silly in the extreme. In the first place, he teaches this clearly everywhere in that he puts God
25   in control of the creation of the universe and explains the reasons for God's having made each thing the way it is. What need would he have had of a false hypothesis to teach what he had been teaching without
191,1   it? And, secondly, their hypothesis will involve his leading men into the worst kind of impiety. For if God must, if the world has not existed from everlasting, have, as they hold, of necessity been neither perfect
5   nor good before the world existed, and if Plato, as they claim, adopts the hypothesis that the world has come to be from some beginning, and indeed prays that this will be believed, without anywhere indi-
10   cating his reasons for doing so, then, by refraining from saying in any of the dialogues that the world is ungenerated but on the contrary everywhere loudly proclaiming its generation, he is persuading those who believe him to accept impious notions. And, moreover, although he also wishes rational souls to be governed by God's providence, he loudly and clearly proclaims in the *Phaedrus*[272] that they are ungenerated without the least fear that they will be deemed to be bereft of it.

15   **22.** Moreover, it is extremely audacious to alter the meanings of[273] words so readily. For in fact [this] Platonic commentator[274] thinks that the disjunctive or interrogative conjunction 'or' is being used for[275] the hypothetical conjunction 'if' in accord with a poetic usage.
20   Later[276] I shall quote a passage in which the Aristotelian commentator Alexander [of Aphrodisias] refutes [the claim that there is] such a substitution of conjunctions,[277] and in my opinion its absurdity is self-evident. In the first place, to accept poetic substitutions as a feature of Platonic[278] prose[279] is one of the most absurd things imag-
25   inable, especially when the Poet [sc. Homer] used such substitutions of conjunctions rarely or even just once, as those who have scrutinised his writings indicate.[280] And besides, even though this violent substitution of conjunctions would have been possible in the present
192,1   passage, what follows could not be treated in the same way. For just as Plato opposes the ungenerated to the generated in the present passage when he says,[281] defining the goal he has set himself, that he is going to consider whether the universe has come to be or is

ungenerated, so does he immediately afterwards express this [same 5
question] in the form of a [dialectical] problem[282] when he asks[283]
'whether it has always been, having no beginning [to its] generation,
or has come to be, having started from some beginning'. So if in this
latter passage he is clearly stating that he is considering whether the
world always is, having no beginning [to its] generation, or has come 10
to be, having started from some beginning, expressing these alternatives in the form of a puzzle without subscribing to the view that the
world is ungenerated, then even more surely is it the case that in the
earlier passage, where he gives notice that he is going to investigate
in this work 'whether the universe has come to be or is ungenerated', 15
he is not using 'or is ungenerated' for 'even though it is ungenerated'
and the conjunction 'or' has the sense that it properly bears in a
puzzle[284] and disjoins ungenerated and generated, so that only one of
them, and not, as Taurus believes, both, is being hypothesised of the 20
world.

And besides, if one were to take 'it has come to be'[285] in one of the
senses listed by Taurus, one would, I assume, also have to take 'not
having come to be' as the negation of that same sense; for a negation
denies what an affirmation asserts. So if they take 'it has come to be' 25
as equivalent to 'it has come to be with respect to causation', then 'not
having come to be' ('not having come to be' is equivalent to 'ungenerated') must be understood to mean 'not having come to be with respect
to causation'. The whole sentence would then read 'we who are about
to discuss with regard to the universe whether it has come to be with 193,1
respect to causation or is ungenerated with respect to causation'. And
the same [would apply] in the case of the other senses [so that we
would get] 'whether it is composite or is not composite', [or] 'whether
it has its being in coming to be or does not have its being in coming to 5
be'. But what could be more ridiculous than this? The man has,
without due consideration, changed the [meaning of the] phrase[286]
straight off,[287] without first checking to see whether his interpretation is going to be in every respect consistent in what is said by Plato
later as well.

And those who alter[288] 'or is ungenerated' to 'or is always coming 10
to be' involve themselves in the same absurdity. For by changing
'ungenerated' to 'always coming to be' they too are in their turn
introducing something that is not present [in the text].[289] But, ironi-
cally, as a result of this addition, they are unwittingly advocating
something closer to the truth and arguing the opposite of what they 15
intend. If the question that Plato is putting is 'whether the universe
has come to be or is perhaps always coming to be', there is every
necessity that when he opposes 'having come to be' and 'always
coming to be' he means by 'having come to be' having come to be from
a [point of] time and not always existing. So when, in what [immedi- 20
ately] follows, Plato looks at this problem and determines that the

world has come to be (he says[290] 'it has come to be; for it is visible and tangible, etc.'), it is clear, even after their shameless tampering with the text, that he is denying the continuous becoming of the world.

25

194,1

23. To the senses of 'generated' enumerated [above] some add the following [additional one]. They say that the universe is described as generated by Plato because it is in everlasting movement. Hence, they say, he describes it as coming to be and perishing but never truly being[291] for none of the heavenly bodies ever remains in the same place.

The reply to this is brief.

5

In the first place, Plato is concerned with the whole world and not just the heavenly bodies, and the universe, as long as it is in existence, does not move or change in any way at all as a whole but remains in the same place. And so Plato is not using 'come to be' instead of 'be in movement'.

10

15

20

Secondly, the fact that the heavenly bodies are in continuous movement is recognised by our senses and we need nothing but our eyes to grasp it. Surely Plato is making himself ridiculous if he says, as though about to tell us of secrets that have neither been comprehended by nor revealed to any of his predecessors, that he must invoke the gods and goddesses to join him in investigating the universe in order to determine whether the heavenly bodies exhibit local movement or are motionless,[292] being so unobservant that he makes things which, because they are known through sense-perception, have stronger warrant than any deductive proof [can provide] the subject of a [dialectical] problem. Who with any sense would ask whether fire burns or if white lead is white? And so Plato is not describing the world as generated in this sense either. So, since all of [their] hypotheses as to [the meaning of] 'generated' have been re-

25

195,1

futed, and the only one that is left is the normal, everyday one, I mean [that it is] generation with respect to time, and since Plato explicitly declares that the world is generated and has come to be, the only remaining possibility is that Plato describes it as generated with respect to time, that is, as having had a beginning to its being – for

5

this, as we have often stated, is what '[generated] with respect to time' means in the case of the world.

24. Since they advance as a factor which is strong evidence[293] that the world is not [really] being said by Plato to be generated with

10

respect to time but [only] hypothetically the fact that in the *Timaeus*[294] soul is similarly represented as coming to be but in the *Phaedrus*[295] is clearly affirmed to be ungenerated, I consider it reasonable to devote a few words to the dismantling of this ingenious [fabrication] of theirs as well.

Now, it is plain to everyone that the rational soul is part of intelligible substance and therefore has a being (*ousian*) which is

15

separable from all body; when it submits to a relation with body, it is

potentially intellect, but the status and name of soul accrue to it
through its relation to body – for it is called soul because it animates[296]
body and gives it life; but when it has been separated from the body,   20
whether through [an acquired] capacity[297] or through being unyoked
from the physical bond[298] at the same time, and thereafter operates
on the intellectual plane and grasps the nature of things by direct
apprehension, it is from that very moment intellect in actuality and
referred to as such. And so it is soul in one respect, intellect in   25
another, and at one time exists in relation with body, at another by
itself, without any relation and freed from the body, just as, for   196,1
instance, the same person is both a man and a helmsman, but the
former in his own right, the latter through the relation that he has to
a ship.[299] This being so, if the *Timaeus* teaches the generation of soul
in so far as it is intellect and without relation to body, we shall, since 5
he declares in the *Phaedrus* that this is ungenerated, concede that he
is describing it as having come to be [purely] hypothetically. But if, in
the *Timaeus*, he is explaining the nature of the relation that it has to   10
body *qua* soul, in virtue of which it orders and moves the heavenly
bodies in this way or that, what need is there in that case for him to
be speaking hypothetically when, in the *Timaeus*, he describes it as
coming to be, if, as we have shown,[300] Plato assigns a beginning of
being to the whole world? As soon, then, as the bodily element in the
universe came into existence the soul entered into a relation with it;   15
for even when they talk of *our* soul coming to be in the body they are
not, I assume, predicating generation of its substance but of the
relation within the body, which takes its beginning from a [point] of
time.

And that what is written in the *Timaeus* about the generation of   20
the soul is doing nothing else but teaching the movements of the
heavenly bodies and the relations to one another which they derive
(if they are indeed, as Plato believes, animate) from soul, can be
proved from the words of the *Timaeus* itself. For Plato says there[301]   25
that God, taking the being that is midway between the being which
is indivisible and is always in the same state and the being which is
divisible in the region of bodies and along with it sameness and
otherness, mixed these three together and stretched them out into a   197,1
straight [strip] and then, cutting this [strip] up according to harmonic
ratios, split it lengthwise into two, then having joined these two strips
together to form a cross, bent [each of] them round and joined their
ends together to make two circles, an outer one and an inner one,   5
joined to each other at two points, and then started the outer circle
moving to the right, the inner to the left and, he says, called the outer
one the revolution of the Same, the inner [the revolution] of the   10
Other, and left the outer circle unsplit but split the inner at six places
to make seven unequal circles, exceeding each other by the double
and triple intervals, making three of them equal in speed (*tôi takhei*

15   *tês kinêseôs*) but the other four unequal in speed (*têi kinêsei*) both to
each other and to the three. Given that this is what Plato has to say
in the *Timaeus* about the generation of the soul, is anyone so inept at
distinguishing the truth that they will not concede from [these] words
alone[302] that Plato is here teaching the movement of the heavenly
20   spheres and their relations to one another, which he believes derives
from soul which is mounted upon them – especially when in other
living creatures both movement and the arrangement and relation to
25   one another of the parts of the body originate from the soul within
them? So Plato is, in the riddling manner of the Pythagoreans,
referring everything in the effect that comes about through the
agency of the cause back to the cause, just as we often say that the
198,1   soul hungers or thirsts, referring the awareness of a lack which arises
in the body through the agency of the soul back to the soul itself.

For those who are interested, a more detailed examination of these
matters may be found in the earlier commentators we mentioned
5   above.[303] They too, even though they claim that the world is everlasting and that it is [merely] hypothetically that Plato teaches the
generation of the soul, nevertheless understand the outer circle in
this passage as the sphere of the fixed stars and the inner, by splitting
which at six points [God] made the seven circles of the planets, as
10   those of the planets.[304] (Some understand the outer circle as the
celestial equator and the inner as the zodiac, which, cutting each
other crosswise, touch at two points [in] Aries and Libra. This is
15   because the sphere of the fixed stars has the same axis as the celestial
equator and moves around its poles while the planetary spheres move
around those of the zodiac). The outer of these circles, namely, the
sphere of the fixed stars, God, says Plato, set in movement to the
20   right, and the inner, that is to say, the planetary spheres, to the left,
calling the eastern parts the right and the western the left as does
Homer, who for his part writes:

whether they go to the right, towards the east and the sun,
or to the left, towards the murky gloom.[305]

25   For the sphere of the fixed stars does move from east to west and the
planetary spheres vice versa. He calls the movement of the outer
circle that of the Same because of the sameness of the movement of
199,1   the fixed stars; for all of the fixed stars carry out movements of equal
duration and travel around the same circle, always rising from the
same points and setting at the same points. The inner movement, on
5   the other hand, that is to say, that of the planets, [God] called, says
[Plato], that of the Other, evidently because of the differences in the
movements of the planets. Their movements are not of equal duration
and not the same for each. They do not each travel around one and
10   the same circle nor does a given planet always have its risings and

settings at the same points. He says that of the seven inner circles three are equal to each other in speed (he means that of the sun, that of the morning star, and the one that is named for Hermes; for these planets, keeping pace [with one another], travel around the whole   15
circle in a year) and the remaining four (that is the spheres that are named for Kronos and Ares and Zeus and that of the moon) unequal both to each other and to these [sc. the three], that of Kronos traveling around its circle in approximately thirty years, that of Zeus in almost   20
twelve, that of Ares, for its part, in approximately two and that of the moon in a month.

They need, then, to take care that they are not creating difficulties for Plato in regard to his account of the generation of the soul when they persist in trying to persuade us that Plato believes that the world is ungenerated and is giving us a [merely] hypothetical account of its generation. And besides, if this were true, why has he not, just   25
as he elsewhere explicitly declares the soul to be ungenerated,[306] brought himself to tell us in one or other of his works that the world   200,1
too is ungenerated, but on the contrary everywhere loudly declared that it is generated and has come to be and is by nature dissoluble?

25. Since Porphyry claims that Plato's proofs relating to the coming to be of the world are not such as to prove that the world has   5
come to be with respect to time and from this draws the conclusion that Plato does not in fact mean that it has come to be with respect to time, I think it makes sense to consider this question too, beginning by quoting Porphyry's own words. This is what he says: 10

Further, let us see which sense [of 'generated'] Plato predicates of the world and what his question is and which [sense of 'generated'] it best fits. [For argument's sake,] let us suppose that he is employing [the sense] that indicates generation from a [point of] time, that the question he is asking is 'whether [the world] has always existed, never having come to be from a [point   15
of] time, or has come to be, having started from some begin-ning',[307] and that his answer is that it has, on account of the proofs he provides, come to be from some temporal beginning. What, then, are these [proofs]? 'For it is visible and tangible', he says, 'and has body, and, [as we have seen], all such perceptible things, since they may be grasped by belief along with sensation,   20
clearly come to be and are generated'. What could be more ridiculous than this? How does it necessarily follow that if it is visible and tangible and has body, it came to be with the begin-ning of time?

Self-evidence constitutes the strongest necessity of all, stronger than any deductive proof. Tell me, my fine fellow (*ô thaumasie*), how   25
you establish the necessity of *your* argument when you claim that

Plato holds that the world is generated in that it is composite and
assert that he offers as proof of this the fact that it is visible, tangible
201,1   and has body? By what necessity is everything visible immediately
5   also composite? Surely you invoke the senses as your witnesses,
which for us human beings are certainly more to be relied upon than
any argument? But we too agree that anything visible is composite.
But just because visibility implies composition and, moreover, according to Plato everything that is visible is also generated, it does not
necessarily follow that Plato uses 'generated' as a synonym for 'composite'. Anything that is visible and tangible and corporeal will also
10   as a consequence necessarily be three-dimensional, of finite size,
always have shape, whether that shape be regular or irregular, and
be continuous, and nobody would on that account believe that Plato
15   uses 'generated' to mean any of these. For why should one use
'generated' to mean 'composite' any more than 'finite' or 'continuous'
or 'having shape' or any of the other necessary attributes of every
20   thing that has body? Each of these other things follows from being
perceptible just as much as does being composite.

  And we have only recently[308] demonstrated that the world cannot
possibly be described as generated by Plato on the ground that it is
composite.

  And we also affirm that Plato drew his evidence that not only
composition but generation with respect to time as well is invariably
associated with visibility and perceptibility in general from the ob-
25   served facts. For Plato expressly states[309] that the whole world is
composed of the four elements – and Porphyry himself agrees with
202,1   this, as we shall show[310] when we get to the thirteenth proof[311] of
5   Proclus. For those with eyes, simple observation provides proof that
all of the elements in all of their particular manifestations are generated and perishable. Any part of water or fire or earth or air that one
cares to consider has invariably come to be in time and had a
beginning to its being. And if all of the parts of water have come to be
10   in time, and if the whole is nothing other than all its parts, then the
whole too has come into existence at some point in time, with the
result that the elemental masses[312] are numerically different at different times. [It is true that] the transition of the elements into each
other, which, because of the stability of the universe, takes place by
15   replacement of what is lost, always seems to keep the elemental mass
numerically the same: as water perishes it changes into, say, air, and
air as it perishes in turn changes to water and restores the deficit of
water, and the same applies to all [such alterations]. But just as a
20   shipwright may from time to time replace damaged planking on a
ship until he has eventually replaced the whole ship and turned it
into a numerically different whole, so is it with an elemental mass;
one part or other is always perishing and another coming to be in its
25   place, with the result that over a long period of time the whole

elemental mass changes. So if not even the elemental masses remain numerically the same, and if that which does not remain numerically the same has both begun to exist in time and perishes in time, it is clear that the elemental masses are, along with their parts, generated   203,1
and perishable with respect to time.

And if we do not have knowledge of the original formation of the elements, that does not make it reasonable for us to think that they   5
have not had a beginning to their existence; the fact that they are currently subject to passing in and out of existence in their individual parts constitutes very adequate evidence that they have also had a beginning to their existence. And, further, everything which is, like plants, animals, minerals or anything else corporeal, composed of the elements both comes to be and perishes in time. Therefore if every visible and tangible (or, [to put it more] generally, perceptible) corpo-   10
real entity is either an element or [formed] from the elements, and if these have been shown to be generated with respect to time, then every perceptible corporeal entity is generated with respect to time. So if the heaven, which, according to Plato, consists of these same   15
elements, is a visible and tangible corporeal entity, then the heaven too should be generated with respect to time; for [the nature of] what is hidden becomes clear through [observation of] what is visible.

And for the same reason it will, according to Plato, also be, as far as the law of nature goes, perishable.

And, besides, it would seem to be irrational that, whereas the   20
elements of the universe always have a temporal beginning and are numerically different at different times, the heaven, which is composed of them, should never have had a beginning to its existence, never have an end to it, and in between never undergo any change or alteration to its substance. It is on the basis of this [logical] necessity   25
that Plato says that being generated with respect to time follows from being visible and from this infers that the world, being visible, is also generated.

And Plato could have reached this same conclusion by induction. If   204,1
each individual perceptible thing (an animal, say, or water, or fire) is generated with respect to time, and after it another and another [of the same kind], and if all particular instances of the elements and their masses [behave] in this way, then all visible things are gener-   5
ated. But the world too is visible. Therefore it too must be generated with respect to time.

Another argument: If we have shown[313] that Plato does not employ 'generated' in any of the senses that they have come up with (for he is referring to generation with respect to time), and if he defines all things that have not come to be (that is, have not come to be *with*   10
respect to time), as capable of being grasped by thought with the aid of reason, then it follows by conversion[314] by negation that everything that is *not* intelligible undergoes generation with respect to time. And

15   everything that is not intelligible is perceptible and tangible. Therefore everything that is perceptible and tangible is generated with
respect to time. And therefore in what comes next Plato is arguing
consistently with his initial hypothesis; for having said that everything that does not come to be with respect to time is intelligible, he
[quite] consistently says that everything that is perceptible rather
20   than intelligible is generated with respect to time.

      Therefore one must either refute the above [arguments] (I mean
[those to the effect] that the generation which he denies to things that
always exist is generation with respect to time and not some other
kind,[315] a point which we have proved[316] by many arguments), or,
should they remain unrefuted, if he says that a thing which is
25   ungenerated with respect to time is intelligible, then it will certainly
follow that everything that is perceptible rather than intelligible is
generated with respect to time.

      Therefore it is [quite] cogently and not [at all] invalidly that Plato
concludes from the fact that the world is perceptible that it also has
a temporal beginning.

205,1   **26.** It was adequately demonstrated earlier that when Plato
states that that which always is has no generation, the generation
that he is denying to it is none other than generation with respect to
time, but one might reach the same conclusion equally well from what
follows.

5   I imagine that it is clear to everyone that it is that which is
absolutely unchanging because it always remains exactly the same[317]
that Plato refers to as 'always being'. Anything that is observed to
undergo change or alteration he refers to as 'never being'. For a thing
10   that is changing is no longer what it is changing from and not yet
what it is changing into. So if a thing is observed in a state of
continuous change, it will never be but always be coming to be. That
this is what 'that which always is' means in Plato he explicitly tells
us himself when defining it. His words are '[the former], always
remaining the same and unchanging, may be grasped by thought
15   with the aid of reason'.[318] And it is also clear from the passage where
he says that that which comes to be never is; 'What', he [there] asks,
'is that which comes to be but never is?'[319] So, if 'that which comes to
be' (i.e. that which is in [a state of] change) 'never is', then 'that which
20   always is' is in every way unchanging. This means that [the phrase]
'and has no generation' is a clarification of 'that which always is', just
as 'but never is' [is a clarification] of 'that which comes to be'.

      This being the case, we should ask what kind of generation it is
that Plato denies of that which always is. My answer is that it is
25   generation with respect to time. A thing which is in every regard
devoid of temporal origin (*arkhê*)[320] is in every way unchanging, and,
conversely, if a thing has had a temporal origin with respect to
206,1   anything seen to be connected with it,[321] it is not absolutely unchang-

ing: in so far as it has had a beginning it has to that extent changed from not being to being. And so anything which is absolutely unchanging must be without a beginning with respect to time, for all change both takes place in time and takes its beginning from a [point of] time. And so anything which is without temporal origin is also devoid of all change. These terms, then, are convertible, and if something is completely unchanging, it is also above all temporal origin, and what[322] is devoid of all temporal origin is in all respects unchanging.

It is with reason, then, that he says that that which always is (i.e. that which is in every way unchanging) has no generation with respect to time. And if someone should take 'having no generation' to mean 'lacking composition', let him explain by what logic someone who has asked 'what is that which always is' (that is, that which always remains the same and unchanging) would add 'and lacks composition'. Even if one were to concede a thousand times over that that which always is (i.e. that which always remains the same and unchanging) is simple and incomposite, it will still not be the case that everything simple and incomposite always remains the same and unchanging. The primary components of corporeal things are simple, namely, matter and form – for the analysis of composite [entities] does not proceed *ad infinitum*, but in analysing anything we of necessity always descend to simple [entities] – and one would not claim that these simple [entities] are in the class of things which always remain the same. For enmattered forms, as we shall show a little further on,[323] dissolve into non-being and come back into existence again out of non-being, while matter takes on and casts off different forms at different times; so matter and form, although simple, are not in the class of things which always remain the same and unchanging. And even if enmattered forms were everlasting (which is impossible), because they appear in different substrata at different times (just as matter takes on different forms at different times), they still would not, any more than does the human soul, have the characteristic of always remaining the same and unchanging. And colours too are simple but do not always remain the same and unchanging. So if Plato takes 'always being' and 'having no generation' as equivalent and meaning the same thing (for if a thing is altogether without generation, and if 'simple and incomposite' is not equivalent to 'always being' – since not all things which are simple are things that always are – then 'always being' is not in every case consequent upon being simple and is not in a sense[324] convertible with it as 'always being' is with 'ungenerated'), then when he writes 'having no generation' he does not mean 'having no composition'.

And that it does not refer to generation with respect to causation we have adequately demonstrated earlier.[325] For Plato states that the first cause is [the cause] not only of perceptible things but of all

20   intelligibles as well, for the cause and origin (*arkhê*) of all things is
one; so if that which always is does not have a generation with respect
to causation, and if he says that everything intelligible and free of
generation always is, the first cause will not be [the cause] of all
25   things and the origin (*arkhê*) of things will be not one but many, which
is absurd. Therefore neither is it generation with respect to causation
that he is denying of things which always[326] are.

208,1   And that he does not by 'having no generation' mean 'having its
being in coming to be' is clear from his not saying 'not coming to be'
rather than 'having no generation' – for he refers to things that are in
continuous generation and change as coming to be rather than as
5   having generation, writing: 'What is that which comes to be but never
is?'

And besides, it is not the case that if something began its existence
from a [point in] time, it always has its being in coming to be and in
continuous change. Take, for example, the centre of a [geometrically]
constructed sphere or of a [geometrically] constructed circle. This has
10   had a beginning to its existence, but as long as it remains a centre is
qua such (*hêi toiouton estin*) completely motionless and unchanging.
Again, the knowledge that the three angles of a triangle are equal to
two right angles has a beginning to its existence in a particular mind,
15   in the mind of Plato, for example, and, as long as loss of memory does
not occur, remains the same and does not undergo change of any
kind.[327] And the particular triangle itself ([in] wood, for example, or
one drawn on the board [by the geometer]) with its three angles equal
to two right angles has similarly had a beginning to its existence, but
20   as long as it exists does not change *qua* triangle or in having its three
angles equal to two right angles. And so a triangle does not have its
being (that is, its [having its] three angles equal to two right[328] angles)
in coming to be. And the same could be shown of many other things.
Therefore it is not the case that everything which has a beginning to
25   its existence always has its being in continuous generation and
209,1   change. However, if a thing is completely *without* temporal origin, it
is also, as we have recently shown,[329] above all change.

Given [all of] this, if when he says that that which always is has no
generation, Plato means by denying generation of it to deny all
5   alteration and change of it, and if it is possible for a thing not to have
its being in coming to be and not to be in continuous alteration but
nevertheless have a beginning and an end to its existence and in that
respect not be inalterable, and if such a thing is not in the class of
10   things that always are or of things that always remain the same and
unchanging, then it was not this kind of generation (I mean [the kind
whereby a thing] has its being in coming to be) that Plato denied of
things that always are. So if, when he says that that which always is
has no generation, Plato is not denying generation of it in any of its
15   other senses, [the only alternative that] remains is that he is denying

generation with respect to time of it, which is what we set out to prove.

It is so as to rule out *a fortiori* all thought of change in regard to eternal things that he rules out a temporal origin for them. We observe that all change takes place in time and begins from some   20
point in time. So a thing which is outside all temporal origin is also outside all time, and a thing that is outside all time is also excluded from all change, since all change is with respect to time. So if [1] that which always is, is intelligible, and is eternal has no generation, while that which is perceptible, never is, and is not eternal is generated,   25
and if [2] the following [pairs] are opposed to one another: the intelligible to the perceptible; the non-eternal to the eternal; that which never is to that which always is; that which is ungenerated in any given sense to that which is in that same sense generated, and if   210,1
[3] the intelligible and the eternal do not have a generation with respect to time, then the perceptible and the non-eternal do have a generation with respect to time. For, as was shown in the *Topics*,[330] opposite [qualifications] belong to [each of a pair of] opposites in so   5
far as each is such. For example, if combining is a feature of black, separating is of white; if ruling is of a master, being ruled is of a slave; if seeing is of the possession of vision, not-seeing is of the lack of it; if unimpeded natural functioning is of being in good health, the failure   10
to perform natural functions in an unimpeded manner is of not being in good health. I said 'in so far as each is such' so as to include things [only] *qua* opposites. Master and slave are opposed as relatives, but each of them breathes and lives and is sentient not *qua* slave or *qua*   15
master but *qua* man; ruling, on the other hand, is a feature of being a master *qua* master, and being ruled likewise of a slave *qua* such. And being a quality[331] is associated with being white or black al-   20
though not by virtue of their being opposites. Separating and combining [are the features which belong to them] by virtue of their being opposites. Similarly, if loving is [characteristic] of a father, being loved is [characteristic] of a son. Father and son are not contraries but relative terms and so it is not the contraries that follow upon them but the relative terms. But loving and hating are opposed as contraries, loving and being loved as relative terms. And so if   25
loving follows upon [being] a father, being loved will follow upon [being] a son. And the same applies in all other cases. Thus if that which changes and is never the same and is perceptible is opposed[332] to that which is unchanging and is always the same and is intelligible,   211,1
and if the unchanging, *qua* unchanging, is without a beginning with respect to time, then that which changes as such will not be without   5
a beginning with respect to time.

27. Since, then, our argument has adequately demonstrated that Plato's meaning is that the world has come to be with respect to time, that is, that it has a beginning to its existence and did not exist before

10   it came to be, it may now *(loipon)* be the appropriate time to bring
       forward the evidence of the philosophers in regard to him.

       I shall pass over the circle of Plutarch and Atticus, who are agreed
       by all to have explicitly affirmed that Plato believed the world to be
       generated with respect to time and to have taken issue with those of
       the contrary opinion. Past teachers of our gospel,[333] among them
15   Eusebius, who led the Church in Caesarea, have already cited
       lengthy extracts from them in their own works.[334] This being so, I
       shall pass them over on this occasion and produce Plato's [own] pupil
20   as a witness [in favour of] our argument. And who could be a more
       credible witness to Plato's views than Aristotle, who is said to have
       been Plato's student for some twenty years, who surpassed all earlier
       Greeks in sagacity, and whom Plato so admired for that sagacity that
25   he used to call him the Brain of the School? When I cite his words I
       shall at the same time cite Alexander of Aphrodisias' explanatory
       comments on them. By doing so I shall be at once clarifying Aristotle's
212,1 meaning, [which is necessary] because of the convoluted nature of the
       man's style, and bringing on another witness to the matter in hand.

       From Aristotle, *On the Heaven*, Book 1:[335]

5   Now that these distinctions have been established, let us, after
       first reviewing the ideas of other thinkers, go on to ask whether
       the heaven is ungenerated or generated, imperishable or perish-
       able.

       And a few lines later:[336]

       All agree that it was generated, but some say that, once gener-
10   ated, it is eternal, others that, like everything else which is
       composite by nature, it is perishable, yet others, including Em-
       pedocles of Acragas and Heraclitus of Ephesus, that it is by
       turns as it is now and in a different condition when it perishes,
       and that this continues for ever.

15   From Alexander of Aphrodisias' comments on the [above] passages:[337]

       He states that all parties, theologians and natural philosophers
       alike, are of one mind as far as the generation *(tou gegonenai)* of
       the world is concerned and that it is in regard to what happens
       subsequently that there is discord among them. Some of those
20   who hold that it has been generated assert that it is everlasting.
       Orpheus and Hesiod and most of the theologians were of this
       opinion and following them Plato.[338] But some of those who hold
       that it has been generated at the same time declare that it is
25   perishable, as is everything else that is composite;[339] for all
       things are seen to come to be and to perish. Others, such as

Empedocles and Heraclitus, say that it by turns comes to be in
the same form and perishes, and that it comes to be and perishes   213,1
again and again according to certain cycles and that this [alter-
nation] is everlasting and goes on for ever.[340]

And a little further on:

Those who hold that it is generated and perishable like anything   5
else that is composite will be Democritus and his followers. For
just as everything else comes to be and perishes in their view,
so does each of the infinite worlds.

From Aristotle (the continuation of the previous passage):   10

To assert that it has come to be but is nevertheless everlasting
is an impossibility. We can only reasonably assume those char-
acteristics which we see to be present in many or all instances
[of a phenomenon], but in regard to this [phenomenon] the
opposite is the case: everything that comes to be clearly per-   15
ishes.[341]

Alexander's comment:

Having expounded the views of his predecessors on the world,
he [now] enquires which of their assertions are correct and
which incorrect. He begins by arguing against those who make
it generated but imperishable. In this group were, as I said   20
[earlier], the theologians and Plato, and theirs was the position
he described first.
    That Plato is indeed of this persuasion, and that the world is
not, as some of the Platonists claim, being described as generated on the ground that it has its being in coming to be, despite   25
being in his view ungenerated, the reader may ascertain from
Plato's own words in the *Timaeus*. Anything that is generated
in the sense in which they understand him to be describing the   214,1
world as generated is [continually] coming to be and ceasing to
be but has not ever come into existence. At any rate, when
carrying out a division of existing things, he asks 'what is that
which always is and has no generation and what is that which
comes to be but never is?'[342] But [when talking] of the world he
does not use [the present tense] 'comes to be' but [the past tense]   5
'has come to be', and at the outset [of the inquiry] the question
he poses is not whether it *comes* to be but whether it *has come*
to be or is ungenerated. His actual words are 'we who are about
to discuss with regard to the universe whether it has come to be
or is ungenerated';[343] [clearly] the question he is posing is not

10   whether it *is* coming to be but whether it *has* come to be or is
ungenerated.

Those[344] who attempt to alter (*metagraphein*)[345] 'or' to 'even
though'[346] [in this last passage] and to read 'whether it came to
be even though it is ungenerated' are [making themselves]
ridiculous. Quite apart from the absurdity of writing (*metagraphein*) what is not the case,[347] their suggestion is nonsensical

15   and totally fails to square with what follows, for soon afterwards, in the course of further defining the same question, he
writes[348] 'whether it has always been, having no beginning [to
its] generation, or has come to be, having started from some

20   beginning'. [Here] the words 'having started from some beginning' will no longer leave room for those[349] who [would] write
(*metagraphousin*)[350] 'even though it is ungenerated'.[351] And no
sooner has he set himself the task of investigating this question
than he goes on to show that it has come to be, evidently
[meaning] 'having started from some beginning' (for that was
the question being posed), [a beginning] which could not be any
other than a beginning with respect to time. And indeed if that
which is still coming to be has not yet come to be, it is clear that

215,1   that which has come to be is no longer coming to be. But he
states that the world has come to be. Therefore it is not, in his
view, [in the process of] coming to be. For since it has come to
be, it has started upon its existence[352] and already come to the
end of its generation.

5   And even if he had described the world as being generated in
the sense that it has its being in coming to be, he would have
had to accept that it is also perishable. It is the lot of a thing that
comes to be in that sense to perish in the same way as it comes
to be,[353] and by claiming that it is generated he leaves no room
(*ouketi sunkhôrei*) for it to be at the same time imperishable. For

10   in what way is it that they claim that he describes it as imperishable? If they claim that it is in not having its being in
perishing, perhaps one who claims that it is imperishable in a
way that[354] involves denying that it has its being in perishing
would also deny that it comes to be on that basis;[355] for a given

15   kind of generation goes hand in hand with a like kind of passing
out of existence. And should he be describing it as imperishable
with respect to time, it is clear that he would also be using
'generated' with respect to time, for that is the kind of generation that must be opposed to that kind of imperishability.

20   Further, it is out of a desire to eliminate the perishability that
appears to follow for something that is generated that he describes [the world] as imperishable. And if he describes it as
imperishable with respect to time, he is assuming that that
[kind of perishability] follows for something that is generated.

But it does not follow for something that is generated in the sense that it has its being in coming to be but for something that has come to be from a temporal beginning. And so[356] clearly this world has, in his opinion, come to be.

But even to seek a reason for its[357] imperishability, as Plato   25
does, is the act of one who agrees to describe it as having come
to be from a temporal beginning. For if it were ungenerated, it   216,1
would have the cause and origin (*arkhê*) of its imperishability
within itself, since it is conceded by him that that which is
ungenerated is of its own nature imperishable. But since the
world is not of its own nature imperishable, he attributes[358] its   5
imperishability to the will of God.[359]

Moreover, the fact that he frequently uses [the verb] 'is' of the
world is a sign that he is not describing it as having come to be
in the sense that it has its being in coming to be. If it 'was not'
before it came to be but 'is' once it has come to be, it is not being   10
said to have come to be in the sense that it has its being in
coming to be.

Nor is it consistent with Plato's position to claim that its
generation is being hypothesised for the sake of clarity on the
ground that we shall understand its precise nature more readily   15
as a result of this imaginary generation. [Had this been so], he
would not have immediately stated this problem at the outset,
as though he would be inquiring into it as his first priority, and
would not have omitted to explain why he describes it as generated when it is ungenerated; in the *Republic*,[360] when he gives
an account of the formation of the state and its government
because it contributes something to his account of justice, he   20
begins by telling us why he is talking about such matters, and
he would have done the same in the case of the world.

From the same [work] of Aristotle, shortly after the previous   25
passages:

[The parallel] which some of those who claim that [the world] is
imperishable even though it has come to be adduce in an attempt to support their position is not a genuine one. They say   217,1
that they speak of [its] generation in the same way as those who
draw [geometrical] diagrams; they are not saying that it ever
came to be but, for the sake of exposition [and] to advance   5
understanding, viewing it under construction (*ginomenon*) like
a diagram. But this is not in my opinion the same. In the
constructing of diagrams, once all [the lines] have been added,
what at once emerges is identical [with the lines],[361] but in their
demonstrations it is not something identical but an impossibil-   10
ity.[362] The initial and subsequent states which are assumed are

incompatible (*hupenantia*). They claim that ordered things
arose from unordered, and [something] cannot be unordered and
ordered at the same time; there must be [a process of] generation and [a lapse of] time separating [these states]. In diagrams,
15   on the other hand, nothing is separated by [a lapse of] time.[363]

Alexander's comment:

He will be directing this at certain followers of Plato on the
ground that they too saw the absurd consequences of describing
the world as generated but imperishable and therefore sought
to provide a charitable interpretation (*boêtheian tina*) of what
20   Plato and they themselves had written, denying that he describes the world as having come to be in the sense that [it had]
a temporal beginning and once did not exist, but [only] as an aid
25   in the instruction of learners and in demonstrating its essence
and nature. For they claim that he is carrying out a kind of
analysis of its essence and showing how it would have come to
218,1   be if it had come to be, as mathematicians do by means of their
diagrams. For amongst them too, when someone says, to take
an instance, that a cube[364] is constructed from six squares and
analyses it and shows how its construction [derives] from them,
he is not claiming that it ever did come to be or was ever put
together, but that he is showing by means of this hypothetical
5   generation that its existence depends on them, because if it *had*
come to be, it would have come to be from them in just this way.
They claim, then, that the world is being spoken of in the same
way; it is not that it has come to be but that its being depends
on these [components], and if it had come into existence it would,
10   they claim, have come to be in this manner [and] from these
[components].
    But [Aristotle] says that they do not explain the text success-
fully and that those who take this position cannot successfully
avoid the absurdity to which their interpretation is doomed by
means of this parallel. The case cannot be the same. The mathe-
15   matician who states that a cube consists of six squares and that
it is generated from the components from which he says it has
arisen, or that a triangle [consists of] three lines, is assuming
entities that coexist with that which is being said to be generated from them and that exist in it, but things that have a
20   separate existence have not been brought together. And analysis demonstrates this clearly. For analysis is into internal
components, and things with separate existence or things that
need to undergo some change for something[365] to emerge from
them do not result [from it]. For how do they claim [the world]
219,1   would be generated, had it been generated, out of its present

(*toutôn*) internal components? For the mathematician takes things all of which exist at the same time and tries to show that some of them are composed of others which are their internal [components]. A cube, for example, is not destructive of the squares [of which it is composed] by coming to be as a result of a change in them; they are internal to it. Nor is it necessary that the squares themselves exist ahead of the construction of the cube; as we said, they are coexistent with it and exist within it. For anyone selecting [materials] for a hypothesis rather than for the genuine generation of something selects them from among things which that which is said to have emerged from them does not destroy [by being generated].[366] When we make use of things in the generation of something else, they cannot produce the thing [which is generated] from them while remaining unchanging and intact; it is through a change in them that the thing that is said to be [generated] from them comes to be. In such a case something has come to be and this kind of generation is not just being assumed for the sake of a hypothesis. For such generation is of things that really come to be and it is in this manner that things that come to be in nature come to be. Nor would the mathematician any longer be conceiving of things as coming to be for the sake of a hypothesis if he hypothesised that they came to be from the sort of things that had to change in either quality or arrangement to produce such things; things that are being displayed as in the process of coming to be for the sake of a hypothesis do not have the things from which they have come to be hypothetically and [only] seemingly but, since these really do exist and are present in the things which are being displayed as emerging from them, have only the notional synthesis added [as a result of the hypothesis]. Such is the nature of analysis and of the entities with which it deals.

    The situation is different in the case of things that really come to be. Neither the menses and the embryo, nor a disordered heap (*ataxia*) of bricks and stones and the house that is built from them, exist at the same time. And it is from such components that [Plato and his followers] generate the world. And one who generates the world out of the change of a disordered confusion (*ataxias*) of bodies into orderly movement is saying that it has come out of something whose [continued] existence would make it impossible for the world to exist:[367] disorder is the contrary of order and disorder must be eliminated if order is going to exist. Therefore there is need of genuine change and generation if one is to posit the existence of disorder at all; for disorder must have changed into order by means of [a process] of generation and change. But this is not how it happens with diagrams. Since the elements from which [mathematicians] hypothesise their generation are internal to them, they demonstrate their generation without disturbing any of their components. And indeed it is an indication that they are not speaking soundly or, despite what they claim, producing an analysis in the manner of the mathematicians, but on the contrary describing a [process of real] generation, that the elements from which they describe the world as having emerged cannot exist at the same time as it does but must pre-exist it in time, as is the case with all things that come to be; things that are destructive of each other cannot also at the same time coexist even hypothetically.

And so the mathematicians for their part are talking reasonably when they say that they do not attribute generation to diagrams but only employ it as a hypothesis for the sake of clarity and exposition; their kind of generation is not out of contraries or from elements that are in any way separate [from the end result]; and accordingly the elements from which [the end results] are derived and of which they are comprised coexist with the [end results] that are said to emerge or have emerged from them. This is why they also say that it is impossible for there to be generation of [mathematical] shapes; but this does not at all mean that they cannot [generate them] even hypothetically.[368] But the [scenario] described by those who generate the world is not even hypothetically possible. The same things cannot be in a state of disorder and of order at the same time. And so for them disorder, if it existed at all, must have pre-existed the world; for when there was [disorder], it was not possible for there to be a world. So for them the world has really come into existence through a [process of] generation and from a temporal beginning and out of a kind of (*tinos*) alteration and passing out of existence. For the things from which they say the world has come to be can neither exist within it nor coexist with it. Otherwise that which comes to be would be an analysis; for analysis is [found] in things which can coexist in this way.[369] But it is not possible for the causes of the generation and existence of the world to coexist with it and to undergo change while still coexisting. If the disordered confusion (*ataxia*) of bodies from which they generate the world neither exists within it nor coexists with it but pre-existed it, and if the generation of the world [took place] as the result of an alteration to them, and not as it does among the mathematicians, [then] the generation should be described as real and not as an analysis of the kind carried out by mathematicians. One who hypothesises the generation of something out of [elements] from which the thing hypothesised could not emerge unless they altered is assuming a real generation and not a merely verbal one.

From the same [work] of Aristotle:

For there are some who believe that it is possible both for what
is ungenerated to perish and for what has come to be to remain   25
unperishing, as is the case in the *Timaeus*; for Plato says there
that the heaven has come to be but will nevertheless exist
throughout the rest of time (*ton loipon aei khronon*).[370]

222,1

Alexander:

It is not that the statements that there is something ungenerated which will perish and that there is something which has
been generated which remains everlasting both occur there – in
fact, as [Aristotle] himself indicates, only the second, [namely],   5
that the world has come to be but is everlasting, does[371] – but
that once the second is made the first also follows for the person
who makes it; for to say that something which has come to be is
imperishable and that something ungenerated is perishable are
part of the same way of thinking. Besides, for someone who says   10
that the world has come to be but will not perish it also follows
that he destroys[372] something that is ungenerated; for the disorder from which, on their view, the world has come to be was, in
spite of being ungenerated, destroyed in [the process of] changing into order and the world. [Aristotle][373] himself makes it clear   15
that only the second statement appears in the *Timaeus* by
indicating what is actually said there; 'for Plato', [he writes],
'says there that the heaven has been generated but will nevertheless exist for the rest of time'.

Aristotle, from Book 8 of the *Physics*:[374]

But as far as time is concerned all with one exception[375] are in   20
clear agreement. They hold that it is ungenerated. Indeed, it is
on this account that Democritus shows that it is impossible for
all things to have come to be, time being [in his opinion] ungenerated. Plato alone generates it. He holds that it came to be
along with the heaven and that the heaven [itself] came to be.[376]

This, then, is what Aristotle and the man who, in his commentaries   223,1
on Aristotle, has better than anyone come to grips with his thought,
[namely,] Alexander, have to say. And although it was made clear
earlier in the passages we quoted from the commentary on the
Timaeus of the Platonist Taurus that many other philosophers have   5
taken the same view of Plato['s position], perhaps it will do no harm
to quote the same passages again.[377]
    This is what Taurus says:

10

There being a question as to whether the world is in Plato's view something ungenerated, philosophers have had different opinions on the matter. Aristotle states that the *Timaeus* describes the world as generated since Timaeus says that it has come to be. And, indeed, there is a work of his [sc. of Timaeus] in circulation on the universe as [something] generated. Theo-

15

phrastus, on the other hand, in *On Physical Opinions*, says that the world is in Plato's opinion generated and criticises him on that basis, but adds that he may be hypothesizing it as generated for the sake of clarity [of exposition].[378] And some others have likewise been of the opinion that it is in Plato's view generated, although others [have thought that he held that it is] ungenerated.[379]

20

We learned, then, from this passage that many other philosophers, including Theophrastus, have said the same things about Plato [as Aristotle and Alexander did]. Admittedly Theophrastus, as [Taurus] states, attempted to defend Plato on the ground that he may have hypothesised that [the world] is generated for clarity's sake. But this

25
224,1

same Taurus later shows us Theophrastus demolishing such a hypothesis. Here is what he says soon after the passage quoted above:

It was Plato's practice to present things in the process of development for the sake of exposition. In the *Republic* too he shows the city as it develops so that the origins of justice will become

5

clearer during its establishment. Theophrastus, after remarking that 'perhaps he describes it as generated for the sake of clarity, in the way that we follow diagrams as they develop', continues 'but perhaps generation is not of the same nature in the case of diagrams'.[380] And he is saying the same thing as Aristotle, for he too asserts that in the case of diagrams it is

10

possible to postulate [the presence of] contraries at the start but that it is not possible in the case of the generation of the world, as though one were postulating [the presence of] movement and rest, and order and disorder [at the same time].[381]

15

In the circumstances I think that both [our own] argument and the testimony of philosophers as to Plato's position have adequately demonstrated to all, save those who are irremediably contentious and put the truth second to their own desires, that Plato did not mean to say that the existence of the world was without a beginning but on the contrary assigned a beginning to its existence.

As for the [arguments] which, again transcribing from Porphyry, Proclus adduces in the work we have [already] cited on a number of

20

occasions in defence of the *Timaeus* against Aristotle in an attempt to demonstrate in a roundabout way that Plato, since he both states

that the pattern for the world is eternal[382] and claims that the
goodness of God is the cause of the existence of the world, believed   25
that the generation of the world is without a beginning – Plato says
'for he was good, and in the good no envy ever arises in regard to   225,1
anything',[383] from which Proclus concludes that if the pattern for the
world always exists, the copy of that pattern, the world, must also   5
always exist, and that if God is always free of envy, [then,] since he
is also always good, the world too will always exist, or if the world
does *not* always exist, then its creator is only potentially [a creator]
and therefore imperfect and in need of time – these and other similar
[arguments] I pass over now as having been adequately dealt with
earlier.[384] It is clear that, having been refuted, they too will not   10
support the view that Plato held the world to be everlasting.

28. It will be in accord with our undertakings at the beginning of
the present chapter[385] to consider next whether Plato can be caught
contradicting himself. If, as he says, there is necessarily a passing out   15
of existence for everything that has come to be,[386] and if it follows from
this by conversion by negation[387] that everything that does not perish
has not come to be, how can the same person hypothesise that the   20
world is both imperishable and generated at the same time?

The reply to this is brief. If what is ungenerated with respect to
time is also imperishable by nature, then if something is not imperishable by nature, it is not ungenerated with respect to time. But
Plato does not hypothesise that the world is imperishable by nature.   25
On the contrary, he says that it is perishable by nature; for, [he
argues,] everything that has been bound can be unbound.

'For since you have come to be', he says,[388] 'you are not immortal   226,1
nor altogether indissoluble. But you shall certainly not be dissolved nor meet with the fate of death since you have in my will
a greater and more authoritative bond than those with which
you were bound when you came to be.'   5

If, then, the world is in Plato's view mortal and dissoluble by nature,
and [if he also holds that] its indissolubility arises from the will of the
Creator (for he says[389] that [his creations] are indissoluble not by
nature but 'as long as I will it'), it clearly would be generated with
respect to time. So Plato is revealed to be entirely consistent through-   10
out. If he had thought that the world was generated by God so as to
be immortal and indissoluble, as he says the intelligibles are, it would
have been consistent for him to hypothesise that it was also ungenerated with respect to time. But if it is dissoluble by nature, and if
nothing that is ungenerated with respect to time is dissoluble by   15
nature, then it is not ungenerated with respect to time; indeed, for
this very reason Plato says that because the world is generated it is

therefore also dissoluble. And so he reaches conclusions which are consistent with his premises.

20   That the words 'you are not indissoluble nor altogether immortal' do not, as some imagine, mean 'you are not simple, but it is notionally possible to analyse you into your components and you are for that reason mortal', but rather 'you are of a nature that is receptive of death and dissolution', is clear from the opposing [statement] 'you

25   shall certainly not be dissolved nor meet with the fate of death, since

227,1   you have in my will a greater and more authoritative bond than those with which you were bound when you came to be'.[390] So if he is referring to a notional dissolution and death and saying that they are

5   mortal as a result of this, then he would, by saying that they will not be dissolved or meet the fate of death, mean that they will not endure these things notionally; for what an affirmation asserts its negation

10   necessarily denies, [and] it is that same dissolution and death which he has said belongs to them of their nature that he later states will not, by God's will, be theirs. So if they have from nature the [attribute of] being *notionally* dissoluble and mortal, then they will also be *notionally* immortal and indissoluble through the will of God. So the

15   gist of the passage will be: 'You will not be notionally indissoluble or immortal, [but] neither will you die.' So the same thing will be both notionally dissoluble and notionally not dissoluble and [both sides of] this contradiction will be true at the same time. So if this is silly and if it makes no sense to say that the same thing is both notionally

20   analysed and notionally not analysed into simples, he is clearly saying that the heavenly bodies are dissoluble and mortal not notionally but by their nature.

              But since, even though this is the nature allotted to them, Plato is

25   nevertheless of the opinion that they remain indissoluble and immortal in perpetuity, being held together not by a physical bond but by the will of God, he says that they are not wholly indissoluble and immortal but mortal and dissoluble as far as their own nature goes

228,1   (because this is the nature of the corporeal and all that has come to be is dissoluble and mortal), but that through the will of the creator, which is stronger than any physical bond, they have obtained an

5   immortality contrived for them in perpetuity by him who created them. For just as a man may, by continually restoring a house or a ship and replacing its worn out parts, maintain it so that it lasts

10   indefinitely, so, says Plato, does God bestow a restored immortality upon the world.

              Listen to his further philosophical speculations on this topic in the *Statesman*.[391] Here is what he says:

              [Eleatic Stranger:] At times God himself joins in guiding this universe as it moves and assists its revolution, at other times,

15   when its circuits have completed the measure of time assigned

to it, he lets it go. It then revolves of its own accord in the opposite direction, for it is a living creature that has been endowed with intelligence by its framer from the beginning. This movement in reverse is, for the following reason, of necessity innate to it.

[Young Socrates:] What is this reason?

[Eleatic Stranger:] Always to be the same and unchanging and to remain identical belongs only to the most divine of all beings. The nature of body is not of this order. That which we have been calling 'the heaven' or 'the world' has certainly received many fine gifts from its begetter, but it has nevertheless been made to partake of body, and for this reason it is impossible for it to be entirely exempt from change.

20

25

So here too, then, Plato, in conformity with the statements that we have cited from the *Timaeus*, ascribes inalterability and remaining the same and unchanging to intelligible and divine substance alone and says that the whole sphere of the bodily is not of this order, whence too he states that it is entirely impossible for the corporeal element in the universe not to share in change, but, 'when its circuits have fully completed the measure of time assigned to it', the universe then undergoes alterations and changes. And this too, as some of our [Christian writers] have correctly pointed out, he derived from the Holy Scriptures.[392] For what else is 'assisting the revolution' of the heaven and then 'letting it go' 'when its circuits have fully completed the measure of time assigned to it' than for 'the heavens to be rolled up and changed like a cloak'?[393]

And listen to how Plato, once he had decided, again after hearing [the biblical words] 'for God did not make death', and 'he created all things that they might exist',[394] that the universe must remain immortal, states, again in this same *Statesman*,[395] that immortality does not belong to the world by nature but comes to it newly acquired from the Creator:

229,1

5

10

15

20

For all these reasons we must not say either that the world always turns itself, or that it is turned in its entirety in two contrary revolutions by a god, or, again, that two gods with contrary intentions turn it, but rather [must we affirm] the only remaining possibility, the one which I just now stated, that at times it is guided by an external, divine, agency, acquiring renewed life and receiving a restored immortality from its creator, while at other times it is released, being let go by that same [creator] at the right moment to be able to revolve in the opposite direction through a countless number of revolutions.

25
230,1

5

Here he clearly states that inasmuch as the heaven, owing to the mutability of all corporeal nature, does not possess immortality of its

10 own nature, it acquires renewed life and a restored immortality comes to it from its creator.

So if Plato believes that the heaven is a living creature, and if the being and substance of every living creature exists in accordance with the form of the life within it, then the heaven as well will possess being

15 and substance in the form of its own life. But he says that the heaven acquires this life again and again and that a restored immortality comes to it from its creator. Therefore Plato does not believe that the substance of the heaven is of its own nature indissoluble and immortal. Nor therefore does he hypothesise that its existence is without a beginning;

20 for there is every necessity that everything without a beginning should also be of its own nature imperishable and that everything which is by nature perishable should also of necessity be generated.

29. If Plato elsewhere[396] describes the world as self-sufficient, in

25 need of nothing, free of disease and ageless, he does not describe it in these terms because its own resources are adequate for its everlasting

231,1 continuance, but because it does not undergo destructive attacks from outside agencies as our bodies do. For there is no body outside

5 the world at whose hands it could suffer anything of the kind that each and every separate thing [within it] does from its environment. The heaven is certainly not like our bodies and all other particular things, [which are] depleted by their environments and [need to] take in replacements for what is lost in the form of [supplementary matter] coming in from outside. There *is* nothing outside it either to deplete

10 it or to nourish it. 'It uses', says[397] Plato, 'its own waste for food'. For the waste from one thing becomes another's nourishment; the passing out of existence of, say, air becomes the generation of water or fire, and similarly with everything else. It is in this way, then, that it is said to be in need of nothing from outside, and it is [said to be] free of disease and ageless because it has nothing outside it at whose hands

15 it might suffer,[398] not because it is naturally self-sufficient and immortal; for he has stated[399] that [the property of] always remaining the same and unchanging belongs to intelligible substance alone and that corporeal nature is not of that order but belongs in its entirety to

20 [the order] of things that come to be and perish and never truly are. So, again, in what sense other than the one I have stated[400] would he call this same [corporeal nature] self-sufficient and in need of nothing?

There is nothing like listening to the philosopher's own words [to convince one] that this is what he has in mind when he says such

25 things of the world. Here is what he says in the *Timaeus*:[401]

From such elements, four in number, the body of the world came to be, achieving harmony through proportion, and received [the

232,1 spirit of] friendship from them, so that, having come together, it was indissoluble by others than him who had bound it together. And the framing of the world took up the whole of each of the

four [elements], for its framer framed it from all the fire and   5
water and air and earth, leaving no portion of any of them nor
any of their powers outside of it. [In this] his intention was first
that it should be in the highest degree a whole living creature,
complete [and formed] from complete constituents, and in addition to this be one, there being nothing left over from which
another such as it might come to be, and also that it should be
ageless and free of disease. For he was aware that when things   10
that are hot or cold, or have [other] powerful [corrosive] proper-
ties, surround and assail a composite body from the outside,
they break it up before its time and cause it to waste away by
afflicting it with diseases and old age. It was for this reason and
on these grounds that he fashioned it to be a whole, out of
[constituents] all of which were wholes, [and therefore] perfect,   15
ageless and free of disease.

In this passage Plato gives three reasons why the creator has left no
aspect of the elements, neither any portion nor any power, outside of the
heaven. (By a portion he means a body, as, for instance, a portion of fire
or water or of the other [elements] – for portions of bodies are   20
[themselves] bodies, – and by a power the formative qualities of the
elements, I mean heat and cold, moisture and dryness, heaviness and
lightness and the rest.) The first [reason] is so that the world might
be complete, having come to be as a whole [formed] from wholes and   25
a complete thing formed from complete things, [namely,] the elements; the second so that there might be one, single world and not,
as Democritus and others held, several or even an infinite number of 233,1
worlds, for if the world is, as Plato holds, a living creature fabricated
from the four elements, and no portion of an element was left outside
the world, then it is not possible for another world to exist, since all   5
of the world-creating elements have been included in this one; and the
third [reason is] so that the world might be free of disease and ageless,
there being nothing outside at whose hands it might also suffer, for
just as our bodies, when they are chilled or heated, or moistened or   10
dried overmuch by their environment or suffer other [such] afflictions, lose their correct temperament and because of this age and
decay, in the same way, he says, if portions or powers of the elements
had been left outside of the heaven to assail the heaven from without, 15
they would, because of the active nature of their power, have had the
same effects on it as befall our bodies at the hands of the environment;
so, in order that the universe might be free of these afflictions, the
creator, he says, enclosed the entire nature of the elements inside it. 20
    And yet, if the heaven were not by nature subject to old age and
dissolution, it would not, even though the entire nature of the elements existed outside of it and attacked it, ever have suffered from
them anything of which its nature was not receptive; for what would

the *rational* substances in the world for their part suffer from the
active power in bodies? He does not, then, hypothesise that the
heaven is unageing and free from disease through its inalterability
and natural immortality. On the contrary, what I said earlier[402] is
shown to be the case by the present passage: because the world was
(since it was also, by virtue of being body, generated) dissoluble and
mortal by nature, and because he wishes it to last for ever, the creator
has, so that it will not be subject to destructive changes of any kind,
left nothing that is of a nature to dissolve it outside of it. But in the
case of a thing which is naturally indissoluble there is nothing
through whose agency it could ever be dissolved. For that reason
Plato's creator did not take any such precaution in the case of the soul
of the world but, weaving it throughout, from the centre to the heaven
on the periphery, had no apprehension that it would undergo any
change or alteration as a result of its association with heating and
cooling agents, for it belonged to the [sphere of] nature that is
intelligible and always remains the same and unchanging. But why
do I talk of the soul of the world? Even when he bound *our* souls to
bodies and interwove the mortal with the immortal he took no precaution against their suffering from any destructive force, for he
claims that they too are of an immortal nature. That which is immortal by nature, then, can suffer nothing from the [four] elements; for
these, in that they share with one another the same matter and have
a nature that is affected in the same way, are alone by nature able to
suffer at each other's hands. And so the heaven too, if it did not consist
of the same matter as the elements, or rather had not been, as Plato
says, composed of them, would, even if the entire might (*phusis*) of
the elements were assailing it from without, undergo nothing at their
hands; but as it is, since its nature is such that it can suffer at the
hands of [the materials] of which it is composed, to prevent it from
suffering the creator has, he says, left nothing outside of it.

But even if there is nothing outside through which the world can
suffer, even so, because Plato knows that every body is controlled by
a finite power and that no body possesses an infinite power (as Plato's
pupil Aristotle shows towards the end of the eighth book of the
Physics[403]) and nothing that does not possess an infinite power can
last in perpetuity, and for this reason both the heaven and the whole
world, being body and possessing a finite power, would not on their
own, even were there nothing damaging them from outside, have the
resources for an everlasting continuance (for a finite power must,
because of the very fact that it is finite, eventually become exhausted
and perish), and because he believes that the world [nevertheless]
remains indissoluble, he for this reason sets the creator himself over
it to [continually] renew its life and immortality so that it may thus
endure for ever.[404] For if Plato did think that it was inalterable and
immortal by nature (as he claims the nature of intelligibles is), how,

again, is it that he hypothesises that its immortality is restored?
These [positions] are incompatible. Or how is it that he leaves nothing
outside of it so that it will not age or decay through being affected by
it, thereby also indicating that it gets its freedom from want not from   25
the self-sufficiency of its own nature but by having need of nothing
outside of itself to fill or repair any deficiency it might have by the
addition [of new material]? Listen to what he says on this subject in   236,1
the *Timaeus*:[405]

> He made the whole of it perfectly smooth on the outside for a
> number of reasons. It had no need of eyes, for nothing was left
> outside of it [for it] to see, nor of hearing, for there was nothing
> [for it] to hear. There was no surrounding air that it had to   5
> breathe, nor did it have need of any organ with which to take
> nourishment into itself or to discharge it again once it had been
> digested; nothing left it or entered it from anywhere else, for
> there *was* nothing. It was designed to use its own residue[s] as   10
> food and to act and be acted upon by itself and within itself, for
> its framer thought that it would be better for it to be self-suffi-
> cient rather than dependent on others.

He is saying, then, that even its absence of need is not the result of
its being naturally free of need but of its not needing anything extra   15
from outside of itself. The world as a whole does not, like our bodies,
have its losses replaced from outside but is acted upon by itself and
acts upon itself (that is to say, one part of it acts, another is acted
upon), and the decay of one part becomes nourishment and growth for   20
another. When the parts of a thing are subject to breakdown and
alteration, the whole of it must, if the whole is nothing other than all
its parts, undergo the same [processes]. Hence it has need of a
restorer and repairer. Therefore the world is not impassible or free of   25
need but, although it needs nothing outside of itself and is affected by   237,1
nothing outside of itself, since there *is* nothing outside of it, is
nevertheless acted upon by itself and decays. Something of this kind
is neither impassible nor immortal by nature. For nothing that is
naturally immortal, like, for example, rational beings, is of a nature
to be affected in any way or to decay even in its parts, since everything   5
that really is naturally immortal is of an indivisible and simple
nature. If, therefore, the world is not naturally immortal but receives
an acquired and restored immortality from outside [itself], it is, one
assumes, mortal by nature. And if it is, as Plato holds, mortal, he with   10
reason assigns a beginning to its existence. And thus in the passages
under discussion Plato is hypothesising nothing that conflicts with
his position when he says that the world is generated and mortal by
nature and that its immortality is communicated [to it] and comes to
it supernaturally from him who created it.   15

And that this did not escape Proclus, and that he too knew perfectly well that the world does not possess everlasting existence as far
as its own nature goes because all bodily nature is held together by
20   finite power, and that everlasting existence comes to it as something
that is acquired from somewhere else, and that he is now deliberately
misleading us by means of fallacious argument when he starts from
the assumption that it is Plato's view that the world does not perish
without qualification and does not further define the sense in which
Plato says this and then concludes from this that he also believes that
25   the world is ungenerated with respect to time, will be clear to us once
we have cited a few out of many[406] [relevant] passages[407] from his
[writings].

In the course of defending Plato because he says that it is only the
intelligible that always is and that everything perceptible comes to be
238,1   and perishes but never is, Proclus, after much else, adds this:

Proclus, from the work entitled *An Examination of Aristotle's*
5   *Criticisms of Plato's Timaeus*:

This assumption, then, should only be made if the body of the
heaven too, and the whole world as well, must be described as
coming to be. And how can it be other than necessary to so
describe it on the basis of the information he gives us? For he
10   states that no finite body has infinite power, and has shown it
to be so in the eighth book of the *Physics*.[408] So if the world is
finite (and he has shown this to be so as well), it necessarily does
not have infinite power. But we have demonstrated that eter-
15   nity is infinite power in our earlier arguments.[409] Therefore the
world, not having infinite power, does not have eternal existence. And if it does not have eternal existence (for a thing that
does has a share in eternity, and a thing which has a share in
eternity shares in infinite power), the world necessarily does not
20   exist for ever. For he states himself[410] that to exist for ever is the
property of eternity and says that eternity even gets its name
from this fact.[411]

Having thus shown that Aristotle's own positions prove that the
world is not among those things that are for ever, he next shows that
239,1   it has the property of for ever coming to be from another source and
not of its own nature. Here is what he says:

Nor is what is true of that which always is also true of that
which is always coming to be: [it is not the case that] infinite
power belongs to the latter on account of its always coming to be
5   in the way that it does to the former on account of its always
being. But it does [belong] to its maker, and on that account it
too is always coming to be, gaining [the property of] always

being thanks to (*dia*) that which always is by the terms of its own existence, and not having the 'always' in its own right. And so the definition of that which comes to be would also fit the world.

And a little further on:

Everything, then, which comes to be is always in its own right   10
also perishing; but, as a result of having been bound by that which is, this whole [universe] remains in [a state of] becoming [and] comes to be [but] does not perish because of the being it has drawn off from that which is. Therefore, because, in its own right, that which comes to be qualifies[412] for the definition, he also refers to it as perishing, since by its own nature it is such.   15

And the same [writer] in what follows:

For since the universe is finite, and what is finite does not, as he has shown, have infinite power, and that which initiates infinite movement initiates it by infinite power, it is clear that the motionless cause of infinite movement for the universe has   20
infinite power itself. And so, if one separates the universe from that [cause] in thought, it will not, since it does not have infinite power, keep moving *ad infinitum* but will experience a cessation of its movement; but if one connects it to that [cause] once more, it will, thanks to it, keep moving *ad infinitum*. And indeed there   25
is nothing inappropriate about notionally separating things that   240,1
are joined so as to see what each has from the other, and so as to know, once this has been observed, what it is that the inferior [partner] possesses of its own nature and what from its associa-tion with the superior.

And soon after: 5

For, generally, since even in this world perishing occurs as a result of lack of power and preservation as a result of power, all the more so is it the case that amongst imperishable things imperishability [holds sway] as a result of power. And this power is obviously something infinite, for all finite [power] perishes.

Now if, as Proclus himself also believes, it necessarily follows from   10
the world's not having infinite power that it does not exist for ever but acquires (*epiktêton ekhei*) everlasting being (or rather, everlasting becoming) from that which always is, [and] does not have everlasting being in its own right but is something that comes to be and perishes,   15

and that, as a result of this, if one were to separate from it the cause of its continuous becoming and of its everlasting movement, it will on account of not itself possessing infinite power experience a cessation of movement and therefore also of existence, since every finite
20   power perishes – if, then, Proclus accepts these Platonic positions, he is clearly saying that the world is naturally perishable and that imperishability belongs to it supernaturally, being furnished by some superior power.

25   And if, as Proclus has demonstrated in the preceding argument, the world is naturally perishable and therefore of necessity also generated, the philosopher is clearly deliberately misleading us at this point by omitting to mention the manner in which Plato says that the world is imperishable; for if something belongs to a thing in excess
241,1 of its own nature,[413] this does not cause it to depart from its own nature and make it of the same nature as the thing from which it has this power. The ether too, which extends above the mountain tops and is carried around with the heavenly element, and which, in Aristotle's
5   opinion, is going beyond its own nature by moving in this way, is nonetheless [formed] of those substances which move in a straight line and will not have [this] movement [as a] characteristic of its own
10   substance and so itself be said to be of the same species as the heavenly element.[414] Indeed, we would not even describe those divinely inspired souls who, transcending their own nature, know 'what is, what will be, and what has gone before'[415] as beings different from others on account of a power which has come to them from God. And
15   in our own times there are some among the Hellenes, people whom they would describe as divinely inspired but whom I would say were possessed by evil spirits, who, as rumour has it, pierce their own bodies with swords and walk through fire but incur, it is said, none of the injuries that bodies normally suffer from fire and iron. But I do
20   not imagine that they would for that reason claim that their bodies are of a different nature and not corporeal or that they are on that account possessed of impassability and imperishability. Thus, even if this universe is, as Plato holds, endowed with indissolubility by some superior power, it will not on that account immediately share in the
25   nature of things that are imperishable and exist for ever; but, since it is naturally perishable, it will of necessity be generated as well.
242,1   As for the arguments directed against Aristotle, who had criticised Plato for claiming that the world is naturally perishable but is imperishable through the will of God, which Proclus includes in the thirteenth section of the previously-mentioned work[416] – Proclus tries to persuade us that the world possesses imperishability both by its
5   own nature and through the will of God – since they have nothing cogent about them and show him contradicting himself and Plato and the truth, I refrain from stating them so as not to introduce excessive complication into the argument; there is no argument [available] to

refute [the positions] that all body has finite power and that a finite   10
[power] is necessarily perishable and cannot last in perpetuity.

Such, then, being the nature of the power of the world, there is
every necessity that it should be perishable as far as concerns the
power of its own nature. And so it is also of necessity generated, if
indeed everything perishable is also of necessity generated. It is,   15
therefore, possible for the world, while being generated with respect
to time and therefore dissoluble and mortal, to receive an acquired
and [continually] restored immortality from a power that is higher
than that which belongs to its own nature – and it will not because it   20
does not perish have to be ungenerated as well, since it does not
possess imperishability by the law (*kata ton logon*) of its own nature.

The End of the Refutation of the Sixth Argument

The Seventh Argument of Proclus the Successor   243,1

The seventh [argument]: If the soul of the universe is ungenerated and imperishable, the world too is ungenerated and
imperishable. For the definition [of the soul of the universe], as
of all soul, is 'that which moves itself'; and everything which   5
moves itself is a fount and source[417] of movement.[418] So if the soul
of the universe is everlasting, the universe must always be being
moved by it. For, despite always being a source of movement and
being unable not to be a source of movement (for it is by its   10
essence self-moved and therefore a source of movement), it
would not be a source for movement should the universe either
previously or subsequently not exist.[419] But soul is, by virtue of
this very self-movement,[420] ungenerated and imperishable.
Therefore the universe too is ungenerated and imperishable.
[And] from this it is quite clear that all soul is in the first   15
instance mounted upon everlasting body[421] and moves it for ever
and that whenever it is present in perishable bodies, it moves
them through the agency of those [sc. the everlasting ones]
which are for ever moved [directly] by it.

The Sections of the Refutation of the Seventh Argument

1. A description of the approach taken in the seventh proof.   20
2. That the present proof is not based on the facts but derives from
an unproved Platonic hypothesis.
3. That if soul has its essence in being[422] the source of movement,   25
it is impossible for its essence to exist apart from body.
4. That if the essence of soul is agreed to be separate from[423] all   244,1
body, it is impossible for it to have its essence in being the source of
movement. And that Proclus himself is aware that it is in one way

5   that soul has its being and essence but in another that it has [the
       property of] being the source of movement.

       5. That it is impossible for the forces in soul which are responsible
       for moving[424] body to be everlasting and for this reason it cannot move
10   body everlastingly and no everlasting body can be for ever attached
       to it.

       6. That no movement or change in body is ungenerated and
       imperishable, and for this reason there is no body that is moved
       everlastingly by soul, even should soul be, as Plato believes, ungen-
       erated.

15   **7.** That Plato is not saying that self-movement is the source of
       circular movement. Including [a demonstration] that no living crea-
       ture in the sublunary sphere has[425] a naturally rotating body and that
20   the local movement of animate bodies does not take place involuntar-
       ily but at the initiative of souls.[426]

       8. That even if it is agreed that soul is, as Plato holds, ungener-
       ated and the source of all movement, there is no necessity that once
       soul exists everlasting body should coexist along with it.

25   **9.** That even though soul, in so far as it endows bodies with life, is
       said by Plato to be the source of movement, it still does not follow that
245,1 someone who claims that soul is ungenerated should also suppose the
       world to be ungenerated. Including [a demonstration] that the life of
       bodies *qua* capacity[427] is rest rather than movement.

       10. That it is not the rational soul but the irrational that is the
5   cause of all bodily life and movement; the rational soul only controls
       and orders the irrational movement of the passions. Hence it is not
       necessary that as soon as there is a source and cause of this kind of
       movement (i.e. of rational movement) there should at once also be
       something which is moved [by it].

       11. That by the affirmation [of the existence] of soul the affirma-
10   tion of body moved by it is not also implied, but, by the rules of logic
       and according to Platonic doctrine, with the denial [of its existence
       the existence of] animate body *qua* animate is simultaneously denied.

       12. That even if soul were involuntarily the cause of life and
15   movement for bodies just by being,[428] there would even so be no
       necessity that once soul exists body moved by it[429] should also exist.

       13. That in the *Phaedrus* itself, just as in the *Timaeus*, Plato
       clearly states that every body experiences a cessation of movement
20   and life and that nothing that is perishable is ungenerated.

       14. That the hypothesis of the Hellenes in regard to an everlast-
       ing body, which they also refer to as the luminous [body and] upon
25   which they say rational souls are in the first instance mounted and
       in addition to[430] moving it also move perishable bodies by means of it,
       is an implausible fiction. Including [a demonstration] that it is impos-
       sible for everlasting body to move perishable body by some natural

force as a magnet does iron while [itself] remaining free of local
movement.[431]

15. That it is impossible for everlasting body to impart rectilinear   246,1
movement to perishable body while itself undergoing circular movement.

16. That if it imparts movement to perishable bodies while itself
undergoing rectilinear movement, it undergoes rectilinear movement   5
either naturally or contrary to nature, and in either case it will be
generated and perishable, not everlasting.

17. That however it is that one assumes that this everlasting body
which they have invented moves, it will not be able to impart movement to perishable [body], whether it be outside it or inside it, and   10
whether [in the latter case] it be in the whole of it or in a part of it.
Including [a demonstration] that no body, whether celestial or sublunary, can permeate [another] body, nor can [bodies] be[432] inside one
another.

18. That it is not possible for the body which is always being said   15
by them to be everlastingly attached to soul to be different both from
bodies which move in a straight line and from those which move in a
circle.

19. That it is not possible, if it is indeed everlasting, for it to be
one of the bodies which move in a straight line.

20. That neither can it be one of the bodies which move in a circle,
that is, one of the heavenly bodies.   20

21. That neither is it possible for this body to be a mixture
compounded of the bodies which move in a straight line and those
which move in a circle, or, as some claim, for it to naturally move
spirally. And that there is no body at all which naturally exhibits   25
spiral movement.

The Refutation of the Seventh Argument

1. In the *Phaedrus*[433] Plato states that soul is ungenerated and
imperishable, defines its essence as self-movement and postulates   247,1
that the self-moved is the source of movement, and our philosopher
[sc. Proclus] for his part attempts to prove that if these things are so,
it is necessary that the world too should be ungenerated and imper-   5
ishable, or if the world is *not* ungenerated and imperishable, that the
soul of the universe too should not be ungenerated and imperishable,
since soul and the body which is moved by it necessarily exist and
perish together. For, since, he says, soul is self-moved and the source   10
of movement just by being and not through choice, and is everlasting,
the universe too must be everlastingly moved by it, or if the universe
were *not* everlastingly moved by it because the world is not everlasting, then it would not be everlasting itself. For it is the source of
movement just by being. And so if it were not everlastingly the source   15

of movement, neither would it be everlasting. But if it *is* everlastingly
the source of movement, there must also be body which is everlastingly moved by it. And so, he says, if the soul of the universe is in
20   Plato's view ungenerated and imperishable, then the world too is
necessarily in his view ungenerated and imperishable.

And then, since our souls too are in Plato's view self-moved and
these are what Plato is chiefly talking about in the *Phaedrus*, because
they are self-moved and the self-moved is the source of movement and
25   the bodies moved by them (I mean *our* bodies) are clearly generated
and perishable, Proclus, in an attempt to get around the refutation
[of his position] that emerges from [these] facts, joins not thread to
thread, as the proverb has it, but fiction to fiction.[434] For, because the
248,1   rational soul, being everlasting, must in his view everlastingly move
body of some kind, he claims that all soul is in the first instance
mounted upon everlasting body and moves this for ever, and if it is in
perishable bodies, moves the perishable [bodies] by means of the
everlasting [body].

5   Such, then, is the approach taken in the present argument, or,
rather, in the present piece of sophistry.

2. I imagine that it is clear to everyone that the present proof is
not based on the facts and that the demonstration of the everlast-
10   ingness of the world in this argument (*en toutois*) is not based on
generally accepted premises but, if on anything, on the opinions of
Plato. And for this reason we ought perhaps to have absolutely
refused[435] assent of any kind to the unproved statements of Plato –
for, as Plato's pupil [Aristotle] says,[436] 'although both [Plato and the
15   truth] are dear, it is pious to everywhere give precedence to the truth'
– [and], even if it really is a logical consequence of Plato's views about
soul that the world is ungenerated and imperishable, ought not have
given much weight to this until someone should establish by clear
20   proofs the truth of [his] premises. For I at any rate would never
consider self-movement the essence and definition of soul. And, except that I would have been getting off the subject, I would have cited
what Proclus has said in his commentary on the *Phaedrus* in advo-
25   cacy of the position that self-movement is the essence of soul and, I
believe, shown quite clearly that there is nothing sound or cogent
about the argument.

But we shall let that pass on this occasion. Let us accept the
249,1   Platonic doctrine which states that self-movement is the definition
and essence of soul and the one [which states that] self-movement is
the source of movement and let us see whether they give rise to any
necessity for Plato, when he says that soul is ungenerated and
5   imperishable, to hold that the world too is ungenerated and imperishable. And, since the entire fabric of this piece of sophistry has its
origin in Plato's saying that self-movement is the source of movement, it is proper to investigate what is meant by this statement itself

and whether the everlastingness of the world necessarily follows from
this hypothesis. For if it is shown that there is no necessity for the   10
one to follow from the other,[437] it is clear that nothing will prevent
Plato from hypothesising that soul is ungenerated and self-movement
the source of movement but that the world is generated.

    3. For soul, then, being the source of movement is either identical   15
with its being and essence,[438] on the basis that soul has its essence in
being the source of movement, or it has its being and essence in one
way, whether it is self-movement that is the essence of soul or
something else, while it is in another that it is the source of move-   20
ment, just as a builder has his being and essence in one way and his
being the source and cause of building in another, and a teacher has
his being in one way and his ability to affect the pupil in another.   25

    Now, if it is the same thing for soul to be soul and to be the source
of movement, and for that reason as soon as there is soul it is in every
case necessary that there also be body that is moved by it [and] of
whose movement it is the source (for a source is the source of   250,1
something), then, since it is not possible either for body moved by
soul, to the extent that it is moved by soul, to exist without the soul
which moves it (for, as Aristotle shows in his writings on movement,[439] everything which moves is moved by something which moves   5
it), soul and the body which is moved by it, to the extent that it is
moved by it, either exist or do not exist together. Therefore soul
cannot exist without body which is moved [by it]; for if it is the source   10
of movement for [such body], and if being the source of movement is
the essence of soul, and if the essence of soul, as long as it is in
existence, is what it is actually and not potentially, then soul is the
source of movement actually and not potentially. But it is impossible
to be an actual source of movement without something which is being   15
moved. Therefore it is impossible for soul to exist without body which
is being moved by it.

    And so it has turned out that the being of soul lies in its relation to
body; for if someone were to say that soul can also exist on its own
apart from body and [still] be the source of movement, it is clear that   20
he will agree that soul has actual existence but suppose that it is
[only] potentially [that it is] the source of movement. And if this is so,
soul will have its being and essence in one way but be the source of
movement in another; for if it were the same thing for soul to be and   25
[for it] to be the source of movement, if either of these were actualised,
the other would necessarily be actualised as well. But if soul does not
have its being in being the source of movement, there will be no
necessity for someone who claims that soul is everlasting to at once   251,1
hold that the world too is everlasting.

    If, then, soul has its essence in being the source of movement, it
could never exist alone without body which is moved [by it]. For just
as it is impossible for the enmattered life of bodies to exist apart from   5

body because it has its being in being the life of *body*, and, speaking
generally, impossible for the irrational soul, which is itself self-moved
and the source of movement in the view of Plato ([a view] to which
10   Proclus himself subscribes in his commentary on the *Phaedrus*), to
exist apart from body because it has its essence in being the source of
life and movement (*zôtikên te kai kinêtikên*) for body, so, one assumes,
is it impossible for the soul of the world,[440] if it has its essence in being
15   the source of movement of body, either to exist apart from body or to
engage in any activity which is separate from body. For if its essence
could not exist apart from body, it would, one assumes, be much more
impossible for its activities to exist apart from body; for it has been
20   well demonstrated by Aristotle in *On the Soul*[441] and is accepted by
all that should there be an essence which is separate from body, it will
in every case also have an activity which is separate from body (for
an essence which has been separated [from body] will exist to no good
purpose if it is deprived of all activity) and that should there be any
activity which is separate from body, then the essence from which
25   such an activity proceeds will in every case be separate from body as
well. For it is not possible for an activity to be superior to the essence
[which gives rise to it]. But it *will* be superior should it be separate
from body while the essence is not separate. And it is agreed that
252,1   things which have an existence separate from bodies are superior to
those which are not separate. So if an essence is a cause but [its]
activity an effect, and if it is impossible for an effect to be superior to
its cause and for a thing which is brought into being to be superior to
5   that which brings it into being, then it is impossible, in the event that
an activity is separate from body, for the essence not to be in every
case separate from body as well. There is, therefore, every necessity
that if the essence of the soul is not separate from body, every activity
of soul should also not be separate from body; but this is clearly false.
10   **4.** For souls are clearly still in the body when they free themselves
of their relation and passionate attachment to it by engaging in
intellectual activities which are separate from and unrelated to all
body; 'for', says Aristotle,[442] 'it is hard even to imagine what kind of
15   part [of the body] thought will hold together or how it will do it'.
Therefore there is every necessity that the essence of soul, from
which such activity proceeds, should also be separate from and unrelated to all body, as indeed Plato and all the best philosophers have
20   believed. For it is from this that Plotinus inferred its immortality as
well, showing from its separate activities that its essence is necessarily separate as well, and on that account immortal.[443] And if the
essence of soul is separate from and unrelated to all body, then it does
25   not have its essence in being the source of movement. For this, as we
have shown,[444] is nothing other than for soul to have its being and
existence in its relation to body.
And besides, it would be absurd to hold that body *qua* body has its

being outside of any relation to soul (if, that is, even for animate 253,1
bodies, being bodies is one thing and being animate another, and they
have no need of a relationship to soul to be bodies), but that incorp- 5
oreal – and intellectual and immortal – soul cannot, since it has its
existence in being the source of movement, exist apart from body.
This is nothing else than to make the intellectual essence of soul
inferior even to bodies.

And that Proclus himself knows that soul has being and essence in 10
one way but is the source of movement in another and that whether
it is engaged in contemplation or is endowing body with life or moving
it in some other fashion, these are all activity of soul and not its
essence, could be proved from many of his works, but it will suffice to 15
quote a single passage from his commentary on the *Phaedrus*; for in
commenting on the present (sc. Plato's[445]) argument about the soul he
expresses himself, to quote his exact words, as follows:

One should be aware that in the *Phaedo* he was attempting to
establish that soul is immortal by means of arguments from
recollection, from its likeness to divine things and from its 20
provision of life to other things. But these are all activities of
soul. And so in the *Phaedo* the proof was drawn from the
activities of soul. Here, on the other hand, he takes his proof
from the essence of soul. So, to the degree that the essence of 25
soul is more perfect than and superior to its activity, to that
degree is the proof of the immortality of soul in this work 254,1
superior to and more exact than that in the *Phaedo*, for the
argument proceeds from the essence of soul, that is, from self-
movement.

If, then, Proclus states that the provision of life to other things
(namely to bodies) – from which life all activity and all movement in 5
animate bodies arises – is an activity of soul rather than its essence
and that its essence is self-movement, then the essence of soul and its
being the cause and source of movement are not the same thing, but
self-movement is, as Plato says, the essence of soul and being the 10
source of movement is a power of soul from which the vital and motor
activity of bodies proceeds.

The above arguments, then, have shown that it is not possible to
say that soul has its essence in being the source of movement. And so 15
even if someone claims that the essence of soul is ungenerated and
imperishable it is not implied that he holds that the world too is
ungenerated and imperishable.

5. But if soul has its being and essence in one way and its being 20
the source of movement in another, [then] it is certainly an activity
or a power of soul that leads to its being the source of movement, just
as the teacher, who is the source of change (*kinêseôs*) in the pupil, is

25   not the source of such change *qua* man (for, if this were so, every man
the moment he was a man would immediately also be a teacher) but
in consequence of one of the powers or activities associated with his
essence. Given that this is so and it has been shown that it is in
consequence of a power or an activity of soul that[446] it is the source of
255,1 movement, if someone is able to show that every power of soul is at
once attended by its actualisation or, at any rate, that all of the
activities of soul are everlasting, we shall concede that soul is also, to
the extent that it is the source of movement, everlastingly active, that
5   is, that it everlastingly moves body of some kind; but if the activities
of soul, whether cognitive or practical, are not everlasting and it
moves from ignorance to knowledge and back from knowledge to
forgetfulness and ignorance, and from vice to virtue and from virtue
10   back to vice, what obvious necessity is there still that the power of
soul which moves bodies should be everlastingly active? It will, then,
sometimes be potentially rather than actually the source of movement, just as it is sometimes potentially rather than actually
possessed of a skill.
15   In particular, it is clear to everyone that the self-reflexive activities
of soul, and still more those which are more intellectual and elevate
it towards the divine, excel beyond comparison those of its activities
which are associated with body, perhaps even as much as soul excels
body, or, better, as much as intelligibles and mind, not to say even
20   God himself, transcend in their incomparable superiority the nature
of bodies, if, as is the case, the intellectual activities of soul connect it
to God but its other [activities] to bodies. If, then, the superior
activities of soul (I mean those which are intellectual and elevate it)
25   are not everlasting, the inferior and debasing ones, one supposes,
would *a fortiori* not be everlasting. For if the better necessarily
belongs to the better and not, contrariwise, the better to the worse,
and if everlastingness is better than perishability, [then] it is, I
assume, clear that if everlastingness does not belong to the intellec-
256,1 tual activities, everlastingness would *a fortiori* not belong to those
activities of soul which move the body and are inferior to them.
And besides, the intellectual activities of soul have, if it is indeed
both intelligible and mind, been agreed by all parties to belong to it
5   even by nature, but those which move bodies are contrary to nature
for reason and are not constitutive of the perfection of its essence; for
10   the essential nature (*idiotês*) of reason is not characterised by the
moving of bodies; for this is more a characteristic of nature and of
irrational power than of rational and intellectual essence. If, then, the
rational and perfective activities of our soul are not everlasting, one
supposes that those which are bodily and contrary to [its] nature and
15   foreign as it were would *a fortiori* not be everlasting.
And if the activities of soul that are associated with body are not
everlasting, then neither can everlasting body be fastened to soul.

6. It is also possible to argue the matter as follows.

All bodily movements, or indeed changes in general, are four in   20
genus.[447] In [the genus of] substance are generation and passing out
of existence, in quantity are increase and diminution, in quality is
alteration, in place is locomotion. Of this last, one kind is in a straight
line, as for example that of the elements (some of which move upwards from below, others downwards from above), and the other kind
is circular movement, as for example that of the heavenly bodies. If,   25
then, soul is the source and cause of the movement of bodies and
therefore, as Proclus believes, everlastingly moves bodies involuntarily and just by being, it is altogether necessary that it also be in
accordance with one or all or several of these movements that soul   257,1
everlastingly moves body. Therefore, if that which moves moves
everlastingly and that which is moved is moved everlastingly, then
the movement too will be everlasting and have no beginning or end
to its existence. We must, then, consider whether any of the movements enumerated [above] is everlasting. For, if none of them is   5
everlasting, that which is moved will not be moved everlastingly and
the soul which moves [it] will not move [it] everlastingly.

That no case of either generation or passing out of existence is
beginningless or endless is clear to everyone. A thing which is coming
to be ceases to at a limit, [namely when it attains its] form. The   10
generation of a house, for example, has as its beginning the [begin-
ning] of the foundations and as its limit the shape of the house. And,
similarly, in the case of things which come to be in nature, the
beginning of their generation is the sowing of the seed and its limit
the perfection of their natural form, for instance, human form. And   15
in the same way something that is perishing stops [perishing] at a
limit, [namely] privation and not-being. In brief, if generation is the
path from not-being to being, and passing out of existence is the path
from being to not-being, it is impossible for generation and passing
out of existence to be beginningless and endless, since they are   20
limited by being and by not-being.

Nor, moreover, can anything alter everlastingly. Rest and definition are present in things and all things are *not*, as Heraclitus held,[448]
in movement. Further, alteration too, being movement, is embraced   25
by two forms, the one from which it is [moving] and the one towards
which [it is moving]. Growing white, for example, is the path from
black to white, and, when the thing which is altering has got there
and become white, it remains in that state thereafter. And, indeed, it   258,1
is plain that actual sensation, since it is a kind of alteration of the
senses, of its nature commences and ceases. For we neither see nor
hear nor employ any other sense continuously and sleep is nothing   5
other than the resting of the senses.

And we say the same things in regard to increase and diminution.
Bodies do not increase [in size] indefinitely but remain at a pre-estab-

lished natural size; and, consequently, diminution too, the contrary
of increase, is also limited.

10   It remains, then, to ask whether one of the [two] types of local
movement is everlasting.

15   Aristotle has adequately demonstrated[449] that things which move
in a straight line have a beginning and an end to their movement and
that they are bracketed by rest on either side of these – I mean before
the beginning and after the end [of their movement]. For if movement
is in magnitude and infinite magnitude does not exist, movement in
a straight line will not be infinite. And nor can objects which are
moving in a straight line reverse direction smoothly (*kata sun-
ekheian*) without coming to rest. For example, if an object which has
been moving downwards from above reverses direction and moves

20   back up from below, there will in every case be [a period of] rest
between these two contrary movements. Aristotle has also demonstrated this.

In regard to the circular movement which the heavenly bodies
exhibit, it will be shown more fully, if God permits, in *Objections*

25   *Against Aristotle On the Everlastingness of the World*,[450] that it too is
not everlasting; for we shall need to produce additional arguments

259,1   against this position. However, if it has been adequately demonstrated in the first chapter that it is impossible for the generation of
the world to be everlasting (something, indeed, which will be demonstrated even more fully [and] in detail when we have got rid of the

5   obstruction[451] arising from all of the puzzles[452]), it is clear that circular movement cannot be everlasting either.

So, if no kind of bodily movement is everlasting, there will be no
body that is moved everlastingly and soul does not move an everlasting[453] body. Therefore it is possible for the soul of the world to be, as

10   Plato holds, everlasting but for the world not to be everlasting.

7. But nor is there any very pressing need for us to give an account
of circular movement at this point. It was in the course of discussing
our souls in the *Phaedrus*[454] and out of a desire to prove their

15   immortality that Plato defined the essence of soul as self-movement
and self-movement as the source of movement in bodies. But it is, I
assume, clear to everyone that no body in us is observed to move with
a circular movement. Every living creature moves from place to place

20   but none of the bodies that rotate changes its position entirely; they
all rotate about their own centres, which [themselves] remain motionless. Therefore no living creature contains any body which moves
with a circular movement. Therefore, when Plato says that self-movement is the source of movement, he does not mean that it is the source

25   of circular movement. For he says that self-movement is the defini-
260,1   tion of all soul. But not every soul moves a body which rotates; for
nothing below the moon naturally moves with a circular movement.

Therefore Plato is not saying that self-movement is the source of circular movement [alone].

And besides, Proclus states that soul is the source and cause of movement involuntarily and just by being, but soul clearly does not cause bodies to move locally involuntarily and just by being but through desire and choice. For if soul moved bodies from place to place merely by existing, their movement would be continuous and the bodies of animals would never be at rest in one place, if soul always possesses the power to move [things] and were it to move [them] through an unconscious natural power. But in fact all movement in a straight line begins from rest and ceases in rest. Therefore soul does not impart rectilinear movement to bodies involuntarily and just by being. And if rectilinear movement, being local movement, takes place as a result of desire and choice on the part of soul, and not involuntarily just by [its] being, it would follow that if there *were* some kind of circular movement arising from soul, it too [would be] at the initiative and choice of soul, since circular movement too is local movement. And surely it would be nothing short of irrational if each individual soul imparted local movement to the body subordinated to it through initiative and choice, while the soul of the universe alone was the source and cause of the movement of the world involuntarily, like irrational nature. But if local movement takes place through choice on the part of soul, and if Proclus states that soul is self-moved and the source of movement not by choice but just by being, then Plato is not claiming that soul is the source of local movement. But circular movement is a local movement. Therefore it has been shown from Proclus' own words that Plato is not claiming that self-movement is the source of circular movement.

But it is agreed by all that none of the other types of movement is everlasting. Therefore Plato is not claiming that self-movement is the source of everlasting movement. And so even if the definition of our souls should fit the soul of the universe, it is not on that account at once necessary that, because soul is said to be ungenerated and imperishable by Plato, the world which is moved by it should also be ungenerated and imperishable.

8. But even should we regard self-movement as the source of all movement, including local movement, even then there is no obvious necessity that once there is soul there should also be body moved by it. When Plato claims[455] that soul, being the source of movement, is ungenerated, on the ground that a source is ungenerated, he does not, it seems to me, express himself correctly. Irrational souls too are sources of movement for irrational bodies, since they also are, as Plato says, self-moved and therefore each a source of movement, but they are nevertheless not ungenerated. The natural constitution (*phusis*) of a stone is the cause and source of its natural downward movement and that of fire of its upward movement but nobody would venture to

claim that the natural constitution of individual bodies is ungenerated.

But even should it be conceded that soul is, as Plato holds, ungen-
262,1   erated and the source of movement, there is no obvious necessity that
as soon as there is a source, the things of which it is the source should
also exist, since, as has been shown,[456] soul does not have its essence
in being the source of movement for body. The builder is responsible
5   for and the source of the movement involved in building, and the
teacher for the movement of the pupil in learning, but there is not at
once something under construction or something being taught the
moment there is a builder or a teacher, because the builder and the
10   teacher do not derive their being from being the source of movement.
Similarly, God is the very first cause and source of all things that are
and will be, but all things have not [always] coexisted along with God,
since there are also generated and perishable things in the universe.

And even more to the point, it is, I suppose, altogether necessary
15   that soul should also be the source and cause of the movement of
generated and perishable bodies as well,[457] for movement in living
creatures originates with soul. Therefore if soul is also the source of
20   the movement of generated and perishable body, and if, as Plato
holds, soul is ungenerated but this body is not ungenerated, then
there is no necessity that once the source and cause of the movement
of body exists, body moved by it should also of necessity exist. Even
should it be agreed that perishable body is not moved by soul imme-
25   diately but, as Proclus states, through the mediation of everlasting
[body], there is every necessity that these people should hold either
that soul itself is the source of movement in perishable body as well,
263,1   or that everlasting body is, or that both of them are. Whichever [of
these positions] one holds, one must concede that the source and
cause of movement in perishable body is, in the view of these people,
everlasting while the thing which actually moves is generated and
perishable.

5   There is, then, no necessity that if the source of a thing is ungenerated, it too should be ungenerated.

9. But if they will claim that soul is said by Plato to be the source
of movement because it gives life to bodies, and that it therefore gives
10   life to body involuntarily and just by being present in it, and that
therefore there must in every case be something which is everlastingly being given life by it, it is worth asking first what kind of life it
is that soul confers upon body and then whether it is possible for that
kind of life to be everlasting.

There is, one supposes, every necessity that the life conferred upon
15   bodies by soul is that by virtue of which living bodies differ from those
which have no share in life. Living bodies differ from those without
life by being sentient and taking nourishment and growing and
20   reproducing themselves, as well as by [experiencing] desire and by

[engaging in] local movement on the initiative of soul. And so all bodily life is encompassed in these. Each of them is observed [to be present] in living bodies either potentially or actually (potentially, clearly, through capacity[458]).

Now, that no such activity of soul (neither sensation, that is, nor local movement; not growth, not diminution, nor any other of those enumerated earlier) is everlasting has recently been proved by us[459] by means of [arguments based on] self-evident fact. And so soul is not the source and cause of the actual life of bodies just by being. And if he claims that soul is from [time] everlasting the source and cause of the capacity for life[460] and that it confers this upon bodies as soon as it exists,[461] in the first place[462] no capacity, nor any potentiality at all, is a movement. For if actual sensation and growth are movements, clearly [sensation and growth] as capacity, and potential [sensation and growth] in general, would be rest from sensation and growth. For the [kind of] change that occurs in things which move in a straight line is not a change from one movement to another but a change from rest to movement – just as there is also change from movement to rest. And the same applies to the other [types of movement]. The potential life of bodies, then, is not movement but rather rest. And so when Plato says that self-movement is the source of movement, he will not be claiming that the potential life of bodies is movement.

Therefore, if the capacity for life in bodies is not movement, and if the actual movements through which their life is expressed (*hai zôtikai autôn kinêseis*) are not everlasting, Plato will not, as a consequence of saying that self-movement is the source of movement and that self-movement is ungenerated and imperishable, be compelled to say that the world too is ungenerated and imperishable.

And so it is because soul is sometimes able to move body that he calls it the source of movement, not because it moves it everlastingly. Otherwise, as we have shown, the hypothesis of Plato cannot be in accord with the nature of things. And so, if Plato is not to be drawing invalid conclusions, he means[463] that self-movement is always potentially the source of movement, but not always actually.

10. And even should one concede that the capacity for life in bodies either is or is said to be, as Proclus believes, a [form of] movement, we can go back to the beginning and simply say that it is obvious that the rational soul is not the cause of this kind of bodily life at all, whether as capacity or actual, for bodies. For if sensation or movement or any of the other vital powers or activities observed in bodies, on the basis of which bodies are said to have life, came to bodies from [the rational soul], nothing would be alive that did not partake of the rational essence. But in fact even those animals which are irrational and have no share of rational soul are seen to share in all of the above-mentioned[464] [vital powers or activities] both in capacity and actually, and many of them have sharper and more

15   accurate senses and share in the other powers of soul [to a greater
degree than we do]. So it is clear that such life does not come to bodies
from the rational essence of the soul. All that has passed from the
20   rational soul to the things which have a share in it is the patterning
and ordering of irrational life by it, and rational life consists precisely
in the orderly movement of the emotive faculties of the irrational soul
according to [the principles of] reason. And just as in the case of a
team of two horses (which Plato in fact used as an image of our soul[465])
25   the horses are the cause of the body simply moving while the charioteer in charge of them is responsible for their trained (*tekhnikês*) and
coordinated movement, so in us, one supposes, is it the role of the
irrational soul to be the cause of our bodies simply having life while
266,1   reason is responsible for order and harmony in the movements of our
emotive faculties.

And if in individual living creatures the rational soul does not
associate immediately with the body, there being need of the irra-
5   tional faculty as a kind of link [between them] through which the body
is given life and becomes fit for the reception of the rational soul, then
there is, one supposes, every necessity that even if some rational soul
really is set over the heaven, it will *a fortiori* not associate immediately with heavenly body but use the irrational faculty as an
10   intermediary through which illumination from the rational soul may
come to the heavenly body. For bodies by themselves, without a share
in life and perception, cannot be immediately illuminated by the
15   rational soul, just as our eyes cannot take in the sun's rays without
the intermediate transparent [medium]. What we have said so far
will meet with the approval of even the pagan philosophers.[466]

Now, if the irrational soul is the cause of life in bodies, it is clear
that even if self-movement, that is to say, the rational soul, is a source
20   of movement, it is not the source of all movement but only of that
which is subordinated to it and associated with reason. [This is
clearly so] since even in inanimate things nature is a source of
movement in them, if indeed, as Aristotle holds,[467] nature is a source
of movement and rest. For nature [present] in fire is the source and
25   cause of the upward movement of fire and nature in water of its
downward movement. And I suppose it is obvious to everyone that
inanimate things are not moved by rational soul given that even those
living creatures which are rational are not. So just as the charioteer
267,1   is the source of the skilled movement of the chariot, and the helmsman likewise of that of the ship, while neither is responsible simply
for their movement, and there need not be any chariot or ship just
5   because there is a charioteer or helmsman (for there can be someone
who possesses the skill to be a helmsman or charioteer[468] without
there being a ship or a chariot), in the same way, since the rational
soul is a source not of all movement but of the kind that is appropriate

to reason, there will be no necessity that once there is rational soul, there must also be[469] body moved by it.

11. The necessity is in fact the other way round. With the elimi- 10 nation of soul, bodies moved by it are also eliminated, since where animate bodies are present there must also be soul; [but][470] animate [body] does not in every case accompany soul, for while the soul is believed to be immortal, animate bodies clearly come to be and perish. 15 For this reason Plato does not say in the *Phaedrus* that because of the existence of soul the heaven of necessity also exists, but [rather] that with its elimination the order that has flowed from it to the universe 20 is at once thrown into confusion. This, at all events, is, to quote his exact words, what he says in that dialogue:

> The self-moved, then, is [the source] of movement. And it is not possible for it either to perish or to come to be, or the whole heaven and the whole earth would collapse and remain immo- bile and never again have a source of movement to bring them 25 [back] into being.[471]

It is important to note that when he says that it is not possible for 268,1 self-movement to either perish or come to be, he does not go on to talk about the consequences of the generation of self-movement but about those of its passing out of existence. The result will be, he says, that the whole heaven and the whole earth will collapse and remain immobile and never again have a source of movement to bring them 5 [back] into being. This does not follow from the generation of self-movement (for when self-movement comes into existence, it in turn provides a source of movement to things which are moved [by it], so that, having been moved, they may come to be), but if self-movement should perish, the things which get their existence from it will have nothing from which to derive their existence because the source [of 10 movement] will have perished. This is clear not only from Plato's statement but by logical entailment and the very nature of the facts; as we said earlier,[472] although soul is believed to be immortal, there is no necessity that our bodies also be immortal. And so it is by no 15 means necessary that because of the existence of soul, body moved by it should also exist. And if [the existence of] soul necessarily follows from the existence of animate body, what will assuredly follow by conversion by negation[473] under the rules of logic is not the existence 20 of soul from the existence of body but the non-existence of body from the non-existence of soul. There is, therefore, no need for someone who claims that soul is ungenerated to claim that the world too is ungenerated.

12. But, since Proclus, as though wishing to add a kind of neces- 25 sity to his argument, claims that soul is by its very being involuntarily the source and cause of life and movement in bodies, let 269,1

us examine this [idea] as well. And let it be conceded by us, even if
this is not what Plato says, that rational souls are by their very being
involuntarily the sources of life and movement in bodies. [When I say]

5   'by their very being' I do not mean that souls have their being and
essence in being sources of movement (this hypothesis has already
been refuted; our current position is that soul has its being in one way
and is the source of movement in another), but that I am proposing
that we assume that (*hupokeisthô*), just as the sun involuntarily

10   illuminates the moment it appears and fire heats the moment it is
present (obviously, that is, provided that things capable of being
heated or illuminated are present; for fire does not have its essence
in heating nor the sun in illuminating, but fire and the sun involun-

15   tarily illuminate and heat if receptive objects are present), so in
exactly the same way too does the rational soul by its very being
involuntarily confer life and movement upon the things to which it is
present. This being so, what necessity would there be, should soul be

20   ungenerated, for body moved by it also to be ungenerated? Light too
has the property of setting a potentially transparent [medium] in
motion the moment it is present, but light assuredly does not, the
moment it exists, light up everything that is potentially transparent
but obviously only what is in existence, and not all of that but [only]

25   what stands in the [required] relation to the source of illumination.
For when the sun is above the earth, all of the air and water beneath
the earth are shielded from it by the earth, and because they do not
stand in the [required] relation to the source of illumination, they

270,1   derive no movement from the light and their potential transparency
is not activated. And, moreover, colours too are by their very being
involuntarily such as to stimulate vision, and sounds hearing, and

5   every other perceptible thing is by its very being such as to stimulate
one or other of the senses, but there is no necessity that as soon as
there is a colour an act of seeing should immediately be stimulated
by it, nor any necessity that as soon as there is a sound an act of
hearing should be caused by that sound; and the same goes for the

10   rest [of the senses and their objects]. For colours hidden at the bottom
of the sea or under the earth, and equally those shrouded in darkness,
are by nature such as to give rise to acts of seeing and give rise to
[these] acts of seeing by their very being and not by conscious decision, but even so no act of seeing is caused by them. For the essence

15   of colours does not lie in their being such as to give rise to an act of
seeing. On the one hand, they exist and have being by virtue of being
colours (hence they are every bit as much colours even if they are
never seen), on the other, it is an essential property of theirs to be able
to stimulate vision – provided, of course, that it falls upon them and

20   stands in the same relation to them as [any] passive principle does to
an active one. So just as an active principle is [only] potentially active
until a passive principle is present (I mean potentially in [the sense

of possessing a] capacity), so are colours [only] potentially able to stimulate vision as long as it [sc. vision] is not present. Sounds too, although involuntarily able to stimulate hearing, are [only] potentially able to stimulate hearing if they occur in an isolated place where there is no sentient creature. And an object of desire (such as, for example, the beauty of a beloved [youth][474]) is by its very being such as to arouse desire, but it is not the case that, the moment an object of desire exists, desire must in every instance be aroused by it, but [only] when [desire] comes into contact with it and comes to stand in [the required] relation to it.

If, then, the thing that is of a nature to be moved by it does not in every case coexist with everything that is capable of moving something else, even if it moves [things] involuntarily and just by being, then it was wrong of Proclus, having reached the conclusion (*labôn*) that self-movement is ungenerated and imperishable and the source of movement in bodies and that it is such as to move bodies just by existing and not by conscious decision, to claim that it follows from this that the world too is ungenerated and imperishable on the ground that once there is a moving cause, the thing that is of a nature to be moved by it of necessity coexists with it. That this is not true we have shown from the facts themselves.

13. And Plato himself states in the *Phaedrus* that being ungenerated and imperishable are consequences of self-movement and of that alone and declares that everything which is externally moved undergoes cessation[475] of movement and of life. The passage goes as follows:

> All soul is immortal, for that which is always in movement is immortal. But that which moves something else and is itself moved by something else undergoes cessation of movement and therefore undergoes cessation of life. Only a thing which moves itself never ceases moving because it does not abandon its own nature, and, moreover, this is the fount and source of movement for everything else which moves.[476]

If, then, it is actually only that which moves itself which, since it cannot depart from its own nature, never ceases moving and is therefore immortal, and everything which is moved by something else, on the other hand, undergoes cessation of movement and life, and if, as Aristotle has shown[477] and Plato had earlier declared,[478] no body is self-moved but each and every one of them is moved by something else, and if the heaven and world, since they are not self-moved but are moved by self-moved soul and move other things as a result of being moved by it, are body, then, according to Plato, the world too will undergo cessation of movement and life. And this is in agreement with the words 'since you have come to be, you are not indissoluble nor altogether immortal' in the *Timaeus*.[479]

25

271,1

5

10

15

20

25
272,1

5

10

But it is impossible for a thing which undergoes cessation of life to be ungenerated. Nothing which is perishable (even if it is not destroyed by being overwhelmed by a power which is stronger than its own nature) is ungenerated, since it is not even possible for a thing
15   which is ungenerated to be perishable. For if something perishable were ungenerated, then, of necessity, something ungenerated will be perishable, which is impossible.

Therefore the heaven is not ungenerated according to Plato, since [according to him] it is not imperishable by nature either. And it is not imperishable because, undergoing cessation of movement, it un-
20   dergoes cessation of life. It undergoes cessation of life and movement because it is not self-moved but moved by another thing, soul, and something else moves everything within it. It is for this reason that he says that, in order that it may remain immortal and indissoluble, a [constantly] restored immortality comes to it from the creator
25   because it does not have immortality from its own nature, as has been shown by many proofs in the sixth [chapter].[480]

14. But, as I said at the outset,[481] Proclus claims that it follows
273,1   from soul's being self-moved that body moved by it is co-everlasting with it. In this he flies in the face of the facts, since all bodies which
5   are moved by souls are clearly generated and perishable. He should have argued from the agreed to the unknown. In other words, starting from the fact that all bodies that are moved by souls are seen to come to be and perish, he should have concluded that not even the body of
10   the world could be ungenerated and imperishable. [Instead,] *he*[482] perverts the nature of demonstration and argues from the non-evident to the non-evident. Assuming without proof that as soon as there is soul there must necessarily also be body which is moved by it, [an assumption] which is not warranted either by the facts or by logic, he
15   claims on this basis that it is clear that every soul is in the first instance mounted upon an everlasting body and everlastingly moves this body, and should it find itself in perishable bodies, moves the perishable ones by means of the everlasting one.

Now, perhaps it is clear to everyone [in view of the above] that, since the antecedent has been refuted, the consequent has been
20   refuted along with it; for if we have shown that there is no necessity that as soon as there is soul there should also be body which is moved by it, then clearly no further argument will render it necessary for souls to be in the first instance mounted upon an everlasting body.
25   But perhaps, on the other hand, it will do no harm to examine this last hypothesis in its own right [and determine] whether [the theory] that there must always be a kind of everlasting body attached to souls and existing alongside them throughout their existence and that souls are in the first instance mounted upon this and move perishable bodies by means of it has any claim to be in conformity with natural or [logical] necessity.[483]

Let us, then, begin our investigation. Local movement in bodies is   274,1
of two kinds: either circular or rectilinear. (The mixed movement
which is referred to as a spiral is not natural. There is no body in
nature that moves with a spiral movement, a fact which, obvious   5
though it is, will be demonstrated below.) Now, quite apart from its
being self-evident, all the pagan philosophers[484] have clearly stated
that bodies which move in a straight line are generated and perishable, for it is impossible to discover a body that moves in a straight
line which is not completely subject to generation and passing out of   10
existence. If, then, there is any body at all which is ungenerated and
imperishable, it will either be entirely motionless or exhibit circular
movement if any at all. (Let us concede for the time being that it is an
open question whether those bodies which move in a circle are
ungenerated and imperishable.) This being so, if there is, as [our   15
opponents] claim, another, everlasting, body upon which soul is in the
first instance mounted [and] by means of which it moves perishable
bodies, then either[485] this moves perishable body by moving locally
itself, as a mule moves when it moves a wagon and a hand moves   20
when it moves something other [than itself], or it moves perishable
bodies by means of a natural power while remaining free of local
movement itself, as a magnet imparts local movement to iron, or
amber to straw, while remaining still itself.

Now, if it imparts movement by means of a natural force while
itself remaining motionless, it will not impart movement at one time   25
and not impart it at another but always impart it as long as body
which is moved by it is present and stands in the [required] relation
to it. That is how active natural powers in bodies work; a magnet
always attracts nearby iron as long as the natural force within it is   275,1
not exhausted and remains intact, and amber likewise straw, and the
hot always draws up moisture and the cold always causes things in
its vicinity to contract. And if [imperishable body] is always impart-   5
ing movement, perishable bodies will always be moved; for a thing
which is moved must always move in the same way as the thing which
moves it does. But perishable bodies are not always in movement. So
if perishable bodies are not always in movement but sometimes move
and sometimes are at rest, then clearly [imperishable body] does not   10
always impart movement. But if it does not always impart movement,
it does not [impart it] by a natural power. And besides,[486] soul would
no longer be imparting movement through the agency of this [ever-
lasting] body if it [sc. the body] really did move perishable bodies by
a natural power while itself remaining motionless; [the body] by itself
would be the primary cause of the movement of perishable bodies,   15
just as the magnet is primarily the cause of movement in the iron and
does not itself move through being moved by soul.

And if it does not impart movement by means of a natural power,
the only remaining possibility is that it is moved locally by soul and

20   moves perishable body in the same way, just as a mule is moved by soul and moves a wagon or some other object [as a consequence]. And if it imparts movement through being moved itself, it imparts this movement by being moved either in a straight line or in a circle by soul.

Now, it is not possible for this body to be moved in a circle and to move perishable [body] in a straight line as a consequence. If it

25   imparts movement by moving [itself], it obviously imparts movement by thrust and force. By moving in a circle, it moves about its own centre, which remains unmoving, and so does not completely change position. So how does it impart movement to a perishable body in such

276,1   a way as to cause it to move in its entirety in a straight line from one position to another? A thing which moves another by means of its own movement and carries it from one position to another by itself passing from one place to another, as this [imperishable body] does, is changing [the position of the other body] along with its own. At any rate, it

5   is by changing their own position that horses change the position of the chariot and of the charioteer as well. Moreover, a thing which moves something else communicates to it the same kind of movement as it exhibits itself. The heaven, for instance, which carries the ether which lies beneath it around with it by means of its own movement,

10   carries it too around in a circle. (It communicates the movement involved in alteration and generation to things here [on earth] not simply through its rotation alone but more by means of the power and particular relation to them of the heavenly bodies. The sun, for example, heats things by coming close to them and, conversely, cools

15   them when it moves away. But at present we are only concerned with local movement). And again, the air, which moves in a straight line, imparts the same kind of movement to a ship, and a mule likewise to a wagon. For [in this latter case] the kind of movement [imparted] is the same even though the manner is different (I mean the manner of

20   the movement) because a mule moves by means of legs and a wagon by means of wheels.[487]

15. And in any case, the movement of wheels is not, as one might suppose, of a different kind. The movement of wheels is rolling, not

25   circular movement, and rolling too is a mode of rectilinear movement. [It is] as though one were to imagine a round stone travelling down an inclined [surface]; the shape is the cause of the different mode of movement, not a difference in the kind of the movement. At any rate,

277,1   if one were to change the shape of the wheels, the mode of the rectilinear movement would be changed along with it. And it is clear that the plane (*megethos*) upon which rolling occurs is extended rectilinearly. And so rolling objects move in a straight line. And so

5   rolling too is a rectilinear movement, differing only in the mode of movement involved, just as creatures that go on foot differ from those

that slither or crawl only in their mode [of locomotion]. And, indeed, none of the bodies that naturally rotate rolls.

And so if perishable body exhibits rectilinear movement, and if, as [our opponents] claim, perishable [body] is moved by the movement of ungenerated and imperishable body, then it is impossible for the latter, while itself rotating, to impart rectilinear movement to perishable body; for that which rotates does not completely change its position.

And since a perishable body moves not only as a whole but also in its parts, as when someone moves just their hand or just their finger or foot or head, let these learned men tell us what the mode of movement of a part is; for if an everlasting body, while rotating, moves a perishable body as a whole by means of its own movement, what is the explanation of the movement of a part [of a perishable body]? For a whole and a part do not move from the same cause. It seems plausible, even necessary, that, just as the rotation of the whole [of an everlasting body] moves the whole [of a perishable body], so must this or that part of the everlasting [body] move this or that part of the perishable one by moving itself. But it is not possible for any part of bodies that rotate to move by itself separately from the whole. So what is the source of the movement of the parts of a perishable body? It is not possible for a part of a perishable [body] to be moved [separately] by the movement of the whole [of an everlasting body]. For if a perishable body is moved by the movement of the whole of an everlasting [body] as though pushed by it, and if the perishable body is a continuous whole (*sunekhes ... auto heautôi*), there is every necessity that the perishable body should when pushed move as a whole along with the movement of the [everlasting body]. So [our opponents] will not be able to explain how a part of a perishable body moves while [the body as a] whole remains motionless.

So if it is necessary that a part be moved by a part in the same way that the whole is moved by the whole, and if it is impossible for a part to be moved by a part because it is not possible for any part of bodies that rotate to move in a circle on its own while the whole is stationary, then neither does the rotation of the whole [of an everlasting body] move a perishable [body] as a whole.

And so it is not possible for this [everlasting body of theirs] to move a perishable body rectilinearly by itself rotating.

16. The only remaining possibility, then, is that, if this body exists at all, it too moves in a straight line. And if it too moves in a straight line, movement in a straight line will either be natural to it or not natural to it.

Now, if movement in a straight line is natural to it, since no body which moves in a straight line is ungenerated and imperishable, neither will this one be ungenerated and imperishable. If, on the

20   other hand, it does not move in a straight line naturally, it moves in a straight line either supernaturally[488] or contrary to its nature and by force.

Now, it is impossible for it to do so supernaturally. [Qualities] which belong to things supernaturally belong naturally to [other] things which are superior to them, as circular movement, which
25   belongs to ethereal body supernaturally, belongs naturally to a superior [body], namely heavenly [body]. Such [qualities] are said to belong to certain things supernaturally precisely because they belong naturally to substances which are superior to those things. For this
277,1 reason we say that those souls that are divinely-inspired and those that receive foreknowledge of the future or acquire insight into other secret matters are supernaturally active because such activity is
5   characteristic of superhuman natures. So if rectilinear movement belongs to perishable bodies naturally, it would not also belong supernaturally to this body upon which they claim soul is primarily
10   mounted, since it is superior to [perishable body]; for they assert both that what is everlasting is superior to what is perishable and that this [body of theirs] is everlasting.

If, then, this body exhibits rectilinear movement neither naturally nor supernaturally, it evidently must do so contrary to its nature and by force. But no body which moves contrary to its nature and by force is ungenerated and imperishable. Both all bodies which move in a
15   straight line (i.e. particular things, [by which] I mean a particular instance of fire or a particular instance of water or of anything else) and everything which moves contrary to nature (as, again, particular things; for fire is [only] carried downwards, or a clod of earth or some water, say, upwards, by force and contrary to their nature), and,
20   [speaking] generally, all things that are receptive of movement which is contrary to their nature, are observed to come to be and to perish, and nothing of this sort is ungenerated and imperishable. And so this body too, if it moves in a straight line contrary to its nature, will not be ungenerated and imperishable. For the very path towards [a condition that is] contrary to [their] nature – in fact even the cause of
25   a movement that is contrary to their nature – is a cause and source of passing out of existence for bodies.

Therefore either let [our opponents] search for yet another[489] ungenerated body which will move this one, and we shall once more
280,1 raise the same puzzles in regard to it, and in this way the argument will proceed *ad infinitum*, or else let them concede[490] that soul is of necessity mounted immediately upon perishable body and moves it directly. (By 'immediately' I mean without there being another, ever-
5   lasting, body between them; for we ourselves concede that nature and the irrational powers, which are themselves generated and perishable, lie between rational soul and body).

17. And besides, if this ungenerated and imperishable body,

through being moved, as [their] hypothesis has it, by soul (whether
one would have this to be in a straight line or in a circle), in its turn   10
moves perishable bodies, and if every body which moves another body
through its own movement moves it by touching and being in contact
with it, then this everlasting [body] also moves perishable [body] by
touching it and being in contact with it. There is, therefore, every
necessity that everlasting body should be in external or internal   15
contact with perishable [body].

But if it moved it by touching it externally, the cause of movement
would be seen to be external too. But we do not in fact observe
anything imparting movement externally; on the contrary, the sin-
ews which move the body are agreed to be inside it. Nor would the air   20
be in continuous external contact with our bodies at every point if
there were another body external to it that was in contact with the
mortal body and moved it. And moreover, when some [other] body
was in external contact with us at all points – this can happen, as it
does when a person is swimming entirely under the water – this   25
[everlasting] body would have been separated from us and would not
be imparting movement [to us] because it would not be touching us
externally. [This would be so] because it is not possible for both water
and some other body to be in contact with us at all points at the same   281,1
time. [In such a case] body would be permeating body, which is agreed
to be impossible and which we shall shortly[491] demonstrate to be so.
Therefore when we swim we must be moved directly by soul and not   5
as a result of this [everlasting] body being in external contact with us
and imparting movement [to us].[492] So this hypothesis should be
avoided as transparently false.

But if the everlasting [body] is in contact with the generated body
through being within it, there is every necessity that either the whole
of the everlasting [body] should permeate the whole of the perishable   10
one, or that they should [only] be in partial contact with one another
– more specifically, [only] at the surfaces (*perata*) of the touching
parts, which is how all touching bodies actually do touch one another.

Now, it is impossible for a whole to permeate a whole, for it has
been shown by the natural philosophers that for one body to permeate   15
another is an impossibility. Otherwise, the sea could be contained in
a wine ladle. For if it were possible to hold two equal ladlefuls in the
same [ladle], why not three, or an infinite number? Because everything that is finite may be measured out by everything [else] that is
finite, it would be possible, if the greater [quantity] were measured   20
out by the lesser, to hold the whole sea in a wine ladle. So if this is
absurd and impossible, it is impossible for body to permeate body. Nor
is it any more the case that it is impossible for this particular body to
permeate that but possible for others to permeate another [body].[493]
None of them can permeate any other, if even the heavenly bodies   25
clearly do not permeate[494] one another but are only in contact with

one another. It is for this reason that the stars eclipse one another.

282,1 Not only are their bodies unable to permeate one another but neither can the light of the higher stars permeate the lower ones because the bodies of stars are not transparent. If their bodies had been equipped

5 by nature to permeate one another, they would not eclipse one another, since the light within them would illuminate their entire interiors as well as their external shape (*sômasin*). If, then, it is impossible for light to permeate them, it is yet more impossible for their bodies to permeate one another. For even though it has been

10 proved that a hemisphere of the moon is always illuminated by the rays of the sun, the light that falls upon that hemisphere of [the moon] does not have the power to permeate its interior and illuminate its

15 other hemisphere. At any rate, when it is five to seven days old, and the part of it which is facing towards the sun, which is the part that the sun's rays are able to touch, is illuminated, and [this] lighted part of it is illuminating everything transparent within range, [the moon] cannot light up the rest of its body because the light which is on [one]

20 part of it cannot permeate its interior. So if not even the brightest and most penetrative light can permeate the bodies of the stars, this constitutes a much stronger demonstration that their bodies will not be able to permeate one another. For if their bodies had been nat-

25 urally equipped to permeate one another, the light in them would also be able to permeate their bodies – if, at any rate, this light has them

283,1 as its substratum[495] and must itself be wherever its substratum is. But if light cannot permeate them, much less can bodies, for the above argument will apply to all cases.[496]

5 And so if it is not possible for the [whole] extent of the heaven to fit into a smaller [space], for example, the space filled by the sun, then nor is it possible for the heavenly bodies to permeate one another.

10 Least of all could the heavenly bodies permeate any of the sublunary bodies, since no sublunary body is able to contain another body because they are denser and more earthy. And so neither will this ungenerated body [of theirs] be able to completely permeate perish-able body. Therefore, if they have entered one another, each must be

15 itself separated into particles and separate [the other into particles], as liquids do when mixed. Therefore neither of them – not the everlasting one nor the perishable – will be continuous with itself. So if this is both false and absurd and all perishable body is continuous

20 with itself, since, as Hippocrates says,[497] 'there is one concord,[498] one conflux, all things are in sympathy', then it is not possible for the imperishable body to be in the whole of the perishable in such a way that they are separated into particles by each other like liquids when they are mixed.

But if anyone wants it to be possible for everlasting body to

25 completely permeate perishable body, even though this has been shown to be impossible, [for argument's sake] let it be so. In that case

the everlasting [body] will certainly have to shape itself to the perish-   284,1
able one in the way that liquids entering a container shape
themselves to those that receive them. And so the everlasting [body]
will have the same set of organs as the perishable one. In that case,
among other things, what use will the everlasting body make of the
reproductive organs and the like? It will be departing from the shape   5
that is its own and natural to it. In my opinion such a hypothesis
transcends all nonsense. A thing which is ungenerated and imperishable must of necessity be resistant to [any] change towards a
condition contrary to its nature. So how could this [body], which
abandons its natural shape and takes on one which is contrary to
nature, be everlasting? And so, even were it a possibility for one body   10
to permeate another, it has been shown that it is impossible for the
hypothesised everlasting body to completely permeate perishable
body.

And if everlasting [body] has not completely permeated perishable   15
[body] but is situated in some part of it, first let them say in which
this is, for one cannot easily picture this. But let the everlasting body
be situated in some part [of the perishable body], if that is what you
want, in the brain, say. Here too the question of *how* it is in it arises.[499]   20
Is it adjacent to it and in contact with it or has it permeated right
through it? It will be pertinent to pose the same puzzles in regard to
the part as we posed in regard to the whole. And, moreover, how does
it bring about the separate movement of the other parts? As has been
stated,[500] it moves the parts even when the whole remains at rest. So   25
how, if it is situated in the brain, does it move a toe? For either it will,
because of their continuity, move the whole by pushing on the part,
and there will be no separate movement of the part, or it will only   285,1
move the part it touches, and if the whole is not moved, neither will
any of the other parts be.

18. And further, there is, one supposes, every necessity that this
body should either be of the [same] substance as bodies that travel in   5
a straight line or those that travel in a circle or be of some other
substance over and above these.

Now, should it be of another [substance], yet another, sixth, kind
(*phusis*) of body has revealed itself to us after the fifth. And if all of
the bodies that are everlastingly attached to rational souls are of the
same substance, let them show to which [elemental] mass (*holotês*)   10
they belong; for each particular and separate body is drawn from an
[elemental] mass, an individual clod, for example, from the mass of
earth and a particular [volume of] water from that of water. But they
will not be able to point to any other corporeal (*sômatos*) mass over   15
and above the four elements familiar to us and the heavenly one.

And if [these bodies] are not all of the same substance, they will,
rather like story-tellers (*muthôdesteron*), be introducing many kinds
of bodies (*sômatôn phuseis*) into the universe. How on earth will these

differ [from one another]?[501] If every physical body is distinguished by
20   sense, either by all [the senses] or by a number or at least by one of
them, [namely] touch – at all events, even the heaven, which [our
opponents] claim is ungenerated and imperishable, is, as Plato
says,[502] visible and tangible – if, then, [as we were saying], every body
is distinguished by sense, and if we have no perception of these bodies
25   [of theirs] through sense, by what means can they distinguish the
peculiar nature of each of them or its difference from the others? For
even though mind is able to distinguish the substance of [different]
286,1 bodies, it cannot do so apart from sense-perception. Hence Aristotle
shows in his writings on demonstration[503] that where sensation
reaches its limit, knowledge[504] must also reach its limit. At all events,
a person deprived from birth of the means of distinguishing afforded
by hearing is also deprived of knowledge in regard to musical harmo-
5   nies. [And], similarly, a person deprived from birth of visual images
is barred from knowledge in the area of colours. So if there has not as
yet been any perception of these bodies through sense even though,
according to [our opponents], they are not separate but interwoven
10   with mortal bodies and in contact with them, there is every necessity
that there should also be no knowledge of them. So on what basis can
anyone demonstrate that there is any such additional kind (*phusis*)
of body over and above the bodies known to us if they have gained
knowledge of them neither through sensation nor (since not through
15   sensation) through science? For knowledge of bodies does not arise
without sensation.

Therefore these bodies cannot be of a constitution (*phuseôs*) other
than [that of] the four [elements] that are familiar to us and the
heavenly one.

19. But if [these bodies] are not of a different constitution, they
20   must by all accounts either be of the same constitution as the four
[sublunary elements] or of that of the heavenly bodies.

But if they are either [composed] of one of the four [elements] or
25   composed of [all four of] them, they must of necessity be perishable;
for every body that has been detached from the mass of the four
[elements] is, whether it be simple or compound, definitely perishable, for nothing that is particular is everlasting. And so these
[bodies] too will of necessity be generated and perishable. And neither, therefore, can they be everlastingly attached to souls. Therefore,
if these bodies are everlasting, it is impossible for them to be of the
constitution of the elements.

287,1 **20.** And if [these bodies] are of the same substance as the heavenly bodies, they will still be perishable because they will have been
detached from their own [elemental] mass; [for] although the Hellenes[505] hold that the elemental masses are everlasting, detached
5   portions of them are nevertheless fated to undergo generation and
passing out of existence in the course of time. And so even if the

heaven were everlasting, detached portions of it would not be everlasting.

And besides, if these bodies were of the same substance as the
heavenly bodies, circular movement would obviously be natural to   10
them, for this is the nature of all of the heavenly bodies. And if this
is so, their natural shape will necessarily be spherical, for it is not
possible for non-spherical [bodies] to naturally show circular movement. And if they are spherical, when they enter perishable bodies,
they must either retain or not retain their natural shape. If, on the   15
one hand, they have not retained it, they must have degenerated into
an unnatural shape. How, in that case, can they still be everlasting?
None of the bodies that are held to be everlasting – I mean, of course,
none of the heavenly bodies – changes its natural shape at any stage
of its existence. [But] if, on the other hand, they do retain [their
natural shape], in view of the fact that it has been shown[506] that it is   20
impossible for one body to permeate another, a kind of empty spherical space has to be imagined in the perishable body to receive this
everlasting body. But there is no empty space in our perishable body
of a spherical shape, or, indeed, any empty space of any kind at all in   25
the solid body (in our tissues, for instance, or bones, or blood) which
is not completely filled with air or breath. And so it would once more
be necessary for one body to permeate another.

And the same goes for circular movement. If these bodies are   288,1
among those which rotate, they will surely exhibit continuous and
uninterrupted circular movement, for all things which rotate do. So
if any circular movement takes place in us, let them identify it; for all   5
perceptible movement in living creatures takes place in a straight
line, as does, for example, that associated with the heart and the
arteries, since systole and diastole are rectilinear movement. And the
psychic pneuma[507] too, since it travels along channels (*neurôn*) of its   10
own which are pierced in straight lines, itself exhibits linear movement.[508] So on what evidence (*pothen*) could they show that there is a
body in us which moves in a circle?

And if an everlasting [body] has ceased its circular movement upon
entering a perishable one, it has obviously abandoned what is natural
[to it]. So how will it be everlasting? Anything which undergoes a   15
cessation of movement undergoes a cessation of life, as we have heard
Plato state in the *Phaedrus*.[509] And so if the luminous [body] has
ceased its natural movement upon entering mortal [body], it has also
ceased its life and existence.

And if all rotating bodies exhibit continuous and uninterrupted   20
circular movement both as wholes and in their parts, and if this body
invented by [our opponents], if it has indeed ceased moving in a circle,
does not, then it does not belong to the class of bodies which rotate.
And consequently neither is it everlasting.

And in addition to the above it is worth considering this. Nature   25

289,1   has determined a proper place for each body. It has installed earth in
the centre of the universe, water above it, next air, after it fire, and
outside of all the rest it has wrapped around the body that moves in
5   a circle, that is, heavenly [body]. But the same place is natural to a
whole and to its part; the natural place of earth as a whole, namely
the centre, is also naturally that of a clod of earth, and the proper
place of the whole heaven is also naturally that of a part of it. And the
same goes for the rest [of the elements]. So if this so-called everlasting
body of theirs, upon which, according to Proclus, every soul is in the
10   first instance mounted, is [composed] of the substance of the bodies
which rotate, in other words of the substance of the heavenly bodies,
then, one supposes, the place which is natural to every heavenly body,
namely, the periphery, will also necessarily be so for it. Therefore, if
15   soul now dwells on the earth's surface[510] and while here controls
perishable body, it must be that this everlasting body, having assumed a relation with the perishable one, now also dwells, contrary
20   to its nature, on the earth's surface. Will, then, these bodies ever
return to their own [elemental] mass and attain their proper place,
or not? If, on the one hand, they[511] are never united with their own
mass and never attain their proper place, they will be in a state which
is contrary to their nature for an infinite time. But it is impossible for
25   anything to be in a state which is contrary to nature for an infinite
time, for not to exist is better than to be for ever in a state contrary
to nature. Therefore they will at some time attain that position and
occupy the same region as the heavenly bodies. And so even before
290,1   soul had come into this world and assumed a relation with perishable
body, this everlasting body was clearly also in existence. And, to
speak generally, if souls receive a different lot depending on the life
5   [they have led] and, just as those who have lived badly are dispatched
to the nether regions, so do those who have achieved purification
escape from the earthly sphere altogether (some of their religious
thinkers, at any rate, have declared that the so-called Milky Way is
the allotted abode and place of rational souls) – if, then, these are the
10   views of the Hellenes,[512] and if soul is in the first instance mounted
upon some kind of everlasting body and this is everlastingly attached
to it, there is every necessity that at the time when [a soul] is
descending to earth (*entautha*), when it is about to put on a mortal
15   body in addition [to the everlasting one], this everlasting body should
move in a straight line on the way down to earth from [its abode]
above. The soul itself when apart from body transcends both place
and movement, but no body, even if it is immortal, can exchange one
place for another without movement. But movement from above to
below is rectilinear movement. And so, even without any relation to
20   this solid body [of ours], this [everlasting body] will, all by itself, move
in a straight line. And, as was shown earlier,[513] nothing that moves
in a straight line is everlasting.

21. Some people, in a rather naive attempt at finding a way to
refute this argument, assert[514] that [this body] moves down from   25
above with a spiral movement. [They do so] so as to disassociate it as
far as possible both from the substance of those bodies which move in   291,1
a circle and from that of the elements. But, if this is so, given that,
according to them, bodies that rotate are everlasting and those that
move in a straight line mortal, and, given that spiral movement is a   5
kind of blend of a straight line and a circle, there is every necessity
that if moving spirally belongs naturally to this body, it must be
composed of everlasting and perishable body. (It is agreed that spiral
movement *is* a blend of a straight line and a circle). But if this is so, 10
it will either fall somehow between the two and be neither everlasting
nor perishable, which amounts to saying that it will be neither
perishable nor not perishable and neither everlasting nor not everlasting, and [both sides of] a contradiction will be true at the same
time; or part of it will be perishable, part imperishable, and so once
more the whole will not be everlasting, since one of the components   15
will have perished and destroyed the integrity of the whole.

But this is tedious nonsense and a baseless fabrication of the
imagination. There is no body in nature that moves with a spiral
movement. Since all things in the sublunary sphere are either heavy   20
or light, some of them – the heavy ones – travel from high to low, and
others – the light ones – from low to high, while all heavenly things,
on the other hand, both collectively and as individual [bodies] (by
individual [bodies] I mean the sun and the moon and so on), revolve
in perfect circles. So what other body over and above these can they   25
point to that naturally moves spirally? For even though the movement of the sun, or of some other planets, is said to trace out a spiral,
it is nevertheless clear to everyone who studies these phenomena that
it is the human mind that makes up this figure by combining the   292,1
various movements of the heavenly bodies. For the movement of the
planets is twofold. All of them are carried around with the sphere of
the fixed stars as it moves in the plane of the celestial equator, and
each of them revolves with its own movement in the plane of the   5
ecliptic and the so-called zodiac. The human mind combines these two
movements (that is, the diurnal revolution of the sun along with the
whole [universe] as well as the slight oblique movement of the same   10
body to the north or south of the celestial equator) and, even though
each of the heavenly bodies in its own right clearly revolves in a
perfect circle, makes up an imaginary spiral.

And even if some sublunary body should move in a spiral because
of the shape of the object (*megethos*) on which the movement takes
place, as happens on so-called spiral staircases, or should move in this   15
way even without such aids (*kai allôs*) on its own initiative, nobody
would have the effrontery to claim that such movement is natural to
these bodies. Even trumpet shells and the purple fish and other

20   similar creatures do not produce spiral movement through a natural
       propensity of the body but by means of a faculty of the soul reacting
       to (*dia*) the shape of the shell which encloses them. If an ant were
       moving on a sphere, no one would claim that its circular movement
       was natural, and nor do we claim that the sideways movement of
25   living creatures is natural to their bodies – for nature moves heavy
       bodies downwards. It is their shape or an impulse of the soul that is
293,1 the cause of such movement. And, consistently with this, if the shape
       of the object on which the movement [is taking place] or an impulse
       of the soul should become a cause of spiral movement for some
       [creatures], we do not claim that this kind of movement is natural to
       bodies.
5   And so no body moves with natural spiral movement. And there-
       fore nor can this body move naturally in a spiral as it travels down
       from on high.
           It would have been possible to produce countless other arguments
10   in refutation of this fictional body; but, since what has been said will
       suffice and it has been demonstrated that it is impossible for an
       everlasting body to be attached to the soul (since it cannot be one of
       the bodies that travel in a straight line or one of those that rotate or
       a combination of these or of a different nature from these, and, since
15   Plato nowhere delivers an opinion on such bodies), there remains no
       necessity that just because the soul of the world is in Plato's opinion
       ungenerated and imperishable, the world should therefore immedi-
       ately be ungenerated and imperishable as well; for, even though the
       bodies that are moved by them have a beginning and an end to their
20   existence, he wants our souls too to be ungenerated and imperishable.

The End of the Refutation of the Seventh Argument

294,1   **The Eighth Argument of Proclus the Successor**

       The eighth [argument]: If everything that perishes perishes as
       a result of something else[515] attacking it from outside and [per-
       ishes] into something else, and if there is nothing outside of the
5   universe nor anything other [than it], but, coming to be as a
       whole [made up] of wholes and a perfect thing [made up] of
       perfect things,[516] it has encompassed everything, then neither
       would there be anything other than the universe nor would it
       perish into anything else or through the agency of anything
       else.[517] And so it is imperishable.
           And for the same reason it is also ungenerated. For every-
10   thing generated comes to be from something previously other
       [than itself]. And so there would be something other than the
       universe. And this would be outside what comes to be. And so
       there will be something outside of the universe before the uni-

verse comes to be which is other than the universe. And if this
were so, there would be something contrary to the universe out
of which it has come to be. But contraries derive from one   15
another and change into one another, and since they occur in
pairs, there are, as is established by many [examples] in the
Phaedo, two paths between them to return each contrary to the
other so that nature will not be defective.[518]

Now, that the disorderly (*to atakton*) and the ordered (*to*   20
tetagmenon) are opposed is clear. But if, on the one hand, this is
as privation and possession, and if they change from privation
to possession, much more do they also change from possession
to privation;[519] for the former [change] is more impossible because there are some privations that cannot change into   295,1
possessions.[520] So if the former [change], although it was more
impossible for it to take place, has occurred, much more so will
the more possible take place, and the ordered changes into the
disorderly, and this will be in accord with nature and with the   5
will of God; for one who has done what is less possible will [all
the] more do what is more possible.

And if, on the other hand, these are contraries, governed by
the law of contraries, then the universe too changes into the
contrary from which it came to be.

But the universe has been shown to be imperishable. There-
fore it does not change into a contrary. And so neither has it   10
come to be.

And so the universe is everlasting; for it is not possible that
when there are two contraries, there should be a path from the
first to the second but not from the second to the first, nor that
when there is privation and possession, there should be a path
from privation to possession but not from possession to priva-   15
tion; for some things there is no path from privation to
possession, and for contraries there is, as Socrates says in the
Phaedo,[521] [a path] from each to the other.

And so, whether the disorderly and the ordered are contraries   20
or the disorderly is the privation of the ordered, either the
universe is not imperishable or the case for its being ungenerated is stronger than that for its being imperishable.[522]

The Sections of the Refutation of the Eighth Argument

1. That the statement 'everything that perishes perishes as a
result of something else attacking it from outside' is shown to be false 296,1
from doctrines held by Proclus himself and professed [by him] both
elsewhere and here.[523] And that the world is perishable by nature
even if there is nothing outside of it.

2. That, even if it be agreed that it is true that everything that   5

comes to be does so from something that was previously other [than
it], and, further, that there is nothing outside the world or other [than
it], nothing stands in the way of the world having come to be. And that
the hypothesis which states that if the world has come to be there
10   either is or was something other than it and outside of it is a silly one.

3. That not everything that comes to be necessarily comes to be
from a contrary. And so neither has the world, if it has come to be,
necessarily come to be from a contrary.

15   **4.** That, even though it is possible for possession to turn into
privation, Proclus is none the less expounding a position opposed to
Plato's when he says that if the world has indeed, as Plato holds, come
to be out of the disorderly, it will inevitably follow, both in the natural
course of events and by the will of God, that it changes back into the
20   disorderly, that is to say, into its own privation, from which it has
come to be.

The Refutation of the Eighth Argument

1. Of refutations those seem best which have proceeded from
premises that are both credible in themselves and accepted before-
25   hand by one's opponents. Accordingly, we shall refute the source and
root of the present proof (which is the making of the assumption that
297,1   everything that perishes perishes as a result of something else attacking it from outside – from which he infers that the world may not
perish because there is nothing outside of the world and nothing other
5   [than it]) using no other premises than those correctly accepted
beforehand by Proclus himself.

I shall cite the passages from Proclus that I earlier cited in the
sixth chapter.[524] For, Plato having stated[525] that everything perceptible comes to be and perishes, and Aristotle having objected that this
10   is not true, [arguing that] although the heaven and the whole world
are perceptible, they neither come to be nor perish,[526] Proclus [there]
defends Plato's position with, amongst others, arguments accepted by
Aristotle himself, [and] establishes [its truth]. [For] it is Aristotle's
15   view that no body possesses infinite power, but that each [of them] is
maintained by a finite power, and from this Proclus, on the basis that
a finite power is necessarily perishable, infers that every body, by the
20   law proper to its nature, comes to be and perishes.[527] Proclus' words
are, to quote them exactly, as follows.[528]

Proclus, from the work entitled *An Examination of Aristotle's
Criticisms of Plato's Timaeus*:

This assumption, then, should only be made if the body of the
25   heaven too, and the whole world as well, must be described as
coming to be. And how can it be other than necessary to so
describe it on the basis of the information he gives us? For he

states that no finite body has infinite power, and has shown it
to be so in the eighth book of the *Physics*. So if the world is finite
(and he has shown this to be so as well), it necessarily does not
have infinite power. But we have demonstrated that eternity is   5
infinite power in our earlier arguments. Therefore the world,
not having infinite power, does not have eternal existence. And
if it does not have eternal existence (for a thing that does has a
share in eternity, and a thing which has a share in eternity
shares in infinite power), the world necessarily does not exist   10
forever. For he states himself that to exist forever is the property
of eternity and says that eternity gets its name from this fact.

Having thus shown that even Aristotle's own positions prove that
the world is not among those things that are forever, Proclus next   15
shows that it has the property of existing forever from an outside
source and not of its own nature. Here is what he says:

Nor is what is true of that which always is also true of that
which is always coming to be: [it is not the case that] infinite
power belongs to the latter on account of its always coming to be
as it does to the former on account of its always being. But it does   20
[belong] to its maker, and on that account it too is always coming
to be, for ever gaining [the property of] being[529] thanks to (*dia*)
that which always is by the terms of its own existence, and not
having the 'always' in its own right. And so the definition of that
which comes to be would also fit the world.

And a little further on:

Everything, then, which comes to be is in its own right always   299,1
also perishing; but, as a result of having been bound by that
which is, this whole [universe] remains in [a state of] becoming
[and] comes to be [but] does not perish because of the being it
has drawn off from that which is. Therefore, because in its own
right that which comes to be qualifies for the definition, he also   5
refers to it as perishing, since by its own nature it is such.

And the same writer in what immediately follows:

For since the universe is finite, and what is finite does not, as he
has shown, have infinite power, and that which initiates infinite
movement initiates it by infinite power, it is clear that the   10
motionless cause of infinite movement for the universe has
infinite power itself. And so, if one separates the universe from
that [cause] in thought, it will not, since it does not have infinite
power, keep moving *ad infinitum* but will experience a cessation

15   of its movement; but if one connects it to that [cause] once more,
        it will, thanks to it, keep moving *ad infinitum*. And indeed there
        is nothing inappropriate about notionally separating things
        which are joined so as to see what each has from the other, and
        so as to know, once this has been observed, what it is that the
        inferior [partner] possesses of its own nature and what from its
20   association with the superior.

        And soon after:

        For, generally, since even in this world perishing occurs as a
        result of lack of power and preservation as a result of power, all
        the more so is it the case that amongst imperishable things
300,1   imperishability [holds sway] as a result of power. And this
        power is obviously something infinite, for all finite [power]
        perishes.

        If, then, because the world, being body, does not partake of infinite
5   power, and all finite power is perishable, since it eventually perishes
        through weakness (for if [power] is not infinite, it [must be] weak),
        the world must on that account cease to exist and be perishable and
        not last for ever, and if this [susceptibility] belongs to it as a conse-
        quence of its own nature, whereas everlasting existence comes to it
10   as a result of its participation in being, since its immortality is
        acquired, – if this is how things are, and how Plato and Proclus believe
        they are, how could it still be true that everything that perishes
        perishes as a result of something else attacking it from outside? For
15   even should there be nothing to attack the world and destroy it, the
        very finite [nature] of its power, which grows weak on account of the
        very circumstance of its being finite, becomes the cause of its passing
        out of existence; for if the world does not perish (and let one concede
20   this too to them), it is not on account of there being nothing else
        outside of it that it does not perish but because immortality[530] comes
        to it from that which always is.
            So if Proclus, rightly, believes that 'there is nothing inappropriate
        about notionally separating things which are joined so as to see what
        each has from the other, and so as to know, once this has been
25   observed, what it is that the inferior [partner] possesses of its own
        nature and what from its association with the superior',[531] let the
301,1   immortality which comes to the world from that which always is, and,
        indeed, even that which furnishes it with this [immortality], be
        separated [from it] in thought. Once this is done, will the world perish
        on account of the weakness of its own power, which is finite, or not
5   perish because there is nothing else outside [of it]?
            Should the second [of these alternatives] be the truth, it is no
        longer the case that its everlasting existence is acquired from that

which always is. At all events, if that which always is is separated off
in thought, the world is, on Proclus' [present] hypothesis, every bit as
imperishable by virtue of having nothing outside it to destroy it. And   10
if it is imperishable, it exists for ever. And, moreover, if the power of
the world is finite but it is nevertheless imperishable on account of
there being nothing outside of it, not even finite power will be
perishable.

But if it is true that finite power is perishable, the second [alterna-   15
tive] – I mean that the world does not perish because nothing else
attacks it from outside – is necessarily false, if, that is, even though
there is nothing outside the world, it must perish on account of the
finite [nature] of its own power once that which always is has been
separated from it. And so it is not true that everything that perishes   20
perishes through something else attacking it from outside.

Further, if it were the case that the world, having come to be as a
whole [composed] of wholes and a perfect thing [composed] of perfect
things and encompassing all things within itself, does not perish   25
because nothing else attacks it from outside,[532] imperishability
clearly belongs to it of its own nature; for, by encompassing all things
within itself, it has left none of the causes of destruction outside [of
itself]; so, if there is nothing able to destroy it, nor will it be able to
perish of itself; and what cannot perish because nothing exists that   302,1
could destroy it is imperishable by nature; and so the world is
imperishable by nature. But again, if the world, because it is body, is   5
of naturally finite power, and if finite power is perishable, the world
would be perishable by nature. So one and the same thing will be both
naturally perishable because it is of finite power and naturally imperishable because it has nothing else outside [of itself] to attack and   10
destroy it. So if it is impossible for [both sides of] a contradiction to be
true at the same time, and if it is true that the world is of finite power,
then it will be naturally perishable. But if it is naturally perishable,
it will be false that it is naturally imperishable. But it would be
naturally imperishable if everything that perishes perished as a   15
result of something else attacking it from outside. If, then, it is not
naturally imperishable, and if there is nothing apart from it that
could destroy it, since it contains everything within itself, then,
although perishable,[533] it will not be destroyed by things that are
outside of it.[534] Therefore it is not true that everything that perishes   20
is destroyed by something else attacking it from outside.

Also, right at the beginning of the next proof, the ninth of the
treatise as a whole, Proclus says that everything that perishes perishes[535] through its own defect. But what could the defect of each   25
thing that perishes consist in other than a deviation of each thing   303,1
towards what is contrary to nature that occurs on account of a
weakness of its natural power, which is finite? No thing possesses a
natural power which is destructive of it. Natural powers are preserv-   5

ative of the subjects [in which they exist], for all things strive after existence, and if a subject is preserved, the natural power in it is also preserved. But if everything that perishes perishes through its own defect, which is to say, by its own natural weakness, then it is possible

10 for the world, even though there is nothing else attacking it from outside, to perish by perishing through its own defect, that is, through its natural weakness; for nothing has as a defect something that is outside of it and other [than it]; for even agencies that attack and destroy [things] from outside, whether it be the discordance of the environment that is the cause of destruction or what is taken in

15 through the mouth or something else again, become the cause of their destruction by putting them in a condition that is contrary to their nature. So, even if there is nothing present outside, if a subject's own

20 natural and preservative power cannot, because it is finite, last for ever, it eventually allows the subject to go to its destruction and perishes along with it, like a helmsman who is unable to remain [at his post] while his ship sinks under him as a result of his having lost control of the rudder through exhaustion, not because he has been overcome by the storm but because his strength has given out

25 through prolonged exertion.

304,1   So, now that we have refuted this argument, and given that Plato asserts that the world is not imperishable naturally but [only] by the will of the creator and holds that naturally it comes to be and perishes, one may no longer conclude that the world is in Plato's view

5 ungenerated; for being ungenerated is not a [logical] consequence of being in possession of an acquired imperishability, but, if of anything, of being naturally imperishable, as indeed we have shown in the sixth chapter.[536] So if the world is by the law of nature perishable, it is also of necessity generated.

10   **2.** But [Proclus] says:

> Everything generated comes to be from something previously other [than itself]. And so there would be something other than the universe. And this would be outside what comes to be. And so there will be something outside of the universe before the universe comes to be which is other than the universe.[537]

15   Even should we concede that it is true that everything generated comes to be[538] from something previously other [than itself], and that there was something outside the universe and other than it before it came to be out of which it came to be, this is not[539] in conflict with Plato's doctrine that there is nothing outside the world,[540] which –

20 rejecting [the claim] that the world did not in Plato's view come to be as conflicting [with it] – [I suggest] we should accept; for Plato states that there is nothing outside the world or other than it once it is in existence, and that which we have conceded[541] was other than [the

world] before the world came to be, whether it was imbued with form
or formless and [mere] matter, is, once the world has come to be, no 25
longer other than it or outside of it. For if, on the one hand, it was
imbued with form, it is, by casting off its previous form and making 305,1
its own underlying [substance] available as matter for the world
which has come to be, no longer something other than the world once
it has come into existence, either in respect of its underlying [sub-
stance] (for a thing's own matter, from which it derives its being, is
never something other [than it]), or in respect of its previous form,
which has already perished and departed into non-being. 5

To illustrate this (*hoion*), imagine that there is a bronze horse and
let it be recast into the statue of a man. The form of the horse will
certainly be something other than the envisaged statue of a man, but
when the horse has been melted down and become a statue of a man, 10
the shape of the horse has perished into non-being, and what does not
exist can no longer be something other than that which has come to
be. And nor is the matter of the horse, [that is,] the bronze, which has
become the underlying [material] of the statue of a man, something
other than it, but rather a component (*stoikheion*) of it. In the same 15
way, then, even if there was previously something imbued with form
from which, as it changed, the world came to be, its form, having
perished and no longer existing, would no longer be said to be [some-
thing] other than the world once [the world] exists; for how can a
thing that is already non-existent and nothing [at all] be described as
outside something or other [than it]? For a thing that is outside 20
something or other [than it] is clearly outside of and other than
something which has existence, and [clearly] exists itself.

And should, on the other hand, that from which the world came to
be be formless and [mere] matter, even less would it be described as
[something] other than the world, since it would be a part or component of it. And when Plato says that there is nothing outside of the 25
universe or other [than it], he means that nothing bodily was left
outside it.

And surely it is quite obviously silly to say that if the world came 306,1
to be out of something else, there will [have been] something other
than the universe outside the universe before the universe came to
be. For how could anything be said to be outside of, or for that matter,
other than, a universe that does not yet exist? And so neither is it
possible to refer to anything as being outside [the world] or other than 5
it before the world came to be – for a thing that is 'other' is other than
something that exists – nor, on the other hand, reasonable, once the
world has come to be, to refer to a form which has already perished
as 'other than' the presently existing world, unless one could describe
non-being as other than being on the grounds that it is the opposite 10
and the privation of being; for privation is other than form and thus
outside [of it]. But it is not in this sense that Plato states that there

is nothing outside of the universe, but in the sense that there is nothing of a corporeal nature outside of the convex surface of the
15   heaven. Listen to what Plato himself has to say on this topic in the *Timaeus*. Here is the passage:

> From such elements, four in number, the body of the world came to be, achieving harmony through proportion, and received [the spirit of] friendship from them, so that, having come together, it
20   > was indissoluble by others than him who had bound it together. And the framing of the world took up the whole of each of the four [elements], for its framer framed it from all the fire and water and air and earth, leaving no portion of any of them nor any of their powers outside of it.[542]

And so the statement that there is nothing outside of the universe
25   clearly means that there is no body and no bodily power outside of the heaven. But to say that non-being is both outside of the universe and
307,1   other than being is both true and necessary and not in conflict with Plato's hypotheses; for one who says that there is nothing, whether it be a portion or a power of an element, outside of the universe, is not denying that privation is, in a non-spatial sense, by [its] nature[543]
5   other than form and external to that which is imbued with form – I say 'spatial sense' because non-being is in a spatial sense neither inside nor outside being. And privation is non-being. But portions or powers of elements are not a privation of the world; for a portion or a
10   natural power of anything is not its privation.

         3. And, indeed, even if there was, as we have conceded,[544] something before the generation of the world from which the world came to be, there was no need for this to be contrary to the world, for it is
15   not true that everything that comes to be invariably comes to be from its contrary. For if there is generation not only of accidents but of substances as well, and if everything that comes to be comes to be from its contrary, then there will be a contrary to every generated substance. But, as Aristotle has shown in the *Categories*,[545] there is
20   no contrary to a substance; a substance is that which is self-subsistent, and to that which is self-subsistent, *qua* such, there is no contrary. For what is the contrary of man *qua* man? Or of dog or horse? Or fig tree or grapevine or the like? For it is of the nature of
25   contraries to be present in the same subject by turns, as white and black and hot and cold are in body. No substance is in a subject. And
308,1   so there is no contrary to any substance. So, if a substance comes to be, it will not come to be out of its contrary. I have added the words '*qua* such'[546] because it is possible for contraries to exist *in* substances;
5   for instance, hot and wet are in blood and cold and dry in bone, and hot is contrary to cold and wet to dry, but bone is not contrary to blood; each of them is a substance and their matter the same (*koinê*), and each of

them comes to be not simply by virtue of being dry or by virtue of being wet but by virtue of being bone or by virtue of being blood.   10

If, then, each substance comes to be by virtue of being a substance of this or that kind and not accidentally (for a man comes to be by virtue of being a man and flesh by virtue of being flesh[547]), and if there is nothing that is in itself contrary to these and their like, then a generated substance does not, because it is generated, have its gen-   15
eration from a contrary, but this is seen, if anywhere, among accidents; for when hot comes to be, it has in every case differentiated itself from cold simply by being hot and not in any other respect; and the same applies in other similar cases. But nor is the generation of   20
all accidents invariably out of their contraries, for contrariety is not observed in all accidents. The triangle and the circle and the other shapes come to be, but none of them has its generation from a contrary; for shapelessness is not the contrary of shape but the privation of shape, just as the disorderly is the privation of the   25
ordered. Again, since relatives are opposed to contraries, a thing does not come to be 'on the right' out of a contrary, but simply out of its   309,1
privation, that is, out of what is not on the right. Moreover, one becomes knowledgeable after [previously] being ignorant. But if he changes from a contrary condition, the genesis of the knowledgeable person is out of a contrary, but if from [a state of] pure ignorance, out   5
of a privation. For example, if one, previously believing that air is heavy, were to learn better and come to believe that it is light, the genesis of this knowledge would be out of a contrary, but if, not knowing whether it is heavy or light, one were to learn that it is light, its genesis is out of privation into form. And so not even the generation of accidents   10
is in all cases out of a contrary. So not everything that comes to be comes to be out of a contrary.

But if not everything that comes to be comes to be from a contrary, and if, as Plato holds, the ordered has come to be out of the disorderly, and if the disorderly is the privation and not the contrary of the   15
ordered, there will be no necessity for the ordered to turn back again into the disorderly as Proclus' argument would have it – which is, moreover, a position that is not held by Plato, who supposes that the world is imperishable. For in the *Phaedo*[548] Plato says that the   20
contraries emerge from one another and turn back into one another (for just as hot emerges from cold, so, in order that nature will not, as a result of destroying just one of each pair of contraries, become defective, does cold subsequently from hot;[549] and likewise with all pairs of contraries), but does not also say that just as form emerges from privation, so does form in every case subsequently turn back to   25
privation. Plato quite clearly nowhere says this; on the contrary, when he says that everything ordered has emerged from the disor-   310,1
derly and that the disorderly is the privation of the ordered, he says that the ordered, that is to say, the world, is imperishable.[550] There-

5   fore he does not claim that form invariably turns back to privation.
Therefore it is Plato's view that the world has come to be but does not
perish.

4. 'But', says[551] Proclus,

10   even if the disorderly is the privation of the ordered and it has
changed from privation to possession, much more will it also
change from possession to privation;[552] for the former [change]
is more impossible because there are some privations which
cannot change into possessions. So if the former [change], although it was more impossible for it to take place, has occurred,
much more so will the more possible take place, and the ordered
will change into the disorderly, and this will be in accord both
15   with nature and with the will of God; for one who has done what
is less possible will [all the] more do what is more possible.

That Plato too believes that the ordered can, in the natural order of
20   things, change into the disorderly, is clear from Plato's own [words],
for he would have it that everything that has been bound may be
undone, and says 'since you have come to be, you are not indissoluble
nor altogether immortal'.[553] But when Proclus says that it is also in
accordance with God's will that what comes to be also invariably
25   perishes, what he says is no longer in conformity with the beliefs of
Plato. For Plato's creator declares the exact opposite to the heavenly
311,1   bodies. For, having first stated what befalls the world in the natural
order of things – 'since', he says, 'you have come to be, you are not
indissoluble nor altogether immortal' – the creator next adds what
5   accrues to it through his will: 'you shall not', he says, 'be dissolved nor
meet with the fate of death, since you have in my will a greater and
more authoritative bond than those with which you were bound when
you came to be'.[554] And so Plato too acknowledges that, as far as
nature is concerned, their dissolution follows as a consequence of
10   their generation, but, aware that the will of God is stronger than any
physical bond, he bound the immortality of the world by means of it;
for he does not say that it is because he cannot that God does not undo
the world, which is indeed dissoluble even in the course of nature, but
15   because he does not so will. It is for this reason that he says, as we
indicated above,[555] that its existence is acquired and its immortality
[continually] restored.

So, does Plato's commentator and successor contradict Plato?[556]
[Yes.] Plato says that the ordered has emerged from the disorderly (in
20   the present context the disorderly refers, as I have said,[557] to the
privation of the ordered, not to its contrary), and that the ordered is
on that account in the natural course of events dissoluble, but certainly not also that God wants the ordered to revert to the disorderly.
Proclus, in contrast, says that, if the ordered has indeed emerged

from the disorderly, it will inevitably (*pantôs*) follow, both in the   25
natural course of events and by the will of God, that the ordered will
change back into the disorderly. So he contradicts Plato on two counts: 312,1
by denying that the ordered has emerged from the disorderly, although
Plato explicitly proclaims this, and by stating that, if it has so emerged,
God will wish the ordered to revert once more to the disorderly, even   5
though here too, as we have shown from Plato's own text, he specifically
denies that God wills this.

And so we [Christians] when we profess that the world has come
to be and will perish again, have on our side, along with the truth, the   10
vote of Plato for its having come to be, and [in support of our belief]
that, having come to be, it will certainly perish – and not, as Plato
holds, be indissoluble and immortal because an acquired immortality
has accrued to it through the will of God even though it is by nature
dissoluble – we have Proclus himself as witness when he says that   15
'this is [so] both in the natural course of events and by the will of God'.

But Plato has not completely departed from right thinking on these
issues. [I don't mean] in that he believes that the world is imperishable, but in that, having come to the view that it must be
imperishable, he does not claim that it is the unlimited power of the
world's nature that is the cause of its imperishability but that it is the   20
will of the creator. For, if it were absolutely necessary for something
corporeal to last for ever, it could not be imperishable unless the
power of the creator provided it with everlasting continuance, since,
as far as the law of nature goes, no body has everlasting existence (*to*   25
aei einai).

That the disorderly is not the contrary of the ordered is clear even
from [the concepts] themselves. And if Plato says that the ordered is
nothing other than the world, and if the world is a substance, and if,   313,1
as has been shown,[558] a substance does not have its genesis out of a
contrary, then the ordered and the disorderly are not opposed as
contraries but as form and privation.

The End of the Refutation of the Eighth Argument   5

Notes

1. Something needs to be said about the terminology used to describe the various divisions of *Aet*. In the preserved headings for chapters 2-18, which may or may not be Philoponus' own, Proclus' arguments are *logoi*, Philoponus' replies are *luseis* and the sections into which they are divided are *kephalaia*. In the work itself Philoponus' terminology is less consistent. An argument of Proclus is frequently an *epikheirêma* (26,20, etc.), a *logos* may be either an argument of Proclus (126,23, etc.) or Philoponus' reply (69,5, etc.), and a *kephalaion* may be an argument of Proclus (94,22, etc.), a reply of Philoponus (70,9, etc.), or a section of the last (130,11, etc.), in which case it is always a *kephalaion* of a *logos*. In the chapter headings I translate *logos* 'argument', *kephalaion* 'section' (a good case could be made for translating *kephalaia* 'Summaries of the Main Points' in these headings – see H.D. Saffrey and L.G. Westerink, Proclus, *Théologie platonicienne* (Paris, 1968-94), vol. 1, Notes complémentaires, p. 1, n. 2 – but I have been influenced by Philoponus' usage in the text, which I have outlined above) and *lusis* 'refutation'. In the work itself I translate *epikheirêma* 'proof', *logos* 'argument' when it refers to one of Proclus' arguments, but 'chapter' when it refers to one of Philoponus' replies, and use 'proof', 'chapter' or 'section' for *kephalaion* depending on whether the reference is to an argument of Proclus, a reply of Philoponus or a section of such a reply.

2. Proclus had the title Successor (*Diadokhos*) as head of the Academy at Athens in the line of succession from Plato.

3. Lang and Macro do not accept Rabe's insertion of *sunedêsen monos* at this point, but without it the earlier *monos*, which they ignore in their paraphrase of the sentence in n. 2, is difficult.

4. sc. Plato – at *Tim*. 32C.

5. *Tim*. 41Λ-B.

6. Adding *ara* after *adunaton* at 119,22, as suggested by Rabe in the critical apparatus. (Baltes reports that this has the support of Ishâq ibn Hunayn's Arabic translation.)

7. Punctuating the Greek with a comma instead of a full stop in line 21 and a full stop instead of the first colon in line 22.

8. Literally 'the best creator'. The phrase is probably motivated by *Tim*. 29A, where the creator is described as *ho aristos tôn aitiôn* ('the best of causes').

9. Reading <*epei*> *panti* at 120,6 and deleting *eipen* in the next line. (The Republic has *all' epei panti* ... and the redundant *eipen* could stem from a misplaced *epei*. In his critical apparatus Rabe suggested *panti* <*gar*> *genomenôi phthora estin* <*kata*> *phusin, hôs Sôkratês* , and Baltes reports that <*gar*> has the support of Ishâq ibn Hunayn's Arabic translation, but I imagine that that would also be compatible with *epei*.)

10. Plato, *Rep*. 546A. Proclus clearly assumes (as he likewise does at *in Tim*. 1.8), that we are to understand that the discourse on the institutions and social

organisation of an ideal state delivered by Socrates on the eve of the conversation reported in the *Timaeus* (see *Tim.* 17B-19A) is identical with the conversation reported in the *Republic*. For reasons why this cannot be so, see, for example, Cornford, *Plato's Cosmology* (London, 1937), 4-5.

11. sc. the 'doctrine of the Muses'.

12. On the translation of *aïdios* as 'everlasting', see the introduction. On this argument and Philoponus' reply, see L. Judson, 'God or nature? Philoponus on generability and perishability' in R. Sorabji (ed.), *Philoponus and the Rejection of Aristotelian Science* (London & Ithaca, NY 1987), ch. 10.

In the notes to this translation I normally do no more than identify direct quotations and obvious references, often merely repeating Rabe's identifications from his critical apparatus. In the case of Proclus' arguments, a wider range of comparative material can be found in the notes to H.S. Lang and A.D. Macro (eds.), *On the Eternity of the World* (De Aeternitate Mundi), *Proclus* (Berkeley, etc., 2001).

13. Or 'line of attack'. In military parlance the word means 'assault', whence it is used figuratively of arguments (see H.D. Saffrey and L.G. Westerink, *Proclus, Théologie platonicienne*, vol. 2, Notes complémentaires, p. 1, n. 1).

14. Adding *kai* before *hoti* at 120,20, as suggested by Rabe in the critical apparatus.

15. The 'truth' referred to here and at 127,3 may be Christian doctrine, as it clearly is at 57,7 and 75,7-9. Other instances of *alêtheia* of which this may be so occur at 59,24; 61,8; 98,20; 117,16; 312,10.

16. *Tim.* 41A-B.

17. More literally, 'an exhibiting'.

18. Although the world exists in time (*en khronôi*; cf. 99,25), it cannot be said to be generated in time since time itself only came to be with the world. For this reason Philoponus speaks of it, as here, as generated 'with respect to time' (*kata khronon*) or 'from a [point of] time' (*apo khronou*; first at 149,14). Both phrases first occur in Chapter VI, are used most frequently there (*kata khronon* 86 of 94 occurrences, *apo khronou* 10 of 13), and are for the most part used of the generation of the world. Philoponus probably took both of them from Porphyry, who used them in his commentary on the *Timaeus* (cf. 154,7 for *kata khronon* and 149,14 for *apo khronou*).

19. It is often appropriate to translate *Hellênes* 'Greeks' and in a number of passages in *Aet.* I do, but for Jews and Christians alike, including those of Greek culture like Philoponus himself, the word is often equivalent to 'heathen' or 'pagan', and in contexts where it seems to have that connotation I translate 'Hellenes' rather than 'Greeks'. (For this expedient, cf. L.G. Westerink (ed.), *Anonymous Prolegomena to Platonic Philosophy* (Amsterdam 1962), xiii.) In the present passage, the contrast with 'common usage' suggests that Philoponus has in mind the pagan philosophers and not simply the Greeks or pagans at large.

20. At 156,4 the manuscript reading is *prosaptousin* and perhaps that should be read here.

21. See the note at 159,2 for an explanation of these 'six beginnings'.

22. *Tim.* 28B.

23. More literally 'no beginning of generation'. For Philoponus' interpretation of the phrase, see Section 16, especially 168,16-169,3.

24. i.e. they cannot argue both that 'generated' does not mean generated in time in the *Timaeus* and that it does have this meaning there but Plato does not intend the dialogue to be taken literally.

25. Plato, *Tim.* 27C.

26. Literally 'to write'.

27. The first of these substitutions would involve reading *ei* for *ê* and the second *aeigenes* for *agenes*.

28. The full stop after *ourania* in Rabe is clearly a misprint.

29. Deleting *tôi* before *tên* at 124,24 and reading <*tôi*> *ouk* at 124,23. (In the critical apparatus Rabe suggests either deleting *tôi* altogether or emending it to *autôi* but on balance it seems more likely that it has been displaced.)

30. *Tim.* 33A.

31. Philoponus sometimes puts verbs introducing quotation or report in the present tense and sometimes (as here) in a past tense. In either case I normally use the present tense in the translation.

32. *oikothen* is similarly used at 117,19 and 555,6.

33. Translating *tandikh'*, the reading of some manuscripts of Euripides, rather than *diandikh'* as printed by Rabe.

34. Euripides, *Phoenissae* 469-72.

35. Rabe compares *Phdr.* 245C-246A, but Proclus (at 120,6), and presumably Porphyry before him, is referring to *Rep.* 546A.

36. *kata tên sun antithesei antistrophên.* 'Conversion by negation' is the term preferred by e.g. Joseph (*An Introduction to Logic* (Oxford, 1906), 215). A more literal translation would be 'conversion with opposition', or perhaps 'conversion [with substitution of] the contradictory'. M.J. Edwards (*Philoponus: On Aristotle Physics 3* (London & Ithaca, NY, 1994), 'Greek-English Index' under *antistrophê*) prefers 'inversion with negation'. In conversion by negation a proposition is obverted and the result converted. If the resulting proposition is then obverted, the contrapositive of the original proposition is obtained.

37. 126,10-23 = Sodano 2,39.

38. In other words, commits the fallacy of the Consequent.

39. Changing *ekhei* to *eikhen* at 127,1, as suggested by Rabe in the critical apparatus.

40. More literally 'the account [or word] of truth'. The phrase was sometimes used to refer to the Christian gospel and that may be the intention here.

41. *Tim.* 41A-B.

42. The first part of this programme is fulfilled in Sections 1-6, the second in Sections 7-27, and the third in Sections 28-9.

43. The meaning (and, consequently, the correct translation) of the words translated 'Gods, offspring of gods, works of which I am the creator ...' is far from clear. The rendering adopted here is unlikely to represent Plato's intention but has a better chance of reflecting Philoponus' understanding of it. (Anyone interested in the issues involved should consult Cornford, *Plato's Cosmology*, 367-70.)

44. *Tim.* 41A-B.

45. cf. 119,21-120,5 and notes there.

46. *tôn eirêmenôn* is difficult; it presumably refers back to the gods in the quotation from the *Timaeus* at 128,1, who are probably to be identified with the universe as a whole and the heavenly bodies, so that the whole passage will mean that observation of the world is by itself enough to attest that it has been well put together. Rabe, perhaps rightly, suspects that *eirêmenôn* is corrupt (he writes 'eirêmenôn suspectum' in the critical apparatus). If it is, it may have replaced something like *phainomenôn*, which would give 'observation of the phenomena alone'. Another possibility is that *tôn eirêmenôn* was originally a marginal or interlinear gloss, supplied by a reader who understood *aisthêsis* in the sense 'observation' and asked 'observation of what?' whereas Philoponus had actually intended it to mean 'sense-perception'. We could then delete *tôn eirêmenôn* and translate the phrase *autê hê aisthêsis* by something like 'our senses alone', which would be in accord with Philoponus' usage elsewhere (see Rabe's index under *aisthêsis*, especially 201,3 and 416,17).

47. This second 'all' (*panta*) does not appear in the text of *Genesis*.

48. *Genesis* 1, 31.

49. In Section 10.

50. cf. Plato, *Tim.* 41A-B.

51. cf. Plato, *Tim.* 41C.

52. The comparison which follows is neater in the original because in Greek 'put together' and 'tune' are the same verb (*harmozein*).

53. Adding *dialusai* after *boulêtheiê* at 131,9, one of two possible emendations suggested by Rabe in the critical apparatus.

54. *Tim.* 32C.

55. At 119,16-18.

56. *Metaph.* 1050b7.

57. Because neither 'power' nor 'potentiality' seems to do justice to every occurrence of *dunamis* in this section, I use whichever seems to work best in the immediate context.

58. Plato, *Tim.* 41A-B.

59. We have to wait until 134,2 for the 'on the other hand'.

60. The phrase *hoson epi harmoniâi* ('as far as harmony is concerned'), occurring as it does in the middle of a quotation from *Tim.* 41A-B, is unexpected and adds nothing to the argument and may be a gloss on *kai eu ekhon* ('in a good state') which has found its way into the text.

61. sc. those that the physicist or natural scientist rather than the metaphysician would deal with. ('More natural' would be easier, but cf. 7,25 and 12,7.)

62. The reference, like others at 155,19-24; 258,22-6; 396,24; 399,20-24; 461,1-2; 483,20 (of which the one at 258,22-6 is the most explicit), appears to be to Philoponus' *Against Aristotle on the Eternity of the World*, which seems to have been written soon after *Aet.* The substantial fragments of this work, most of them extracted from Simplicius' commentaries on *Cael.* and *Phys.*, have been translated by C. Wildberg in this series (*Against Aristotle on the Eternity of the World* (London & Ithaca, NY 1987)).

63. For this rendering of *kephalaion* see note 1.

64. This signals the end of the first part of the programme outlined in Section 3.

65. At 127,16-20.

66. At 127,7.

67. Or perhaps 'is only interested in attending to ...'.

68. i.e. to Chapters 7-18.

69. One could perhaps substitute 'very many' for 'the majority' but Philoponus would still be guilty of exaggeration, since in reality only a small minority of Platonists interpreted Plato in this way.

70. cf. *Phys.* 251b19 and *Cael.* 280a30-1.

71. Translating *teleutan*, the reading of the manuscripts of Plato, rather than *teleutaion* (last).

72. *Tim.* 27A.

73. *Tim.* 27C.

74. In Aristotelian dialectic a 'problem' is a question as to whether something is the case or not. (At *Top.* 102b32-3 Aristotle gives as an example of a problem 'Is two-footed terrestrial animal the definition of man or not?')

75. *Tim.* 27C-28A.

76. Literally, 'rewoven'. The word (which occurs again at 138,13; 235,28 and 236,25) is not particularly common and Philoponus may have in mind *Phaedo* 87D, where Cebes uses it of the soul repairing wear and tear to the body.

77. *Pol.* 270A.

78. In VI.28.

79. This work is not extant. Philoponus quotes from it or refers to it some twenty times in *Aet.*, Proclus himself refers to it in his commentary on Plato's *Timaeus* and Simplicius probably draws on it in a number of his commentaries. The quotations in *Aet.* and some probable quotations in Simplicius' *in Cael.* are translated by Thomas Taylor in *The fragments That Remain of the Lost Writings of Proclus, Surnamed the Platonic Successor*, 2-31 and the work is discussed in L. Siorvanes, *Proclus: Neo-Platonic Philosophy and Science* (New Haven and London 1996), 216-23. Philoponus' citations are listed in Rabe's index of proper names under 'Proclus'.

80. e.g. species as opposed to individuals, and perhaps the elemental masses (fire, air, water, earth) as opposed to things composed of the elements.

81. *Tim.* 28B-C.

82. *Tim.* 27D.

83. Plato has 'comes to be', and perhaps that is the correct reading here.

84. *Tim.* 37D-38A.

85. *Tim.* 38B-C.

86. The translation assumes that the article *to* is present to nominalise the adverb *prin*, which is the subject of *prouparkhei*, and that *tês sustaseôs* is in the genitive after the same verb. (Philoponus is taking the phrase *prin ouranon genesthai* at 140,16-17 as evidence that Plato believed that there was a 'before' the creation of the universe and time.) Rabe found *to prin* unacceptable. (He writes 'fort. *ti prin* (vix *to prin*)' in the critical apparatus). Presumably he took *prin* with *tês sustaseôs*, which would make *to* a problem. (His conjecture *ti* would make the sentence read 'And if something exists prior to the framing of the heaven, how could the heaven and time be without beginning?', acceptable Greek but hardly acceptable sense in the context.)

87. *Exodus* 3,14.

88. The (unexpressed) subject of 'brought' is unclear. What precedes suggests that it should be 'time', but 'the heaven and time' or 'the heaven' would better suit what follows.

89. cf. 42,10-12.

90. Changing *hote* to *tote* at 142,23, as suggested by Rabe in the critical apparatus.

91. At 142,23-143,5.

92. In IV.3.

93. *Tim.* 38B.

94. The phrase actually derives from *Rep.* 546A. (cf. the note at 126,19).

95. cf. *Tim.* 41A-B.

96. The saying also occurs at 30,20-1. For Philoponus' part in the development of the topos see L. Tarán, 'Amicus Plato sed magis amica veritas, from Plato and Aristotle to Cervantes', *Antike und Abendland* 30 (1984), 112-15. Verrycken also discusses Philoponus' use of it in 'Philoponus' Interpretation of Plato's Cosmogony', *Documenti e Studi sulla Tradizione Filosofica Medievale* 8 (1997) 274-7.

97. *EN* 1096a16.

98. 'Shaken out every reef' would be rather more literal.

99. The expression *epi lexeôs*, which literally means something like 'verbatim' or 'word for word' and which I here translate 'to quote his exact words', was one method used to mark direct quotations in the absence of typographic indications and a case could be made for not translating it at all.

100. Perhaps he is thinking of *Cael.* 280a30-1.

101. At *Tim.* 28B.

102. Plato's Timaeus, who may well be his own creation, is a Pythagorean from Locri in southern Italy. The work referred to here is presumably the *On the Soul of the World and On Nature,* a late (first-century AD?) fabrication, largely based on the *Timaeus* itself, that circulated under Timaeus' name.

103. This sentence is omitted when Philoponus quotes the first part of this passage again at 223,8-19.

104. cf. Diels, *Doxographi Graeci,* 485.

105. 145,20-4 = Fortenbaugh, fr. 241A.

106. *Tim.* 28B. The sentence continues: 'and has body, and, [as we have seen], all such perceptible things, since they may be grasped by belief along with sensation, clearly come to be and are generated' and what follows is in effect an attempt to defuse what it seems to say.

107. Although I have translated both instances of *genêtos* 'generated' there appears on the face of it to be a play on the ambiguity of the word: the *kosmos* is *genêtos* in the sense that it is, *qua* perceptible, generable by nature, even though it has not actually been generated, while other perceptibles are *genêtos* in that they have actually been generated – or perhaps one should say that they are both generable and generated. However, in *Tim.* 28B (see the previous note) the shared genus is 'perceptible things' and the contention may be simply (if unconvincingly) that all perceptible things are described as 'generated' whether they have come to be or not just as they (or at any rate many of them) are described as 'visible' whether they are seen or not.

108. The *mesê, netê,* and *hupatê* (literally, 'middle', 'lowest' and 'highest') were physically the middle, *lowest and highest* strings of the lyre but in musical theory the middle, *highest and lowest* notes in a scale or attunement. The latter usage seems to be the relevant one here and I have translated accordingly. (The use of these three terms in musical theory is actually more complex than the above suggests. More detail can be found in the entry 'Music' in the third edition of the *Oxford Classical Dictionary.*)

109. More literally 'while being one at bottom [or "in his substratum"] changes into many forms'.

110. Changing *legoito* to *legetai* and omitting *de* at 147,5 (cf. 146,13 and 146,20; Rabe writes '*legoito de* suspecta' in the critical apparatus).

111. 145,24-147,9 are translated and discussed in J. Dillon, *The Middle Platonists: a Study of Platonism, 80 BC to AD 220* (London 1977), 242-4.

112. *Tim.* 28B.

113. The *History* of Ephorus (*c.* 405-330 BC), a 'universal' history in thirty books, has not survived and is only known at second hand. The story of the return of the Heraclidae, or descendants of Heracles, to the Peloponnese served as a charter myth for the division of the Peloponnese between the three Dorian states of Messenia, Argos and Sparta (For more information, see the articles 'Ephorus' and 'Heraclidae' in the *Oxford Classical Dictionary.*)

114. Or 'principles'; cf. the note at 159,2.

115. I have assumed that the words I have bracketed are parenthetic, dismissing an incompatible view of the words under discussion, and that the next sentence is intended as further evidence that Plato is rejecting a 'beginning with respect to time'.

116. *Tim.* 28B.

117. *en tôi ginesthai to einai ekhonta.* The phrase, which is common in Philoponus and Simplicius and is used by a number of the other commentators, goes back at least to Alexander (*Mixt.* 227,22; *in Sens.* 50,25; 154,16; *in Meteor.* 73,1; 83,1). At *in Phys.* 465,25 Philoponus uses it to distinguish processes or events, such as a day or a contest, which unfold little by little and are never present as a whole, from substances such as a man or a horse. However, in the Platonic tradition such substances, and indeed the world as a whole (see *Tim.* 27E ff.), are regarded as ever-changing entities and in *Aet.* the phrase is most commonly used to distinguish the physical from the intelligible and the temporal from the eternal.

118. More literally 'bears the description of [a] generation'.

119. sc. matter and form in the case of things composed of them and other diagrams, it seems, in the case of diagrams.

120. 148,9-23 = Sodano 2,37.

121. sc. Taurus.

122. Aristotle discusses lightning in *Meteor.* 2.9 and the author of the pseudo-Aristotelian *Mund.* at 394a10-28, but neither account contains any suitable statement. The reference must be to *Cael.* 280b6-9, where Aristotle says that 'ungenerated' can be used of things which come into existence without any process of generation (*aneu geneseôs*; cf. same phrase at 149, 5) or change. (His examples are touch and motion.)

123. 'Passing out of existence', my usual rendering of *phthora*, does not work well here.

124. Which shows that Philoponus is no more inclined than Proclus to take the *Timaeus* myth at face value.

125. See note to 121,15.

126. 148,25-149,16 = Sodano 2,36.

127. Changing *tou genêtou* to *tôn genêtôn* at 150,1, as suggested by Rabe in the critical apparatus.

128. Changing *ginomenon* to *genomenon* at 150,11-12, as suggested by Rabe in the critical apparatus.

129. For 'conversion by negation', see the note at 126,20.

130. i.e. anything corporeal, and therefore visible.

131. cf. 152,1; but 'of the earth' is another possible supplement (cf. 151,16). In Philoponus' cosmology the centre of the universe and the centre of the earth of course coincide. The point is that anything 'beneath' the centre is invisible to us.

132. A Greek hero who sailed with Jason and the other Argonauts on the expedition to recover the Golden Fleece. Lynceus was famed for his unnaturally keen eyesight and euhemeristic mythographers explained this on the hypothesis that he was the first miner and that his activities gained him the reputation of being able to see underground. (P. Grimal, *The Dictionary of Classical Mythology* (Oxford, 1996), 266.)

133. Apollonius, *Argonautica* 1.155.

134. Presumably the centre of the earth rather than the centre of the universe is referred to here because of the allusion to Lynceus and his ability to see beneath the surface of the earth.

135. More literally, '... does not have its being visible in this, in being seen'. Philoponus uses expressions of this form very frequently both in *Aet.* and elsewhere when stating a thing's essence. Outside Philoponus they are not very common (a TLG search turns up four in Alexander, two in Porphyry, eight in Simplicius – one of them in a quotation from Philoponus – and a handful in other later commentators), and I cannot account for the mannerism. I have not made any attempt to preserve the construction in translation.

136. *Tim.* 27C.

137. *Tim.* 28B.

138. *Tim.* 38B.

139. sc. of the first of Taurus' suggestions as to possible senses in which *genêtos* might be applied to the world.

140. Or perhaps: 'simple [sc. non-complex] things ...'.

141. = Sodano 2,35.

142. Depending on how 148,7-9 is to be read this could mean either the three attributed to Porphyry at 148,7-149,16, or these together with those cited from Taurus at 146,8-147,9.

143. cf. *Tim.* 28B.

144. Adding *on* after *diastaton* at 155,2, as suggested by Rabe in the critical apparatus.

145. = Sodano 2,38.

146. Literally 'the [views] of the man'.

147. sc. in his *Against Aristotle on the Eternity of the World*, on which see the note at 134,17.

148. *Cael.* 280b1-20. (In the translation I translate all titles into English, but in the notes I normally use the traditional abbreviations, which are frequently formed from the Latin versions of titles).

149. At 52,15-26.

150. Changing the second *kai* to *ei* at 156,13, as suggested by Rabe in the critical apparatus.

151. *Tim.* 27C.

152. *Tim.* 28B.

153. *Tim.* 28B.

154. sc. at *Tim.* 27C.

155. Changing *gar* to *kai* at 157,1, as suggested by Rabe in the critical apparatus.

156. At 153,17-25.

157. i.e. at *Tim.* 28B.

158. This claim is a little puzzling. Perhaps he has in mind 140,2-144,15, where he discusses the passage in the *Timaeus* in which Plato says that time came into being together with the heaven.

159. Changing *onta* to *onti* at 159,1, as suggested by the reader.

160. The word I have been translating 'beginning' (*arkhê*) is used interchangeably with the word 'cause' (*aition* or *aitia*) by Aristotle to describe his famous four causes (form, matter, efficient cause, final cause), the four factors we must take into account when explaining change in the universe. In this context *arkhê* is commonly rendered 'principle', or even 'cause', but in what follows I shall retain the translation 'beginning' in spite of the occasional awkwardness this produces rather than alternate between 'beginning' and 'principle'. (I shall draw attention to the few cases in which I depart from this practice.)

161. Philoponus and Simplicius both attribute the identification of these six causes to Plato in their commentaries on Aristotle's *Physics* (at 5,7-6,8 and 3,13-19 respectively). They are, of course, the four Aristotelian causes plus the paradigmatic and instrumental causes. (Philoponus offers an explanation for the absence of the last two in Aristotle but the details need not concern us here). The six-cause scheme was standard for the late Neoplatonists. For its occurrence in Proclus, see R.J. Hankinson, *Cause and Explanation in Ancient Greek Thought* (Oxford, 1998), 326 and 435, and for the earlier history of the paradigmatic and instrumental causes, follow the references under 'Cause – instrumental' and 'Cause – paradigmatic' in the index to Hankinson.

162. At 159,6-7.

163. At 159,16-18.

164. Changing *elaben* at 161,16 to *estin labein*.

165. cf. 154,17-19.

166. At first sight *Hellênes* here could simply mean 'the Greeks' and the phrase be equivalent to 'unknown to the Greek language', but in the section summary at 122,3 I think the word must refer to the pagan philosophers, which should fix its meaning here.

167. i.e. the extraordinary hypotheses which Porphyry and others attempt to foist upon him.

168. 781E.

169. Editors of the *Laws* agree that the last part of this sentence is not satisfactory Greek, but the general sense is clear.

170. 981E.

171. This material between inverted commas is actually a conflation of the passages that have just been quoted from the *Laws* and the *Epinomis*.

172. Here and in the next sentence Philoponus treats the *Epinomis*, which was regarded as a kind of appendix to the *Laws*, as part of the *Laws*.

173. 28B.

174. cf. 154,18.

175. In VI.24.

176. cf. *Tim.* 27C.

177. *Tim.* 30A.

178. It is tempting to read *epiginomenon <eidos>*, or, in view of *skhêmata* ('shapes') at 165,3, *epiginomenon <skhêma>* but perhaps *to epiginomenon* ('something which supervenes') can stand on its own.

179. = Sodano 2,47.

180. cf. *Tim.* 52B.

181. = Sodano 2,49.

182. Or perhaps 'eyes and the ability to use them'. For the phrase cf. 202,3-5.

183. More literally 'who have diverted Plato into these stupid theories'.

184. Half a dozen times in fact, most recently at 138,20.

185. Emending *eipômen* to *eipomen*. The reference is to 149,12-16.

186. These lines were quoted at 96,7-11, though not in the same sequence. On that occasion Philoponus' paraphrase of the words in parentheses (*hoson gar ... ho khronos*) at 96,20-1 shows that he understands them as I have translated them, but I think that Proclus intended something like 'for whatever is there [sc. in time], is in a particular [part of] time'.

187. More literally 'always existing at a particular moment, [namely,] in the [or: 'at each'] present part of time'. The phrase is a little awkward and it may be that *kata to enestêkos tou khronou meros* ('in the present part of time') is a gloss on *pote* ('at a particular moment') that has found its way into the text.

188. *Tim.* 28A.

189. cf. *Tim.* 28B.

190. Aristotle argues that the universe is ungenerated and imperishable at *Cael.* 279b1-284b5. The only specific reference to Plato is at 280a28-32, which Philoponus quotes below at 221,24-8.

191. *Tim.* 28B.

192. The MSS of Plato have *gennêtos* rather than *genêtos*, but the two words are frequently confused in manuscripts and, at least by Philoponus' day, were probably not clearly distinguished by the Greeks themselves.

193. Changing *ta* to *to* at 170,14, as suggested by Rabe in the critical apparatus.

194. Adding *ei* before *en* and changing *ekhein* to *ekhei* at 170,28, as suggested by Rabe in the critical apparatus.

195. In IV.14.

196. cf. *Tim.* 27D-28B.

197. *Tim.* 28B.

198. At 159,5-7.

199. At 167,24-7.

200. 'Most truly' (*kuriôtata*) looks forward to 'in the truest sense' (*kuriôtatên*) in the quotation at 172,9.

201. Although translators commonly translate along these lines, something like 'this is [its] most supreme ["principal", "ultimate", etc.] cause' would also be possible, but it would then be more difficult to make good sense of *kai tauta kuriôtata* at 172,6.

202. *Tim.* 29E.

203. Or 'If this is the ultimate origin ...' (cf. the note at 172,9).

204. Both here and earlier in the sentence one could translate 'from' rather than 'through the agency of'.

205. *Tim.* 28B.

206. = Smith 172F (omitted by Sodano).

207. *Tim.* 28B.

208. *Tim.* 27C.

209. *Tim.* 28B.

210. sc. in a question as to whether something is the case or not (cf. the note at 136,16).

211. *Tim.* 28B.

212. *Top.* 105a3-7.

213. *Mund.* 397b13-16.

214. 34B-C.

215. *Tim.* 27C.

216. *Tim.* 27C.

217. Actually paraphrase rather than quotation of *Tim.* 27C, but it seems reasonable to retain Rabe's quotation marks.

218. *Tim.* 27D-28A.

219. *Epist.* 2, 312D-E.

220. 715E.

221. = Kern fr. 168; but this passage is not cited there.

222. 174,27-175,2.

223. *Mund.* 397b13-16.

224. The argument that the cause and beginning of all things is one runs from 1070a3 to 1076a4. The Homeric quotation (*Il.* 2.204) constitutes its last line.

225. 34B ff.; 41C.

226. Changing *monôi* at 180,16 to *monon*. (cf. 181,4).

227. Adding *ou* before *ta men* at 180,23.

228. 180,16-18.

229. *Rep.* 534E.

230. *Phdr.* 265E.

231. 27D-28A.

232. Changing *genomenôi* to *ginomenôi* at 182,10, as suggested by Rabe in the critical apparatus.

233. Changing *genomenon ... genomenon* to *ginomenon ... ginomenon* at 182,19, as suggested by Rabe in the critical apparatus.

234. VI.18.

235. *Tim.* 28B.

236. sc. the Presocratics.

237. cf. *Phd.* 97C ff. and Diels-Kranz, 'Anaxagoras' A57 with Diels note. (The phrase 'as though waking from a dream' does not occur in Plato.)

238. That is, that it *has* an efficient cause.

239. This quotation, which is actually an amalgam of two different passages in the *Timaeus*, occurs again at 184,18-21. The words before the semicolon are from 28C, where, as Philoponus states, they immediately follow the quotation earlier in the sentence, but the words following the semicolon are from 28A. The misquotation is not critical for the argument and may be accidental, having arisen because the words from 28A are there preceded by words that are similar to those from 28C.

240. Literally 'run back to'. For the usage, cf. the passages cited at LSJ *anatrekhein* I.3, and Olympiodorus, *in Gorg.* 161,35 (Westerink).

241. 196a28-b5.

242. Aristotle has 'comes about' (*ginomenon*; 196b3) and Rabe's suggestion in the critical apparatus that 'has come about' (*genomenou*) may have replaced 'comes about' (*ginomenou*) is plausible.

243. *Tim.* 28B.

244. cf. 183,17-19 and note there.

245. *Tim.* 27D.

246. *Tim.* 28A.

247. *Tim.* 28B.

248. 145,2, etc.

249. *Tim.* 27C.

250. Homer, *Il.* 3.215.

251. The manuscripts of Homer have *êen* ('he was').

252. When translating the *Timaeus* passage it is natural to render *poieisthai logous* by something like 'to discuss' (as I have a few lines earlier) or 'to engage in dialogue' (cf. LSJ *logos* VI.3.c), but here, where the subject of the infinitive appears to be singular (Plato?) and the phrase is followed by *hôs* ('that'), it makes sense to treat the phrase as periphrastic for the simple verb *legein*, 'to say' (cf. LSJ *poieô* II.5). Alternatively, one might perhaps translate 'will discuss how it has come to be, even though it is ungenerated', but this seems a less natural interpretation of the Greek and less in accord with what Taurus goes on to say.

253. This passage is, as Philoponus says, a comment on the lemma 'we who are about to discuss with regard to the universe whether it has come to be or is ungenerated', and in particular on the words 'or is ungenerated'. Is the first sentence ('Even though it is ungenerated.') intended as (a) a statement that Plato wrote *ei kai* rather than the *ê kai* of the lemma (Verrycken, 'Philoponus' Interpretation of Plato's Cosmogony', 310-17), or (b) a statement that *ê kai* is here synonymous with *ei kai* (Baltes, *Die Weltentstehung des platonischen Timaios nach den antiken Interpreten* (Leiden, 1976), 1,112-115)? The issue is a complex one and any attempt to resolve it must take into account not only the present passage but, at a minimum, Philoponus' comments on it at 191,15-193,9 and the passage from Alexander which he quotes at 214,10 ff., on which those comments are clearly in part based. I cannot go into the matter thoroughly here, but at certain points the translator must (at least implicitly) take a position, so I shall first give a brief indication of the views of Baltes and Verrycken and then, equally briefly, state the position I shall take.

Baltes believes that Taurus read *ê kai* in Plato but interpreted it as equivalent to *ei kai*. Alexander, misunderstanding Taurus' highly abbreviated comment on the *Timaeus* passage, believed that he was changing Plato's *ê kai* to *ei kai* and, in his commentary on Aristotle's *de Caelo* (in the passage quoted below at 214,10ff.), criticised him on that basis. Porphyry, on the other hand, understood Taurus' intention correctly but, in his own commentary on the *Timaeus*, argued that he had misinterpreted Plato. Philoponus, who was familiar with the criticisms of both Alexander and Porphyry, combines them rather awkwardly in his own criticism of Taurus at 191,15-193,9, with the result that, although he clearly believes that Taurus altered the transmitted text of Plato from *ê kai* to *ei kai*, he also accuses him of misinterpreting Plato's *ê kai.*

Verrycken believes that Taurus reads *ei kai* in Plato, either regarding it as one possible solution of an ambiguous unaccented *ê* (Verrycken's preferred position) or as a correction of the transmitted reading. Alexander believed that Taurus had illegitimately changed the transmitted text and criticised him on that basis. Philoponus, like Alexander, believes that Taurus changed the transmitted text and criticises him on that basis. Some of his arguments are taken from Alexander, but those which accuse Taurus of misinterpreting *ê kai* are his own. He is not, as Baltes argues, illegitimately combining incompatible arguments. His position is that it is just because Taurus thinks that *ê kai* is to be understood in the same sense as *ei kai* that he substitutes *ei* for *ê.*

My own belief is that Taurus was, as Baltes holds, interpreting *ê kai* rather than emending it. Philoponus understood this perfectly well and nothing he writes is intended to suggest anything else; in fact, he also seems to believe that Alexander too is criticizing the misinterpretation of *ê kai*, not its emendation. (I am not sure that he was correct in this last belief, but nor am I certain that Alexander's criticism was directed at Taurus.)

Whichever was Taurus' position, he is clearly quoting the line from the *Iliad* to bolster it. The manuscripts of Homer (see M.M. Willcock (ed.) *The Iliad of Homer* (Houndmills & London, 1978-84), 1,85) are divided between *ê* (accented in two different ways) and *ei* and the ancient scholia (see H. Erbse (ed)., *Scholia Graeca in Homeri Iliadem* (Berlin, 1969-83), 1,398-9) show that some commentators read *ê* but argued that it was synonymous with *ei*. If Taurus is proposing emendation, he is adducing the Homeric passage as another case where *ei* should be restored even though (many of) the manuscripts read *ê*, if merely a particular interpretation of *ê kai*, as another case where *ê* is supposedly synonymous with *ei*. To my way of thinking Taurus' quotation of Homer favours the second alternative, since, as far as we can see from the scholia, the scholarly debate was concerned with how *ê* should be understood rather than with whether *ê* or *ei* should be read, and a possible expansion of Taurus' rather cryptic first two sentences would be (retaining *ei kai* at 186,22 rather than emending to *ê kai* as Baltes (113, n. 135) suggests): '[The words *ê kai agenes estin* have here the rather unusual meaning] "even though it is ungenerated". The Poet [likewise means] "even though it were later in birth" [when he writes *ê kai genei husteron eien*].'

254. As the text stands, the subjects of the verbs in this sentence are the two reasons (*aitiai*) mentioned in the previous sentence. This is awkward and there may be something wrong with the text. The sense required seems to be something like 'the first is [that] he is exhorting [us] to piety, the second [that this expedient] is employed for the sake of clarity'; but something more complicated may have gone wrong.

255. i.e. even without a temporally prior cause. (This '*allôs*' looks back to the one in line 7).

256. For this sense of *khôrein* see Lampe C.5.

257. This strikes me as a rather odd thing to say and I am tempted to change *suntethenta* at 187,17 to *suntethentôn* and *ginomena* in the following line to *ginomenôn* and translate '... construct diagrams of things that have not [really] been constructed as though they are in the process of being generated', or to omit *diagrammata* as a gloss and translate '... construct things that have not [really] been constructed as though they are in the process of being generated', but the first part of the sentence is, I think, against it. (Perhaps Taurus would have done better to write 'describe' rather than 'construct'.)

258. *Elements* I, def. 15.

259. Punctuating with a full stop after *ginomena* at 187,18.

260. 369B ff.

261. = Fortenbaugh, fr. 241B.

262. cf. *Cael.* 279b33-280a11.

263. Compare this report of the views of Theophrastus and Aristotle with the earlier one at 145,15-24.

264. sc. in the *Critias*. (For the title *Atlantikos*, cf. Diogenes Laertius 3.51,1 and 3.60,6; Stobaeus 2.28,1; Proclus, *in Tim.* 1.201,14ff.). Another possibility, although I think it is a slim one, is that the reference is, as Verrycken assumes (see 'Philoponus' Interpretation of Plato's Cosmogony', 312), to the summary of the Atlantis story at *Tim.* 20D-25D, in which case I would translate 'from the Atlantis [myth]'.

265. Those who ignored Taurus' advice could in the case of the *Statesman* have pointed to the passage in the myth where it is said that a creator god brought the universe into its present state of order out of a state of disorder (273B-D). It is less clear what evidence they could have found to support their position in the Atlantis myth; perhaps they might have argued that the reference to the division of the earth among the gods at *Critias* 109B (also hinted at at *Timaeus* 23D-E) implies a finite age for the earth, and therefore the world, and that the chronology outlined by the Egyptian priest at *Timaeus* 41E even gives some idea of its age.

266. Rabe writes '*autôi* suspectum' in the critical apparatus, and I have changed *autôi* to *tôi*. Another possibility would be *autôi* <*tôi*>, a suggestion of the reader.

267. cf. 164,24-165,2.

268. Or 'distraction', perhaps. LSJ glosses *okhlêsis* 'disturbance, annoyance, distress', none of which quite works here. The word is used in a similar context at 259,5.

269. *Tim.* 27C, as emended, or interpreted, by Taurus 186,21.

270. Adding *khreia* after *ên* at 189,25, a suggestion of Brinkmann reported by Rabe in the critical apparatus.

271. At VI.8.

272. 246A.

273. Both Baltes and Verrycken base their cases that Philoponus believed that Taurus was proposing to emend *ê kai* at *Tim.* 28C to *ei kai* largely on certain phrases in this section and in the section summary at 123,19-24. The key phrases are *metapherein tas lexeis* (here), which they (on the face of it quite plausibly) take to mean something like 'to alter manuscript readings', the roughly equivalent phrase *metethêke tên lexin* at 193,6, and the phrase *metethêke eis* ('change to') in the section summary, to which Baltes would perhaps add *metalambanesthai* at 191,17 (cf. Baltes, 113, n. 133) and, presumably, other related words in this section, although this would leave it unclear how he would draw the line between Philoponus' criticism of the misinterpretation of *ê kai* and his criticism of its emendation. My own view is that *metapherein* (or *metatithenai*) *tên lexin*, which I take to mean something like 'altering the meaning (cf. LSJ *metapherein* 3) of a word [or phrase]', or perhaps 'altering the literal meaning' (cf. Lampe *lexis* 9), are merely generalised descriptions of the specific crime of which Philoponus is accusing Taurus, sc. claiming that *ê kai* is equivalent to *ei kai*. This has the great advantage that it gives Philoponus' argument a coherence that it lacks as either Baltes or Verrycken understand it. What is required is evidence that the phrases in question are likely to mean what I want them to and that is, I believe, provided by VI.11 above. There Philoponus is attacking an alleged attempt to take *genêtos* ('generated') as equivalent to *sunthetos* ('composite'), or, as Philoponus puts it, to claim that Plato has substituted 'generated' for 'composite'. There is clearly no hint of any proposal to emend the text; the question is purely a semantic one. The verbs used to describe the alleged substitution are *metalambanein anti* (155,11.13; 156,26; 157,3.6.13), and, as in the present section, *metalambanein eis* (155,19; 157,14), and at 156,1 such substitutions are described as *metapherein tên sunêthê tôn onomatôn epi to atribes kai asunêthes* ('changing normal word-usage to the novel and unfamiliar') and at 157,14 as a *metathesis* (the noun is from the same root as *metatithenai*) *tôn onomatôn* ('a substitution [or "interchanging"] of nouns').

274. sc. Taurus.

275. For *metalambanein* in this sense, though in a different construction, cf. LSJ s.v. IV.3.

276. At 214,10-20.

277. If, as I believe, and as Verrycken presumably, and Baltes possibly, would agree, *tên toiautên tou sundesmou metalêpsin* ('such a substitution of conjunctions') refers to the proposal to understand *ê kai* in the sense of *ei kai*, it seems that Philoponus believes that Alexander's criticism, like his own, is directed at the misinterpretation of *ê kai* and not, as Baltes and Verrycken hold, at its emendation.

278. Changing *Platônikas* to *Platônikês* at 191,23, as suggested by Rabe in the critical apparatus.

279. Literally *kuriologia* is either the use of literal rather than figurative language or the precise use of words.

280. The ancient scholia on the *Iliad* (see note at 186,3) do not contain any statement about the frequency of the alleged usage.

281. *Tim.* 27C.

282. On dialectical problems see the note at 136,16.

283. *Tim.* 28B.

284. Here and above in line 11 *en aporiâi* ('in a puzzle') seems to be used synonymously with the technical term *en problêmati* ('in a dialectical problem'), which was used in line 5 and reappears at 193,19. This is a little surprising and a case could be made for emendation.

285. sc. in 27C.

286. Or possibly: 'altered the literal sense'. The phrase (*metethêke tên lexin*) is, I believe, equivalent to *metapherein tas lexeis* ('alter the meanings of words') at 191,15.

287. Although I have retained it in the translation, *hama* at 193,6 looks rather like a gloss on *aperiskeptôs* that has found its way into the text, perhaps at the expense of a particle, whether *ara*, as Rabe suggests, or something else.

288. Changing *metalambanontes* to *metalambanousin* at 193,11, one of two possible corrections suggested by Rabe in the critical apparatus.

289. If this, as it may at first appear, refers specifically to their addition of the letters *ei* to the text of Plato to change *agenes* to *aeigenes*, the parallel with Taurus does not hold up, since his activity, even if it amounted to emendation, could not be described simply as the addition of something. However, the phrase is almost certainly inspired by Alexander's *metagraphein ta mê houtôs ekhonta* at 214,3, which seems to mean something like 'transcribe incorrectly', and probably has much the same meaning. (In fact, I suspect that when Philoponus wrote *palin kai houtoi* ('they too in turn'), he thought that he had, following Alexander, earlier used some such phrase to describe Taurus' activity – and indeed may have in an earlier draft.)

290. *Tim.* 28B.

291. *Tim.* 28A.

292. cf. *Tim.* 27C.

293. More literally 'as something strong towards proof'.

294. 34C ff.

295. 246A.

296. The word translated 'animates' (*psukhoun*) has the same root as the word translated 'soul' (*psukhê*).

297. It is difficult to know how best to translate *kath'hexin* here but a passage from his *in DA* (2,7-15) shows what Philoponus has in mind. 'The function of intellect is to apprehend things better than [is possible] through demonstration by acts of pure intuition. This activity of intellect only takes place in those who have reached the pinnacle of purification and knowledge, in those who through [the practice of] the purificatory virtues have habituated themselves to engaging in [mental] activity without imagery and quite apart from sense perception. For intellect is, as it were, the most perfect condition (*hexis*) of the soul.' (A scholiast put it more economically when he glossed *kath'hexin* 'i.e. philosophically' in the main manuscript of *Aet.*)

298. sc. by dying.

299. Changing *autêi* to *autê* at 196,1 and *en têi* to *en hêi* at 196,3. *autêi* and *tê* may both have arisen under the influence of the phrase *en skhesei têi pros to sôma* at 195,26-7. (In 196,3, one might, as an alternative, delete *ekhei*.)

300. In VI.7.

301. 35A-36D. Cornford's commentary on the *Timaeus* passage will also serve to elucidate Philoponus' paraphrase of it.

302. More literally 'out of the bare text itself' (i.e. without further commentary).

303. i.e. Taurus, Porphyry, and perhaps Proclus himself (cf. 146,1-7).

304. Here and in what follows 'the planets' translates *hoi planômenoi* (sc. *asteres*; for the gender cf. *Aet.* 579,16, for the complete phrase e.g. [Philop.] *in GA* 218,22), and 'the planetary spheres' *hai planômenai* (sc. *sphairai*; for the complete phrase cf. *Aet.* 537,6).

305. *Il.* 12.239-40.

306. e.g. at *Phdr.* 246A.

307. cf. *Tim.* 28B-C.

308. In VI.11.

309. cf. *Tim.* 32C.

310. 521,25-522,22.

311. For this rendering of *kephalaion* see note 1.

312. i.e. the total amount of each of the four elements. (In fact, a more literal rendering of the phrase would be 'the totalities of the elements').

313. VI.9-23.

314. For 'conversion by negation', see the note at 126,20.

315. Deleting *ou* at 204,21 and changing *all'* at 204,22 to *kai ouk*.

316. VI.7-23.

317. I would normally translate the phrase *aei kata ta auta kai hôsautôs ekhein* 'always remains the same and unchanging', but I have used 'unchanging' earlier in the sentence to render *ametablêton*.

318. A slightly inaccurate quotation of *Tim.* 27D-28A, probably under the influence of 29A.

319. *Tim.* 27D.

320. Here and in the rest of this section 'temporal origin' translates *khronikê arkhê*.

321. *kath'hotioun tôn peri auto theôroumenôn*. More literally 'with regard to anything at all observed around it [or perhaps "in it"]'. This is awkward and I am tempted to think that *tôn peri auto theôroumenôn* is a gloss on *kath'hotioun* which has found its way into the text.

322. Adding *to* before *khronikês* at 206,10, as suggested by Rabe in the critical apparatus.

323. Actually almost a hundred pages later in IX.11.

324. Changing *pros* to *pôs* at 207,15, as suggested by Rabe in the critical apparatus.

325. VI.18-20.

326. Adding *aei* before *ontôn* at 207,27.

327. Adding *de* after *lêthês* at 208,14 and changing *autôi* to *autêi* in the following line. (In the critical apparatus Rabe suggests the former change and casts doubt on *autôi*.)

328. Changing *horasthai* to *orthais einai* at 208,23, one of two possible corrections suggested by Rabe in the critical apparatus.

329. 205,25-206,7.

330. 113b15-114a25.

331. Omitting the words *to khrômasin einai*, which look like a gloss on *to poiotêsin einai*. (Rabe writes 'to khrômasin einai vix sana' in the critical apparatus.)

332. The verb (*antikeintai*) is plural, and the sentence could also be translated: 'Thus if that which changes and that which is never the same and that which is perceptible are opposed to that which is unchanging and that which is always the same and that which is intelligible ...'

333. For this sense of *logos* see Lampe s.v. A.12.b. *logos* could, of course, be rendered by something more neutral, say 'position'.

334. Atticus (*c.* AD 150-200) and Plutarch (before AD 50-after AD 120) were both notorious for having supported the literal interpretation of the *Timaeus*. Eusebius quotes them both at length in his *Praeparatio Evangelica* (*Preparation for the Gospel*), although in the case of Plutarch not on creation. The most important work of Plutarch in that connection is his *de Animae Procreatione in Timaeo* (*On the Generation of the Soul in the Timaeus*) and the fragments of Atticus are collected in E. Des Places (ed.), *Atticus: fragments* (Paris 1977), which also has a useful introduction. As I remarked in the introduction to my translation of *Aet.* 1-5, the fact that Philoponus feels able to direct his readers to Christian authors for information about Plutarch and Atticus suggests that he is writing primarily for a Christian audience.

335. 279b4-6.

336. 279b12-17.

337. Alexander's commentary on *Cael.* has not survived.

338. Aristotle attributes this view to Hesiod at *Cael.* 298b25-9 and to Plato at *Cael.* 280a28-32.

339. Changing *tinôn* to *sunistamenôn* at 212,24. (Rabe suggests emending it to *ginomenôn*, but 212,10 and 213,6 seem to favour *sunistamenôn*).

340. As Rabe indicates, the words *tautês de phêsin tês doxês kai tous Stôikous gegonenai* ('He says that the Stoics too were of this opinion') at 213,3-4 cannot stand. It seems probable that they were originally a marginal gloss with 'he' referring to Alexander, and I have deleted them.

341. *Cael.* 279b17-21.

342. *Tim.* 27D.

343. *Tim.* 27C.

344. Although Philoponus' earlier criticism of Taurus' treatment of *Tim.* 27C at 191,15-193,9 is in large measure based on what Alexander says in this passage, it is not necessarily the case that Taurus, whom he does not mention elsewhere in his writings, is one of those Alexander has in mind here.

345. Although, if I am right (cf. the note at 191,19), Philoponus believed that Alexander is attacking an incorrect interpretation of *ê kai* rather than a proposal to emend it, I doubt that this is really the case. A TLG search for the verb *metagraphein* (the key word for present purposes) turns up numerous passages, including the only other one in which Alexander seems to use it (*in Metaph.* 59,7), in which it clearly means 'to emend', and that seems most likely to be its meaning here. However, the verb can be used of various kinds of translation or rewriting, and Philoponus, prompted perhaps by the belief (correct or not) that Alexander's comments were directed at Taurus and by his own understanding of Taurus' intention, seems to have thought that in this case it described (as do, if I am correct, his own phrases *metapherein tas lexeis* and *metethêke tên lexin*) the process of producing an interpretative gloss or paraphrase. (Here, and later in the paragraph, I have tried to render *metagraphein* in a way that is compatible with either 'emendation' or 'interpretation'.)

346. Or, transliterating rather than translating, 'to alter *ê* to *ei*'.

347. Or perhaps: 'copy what is not there'.

348. *Tim.* 28B.

349. Adding *tois eis* after *dôsei* at 214,19, one of two possible emendations suggested by Rabe in the critical apparatus.

350. Literally 'rewrite to'.

351. Although what Philoponus writes at 191,26 in close dependence on the present passage shows that he took the contrary view, it seems to me that Alexander is arguing that what Plato says rules out rewriting 27C rather than that it offers no opportunity for similar rewriting here.

352. Changing *gignesthai* to *einai* at 215,3, as suggested by Rabe in the critical apparatus.

353. Emending *ginesthai* to *ginetai* at 215,7. (Rabe writes '*hôs ginesthai* suspecta' in the critical apparatus.)

354. Emending *toioutos* at 215,12 to *toioutôs* and *ekeinos* at 215,14 to *ekeinôs* and retaining *anairein* at 215,13. (Rabe writes 'fort. *anairôn*' in the critical apparatus.)

355. i.e. on the basis that it has its being in perishing.

356. Adding *hôste* before *dêlonoti* at 215,24, as suggested by Rabe in the critical apparatus.

357. Emending *auton* to *autou* or *autôi* at 215,25.

358. Emending *antitithêsin* to *anatithêsin* at 216,6. (Rabe writes '*antitithêsin* suspectum' in the critical apparatus.)

359. At *Tim.* 41A-B.

360. 368C-369B.

361. In other words, the final figure is complete as soon as the last line has been drawn and is identical with the lines that have entered into its construction.

362. Punctuating with a comma rather than a full stop after *tauton* at 217,9.

363. *Cael.* 279b32-280a10.

364. Adding *ho ton kubon* before *pher'* at 218,1, as suggested by Rabe in the critical apparatus.

365. Adding *ti* before *ex* at 218,22.

366. Literally 'of which that which is said to have emerged from them is not destructive'.

367. Since the literal meaning of *kosmos* is 'order', the point is to a degree a verbal one.

368. 'They' are presumably the mathematicians. It was, of course, an issue whether Plato intended the generation of the five regular solids at *Tim.* 53C-56C to be taken literally.

369. The clause is rather awkward and it is possible that the words *sunupark-hein dunamenois* ('[in] things which can coexist') are a gloss on *en toioutois*, in which case I would translate: 'for analysis is [found] in things of this kind'.

370. *Cael.* 280a28-32.

371. cf. *Tim.* 29B ff.; 41A-B.

372. As Rabe points out in the critical apparatus, we might have expected *phtharênai* (which occurs at 221,25 in the passage quoted from *Cael.*) rather than *phtheirein* at 222,11. The last part of the sentence would then read 'that anything which is ungenerated perishes'.

373. Changing *gar* to *de* at 222,13. (Rabe writes 'expectes *de*' in the critical apparatus.)

374. 251b14-19.

375. Translating Aristotle's *exô henos* at 222,19 rather than the *ex aiônos* ('from eternity') of the manuscripts of *Aet.* (Although the manuscripts also had *ex aiônos* when the passage was quoted at 117,27, the substitution seems more likely to be due to a copyist than to Philoponus.)

376. As Rabe suggests, Alexander's comment on this passage may have been lost at this point. (Like his commentary on *Cael.*, Alexander's commentary on *Phys.* has not survived.)

377. Page references to these earlier citations are given at the end of each extract. Notes and references associated with them are not repeated.

378. = Fortenbaugh, fr. 241A.

379. = 145,13-25.

380. = Fortenbaugh, fr. 241B.

381. = 188,6-18.

382. *Tim.* 29A.

383. *Tim.* 29E.

384. 224,18-225,10 = Smith 456aF. The title of Porphyry's work is not known.

385. 127,20-6. (For *kephalaion* = 'chapter' see note 1.)

386. cf. *Phdr.* 245C-246A.

387. For 'conversion by negation', see the note at 126,20.

388. *Tim.* 41A-B.

389. *Tim.* 41A.

390. As Rabe sees, there is something wrong with this sentence. His solution is to insert *hôs* before *dêlon* at 226,24 and he also suggests in the apparatus that one might have expected *to d'* at the beginning of the sentence (226,19). I would prefer to add *hoti* before *to* at the beginning of the sentence and have translated accordingly. (I have also omitted *phêsin* at 226,25, which seems equally awkward in either case.)

391. 269C-E.

392. The idea that Plato drew his inspiration from Moses and the Bible is a constant theme of Eusebius' *Praeparatio Evangelica*, which Philoponus clearly knew (cf. the note at 211,18).

393. A paraphrase of *Hebrews* 1,12, which is itself an adaptation of *Psalms* 102, 27. (The occurrence of the verb *heilittesthai* ('to be rolled up') shows that Philoponus is citing the *Hebrews* version.) In *The New Oxford Annotated Bible* the whole passage reads: 'In the beginning, Lord, you founded the earth, and the heavens are the work of your hands; they will perish, but you remain; they will all wear out like clothing; like a cloak you will roll them up, and like clothing they will be changed. But you are the same and your years will never end.' (The second 'like clothing' is omitted in some ancient versions, including it seems the one used by Philoponus.) There does not actually seem to be any reference to the revolution of the heavens in the biblical passage.

394. *Wisdom of Solomon* 1, 13 and 14.

395. 269E-270A.

396. cf. *Tim.* 33A; 33D.

397. *Tim.* 33C.

398. *pêsetai* here and at 233,8 seems to be a variant of *peisetai*, the usual future of *paskhô*. Although LSJ does not list *pêsetai*, it does give *pêsis* (which occurs at 62,5) as a late variant of *peisis*, a noun formed from the same root.

399. *Tim.* 27D-28A.

400. 230,23-231,1.

401. 32B-33A.

402. 230,27 ff.

403. 266a24-b24.

404. For a discussion of the role of 'infinite power' arguments in the creation debate in ancient and mediaeval philosophy with references to earlier literature, see R. Sorabji, *Matter, Space and Motion* (London & Ithaca, NY, 1988), ch. 15. For Philoponus' contribution in *Aet.* and elsewhere, see especially pp. 254-9. (The same material appears in abbreviated form in R. Sorabji (ed.), *Aristotle Transformed* (London & Ithaca, NY, 1990), ch. 9.)

405. 33B-D.

406. For the phrase cf. 523,7-8.

407. Or perhaps 'examples'.

408. 266a24-b24.

409. Or perhaps: 'in earlier chapters'.

410. *Cael.* 279a25-8.

411. The reference is to the supposed derivation of *aiôn* (eternity) from *aei ôn* ('always being').

412. Changing *apolabonta* to *apolabon* at 239,14. (Perhaps the copyist unthinkingly took *apolabonta* with *ton horismon*, or even, at least fleetingly, with '*to ginomenon kai apollumenon*', construing the phrase as plural. Alternatively, Philoponus may have written *tou ginomenou apolabontos*, which would make the otherwise seemingly otiose *auto* in the next line easier).

413. *huper tên hautou phusin*. I have until now translated *huper phusin* by 'supernaturally' but the presence of *hautou* makes that impossible here and in the next few lines.

414. The development of Philoponus' ideas on this question of the nature of the rotation of the fire belt is outlined in Sorabji, *Matter, Space and Motion*, 240-1.

415. Homer *Il.* 1.70.

416. sc. *An Examination of Aristotle's Criticisms of Plato's Timaeus.*

417. In the previous chapter I usually translated *arkhê* 'beginning' (see the note at 159,2), but in this one 'origin' or 'source' works better, and I have opted for the latter.

418. At this point the Arabic translation of Isḥâq ibn Ḥunayn has words which Badawi translates 'Car il n'est pas un principe de mouvement par choix, mais dans le sens de ce qui se meut par soi' (A. Badawi, 'Un Proclus perdu est retrouvé en arabe', in *Mélanges L. Massignon I* (Damascus 1956), 150; citation from Baltes), and Baltes, inspired by this but influenced by the phrasing of Philoponus' paraphrase at 247,9-11 (which I translate 'For, since, he says, soul is self-moved and the source of movement just by being and not through choice'), includes the words 'denn es ist nicht aus eigenen Entschluß selbstbewegt und Prinzip der Bewegung, sondern durch sein Sein selbst'. This, or something similar, would fit well enough at this point, and Philoponus certainly appears to attribute some such statement to Proclus on a number of occasions (in addition to 247,9-11, cf. 256,25-8; 260,4-5; 260,28-261,1; 268,25-8). However, the words are not necessary to Proclus' argument and when they first appear at 247,9-12 they look like an interpretative paraphrase of what Proclus says at 243,4-7, designed to introduce terminology (sc. *autôi tôi einai* and *ou proairetikôs*) which Philoponus will use later in the refutation and I am inclined to think that they have been imported into the text of Proclus by someone who felt that Philoponus' language mandated their presence there. (If this were the case, it would suggest that the Arabic text of Proclus is ultimately derived from the tradition of *Aet.*, which, as far as I can see, is perfectly possible.)

419. The sentence is unsatisfactory as it stands, but I am not sure how best to repair it. Baltes, apparently with the support of the Arabic translation, changes the *ê* before *proteron* to *mê* and translates 'denn für die Bewegung des Alls, das nicht vorher oder nachher existiert, ist die immer seiende Seele Ursprung der Bewegung; sie kann gar nicht Ursprung der Bewegung sein, da sie aufgrund ihres Wesens selbstbewegt und eben deshalb Ursprung der Bewegung ist'. But (1) apart from *mê proteron ouk ontos ê husteron* ('not not existing previously or subsequently') being strangely convoluted Greek, the phrase *dia to mê einai ton kosmon aïdion* ('because the world is not eternal') in Philoponus' paraphrase of this passage at 247,13-14 seems to show that he read *ê* rather than *mê*, and (2) the resulting sentence (the syntax of which would still, as far as I can see, be defective) would leave the adversative *alla mên* at the beginning of the next sentence unmotivated. One could go some way towards repairing the syntax of the sentence by changing the participles *ousa* and *dunamenê* in line 10 to finite verbs and translating 'for it is always the origin of movement for the movement of the universe, even if it [sc. the universe] did not previously exist or will not subsequently, and it cannot not be an origin of movement, since it is by its essence self-moved and therefore an origin of movement', but the phrase *ê proteron ouk ontos ê husteron* would then be rather awkward (*tou pantos ê proteron ouk ontos ê husteron* actually looks like a genitive absolute) and Philoponus' paraphrase is, again, against it. I have opted, very tentatively, for inserting *arkhê ouk an eiê* after *kinêseôs* at 243,10, which at least produces something closer to Philoponus' paraphrase (cf. 247,14), but I doubt whether the solution is so simple.

420. If the word existed, 'self-movedness' would be more literal.

421. On the significance and history of these bodies, which are variously called 'astral', 'luminous', 'ethereal' or 'pneumatic', see Dodds, *Proclus, The Elements of Theology*, App. 2 and Siorvanes, *Proclus: Neo-Platonic Philosophy and Science* (New Haven and London 1996), 131-3. (Siorvanes cites some more recent literature in n. 27.)

422. A closer rendering would be 'if soul has its essence in this, in being ...'. Similar phrases occur later in the chapter, when I also telescope the construction.

423. i.e. 'independent of'. *khôristos* may mean either 'separate(d)' or 'separable' and there are passages in Sections 3 and 4 where a case could be made for the latter rendering. However, Philoponus is not just arguing that soul can exist separately from body (i.e. that it is 'separable'), but that it is at all times essentially independent of body, and I have decided to stick to 'separate' throughout – and to 'not separate' rather than 'inseparable' for *akhôristos*.

424. I have been unable to find one or even a small number of suitable equivalents for *kinêtikos* ('responsible for moving') in this chapter. The relevant glosses in LSJ ('of or for putting in motion') and Lampe ('setting in motion, causing to move') are of little help, since not only do they fail to acknowledge that the word, like many other adjectives formed with the suffix *-iko-*, often conveys the idea of fitness or ability to carry out the action expressed, but, as with cognate words such as *kinêsis* ('movement') and *kineô* ('move'), moving or setting in motion is not always the best description of that action. I have opted for looking for a reasonable rendering in each separate context and listing the results in the Greek-English word index.

425. One would expect *ekhei* (from 259,22) rather than *kinei* (from 259,27) at this point. Either the summariser, whether Philoponus himself or someone else, has been careless, or the transmitted text is corrupt. I have assumed that the latter is the case and changed *kinei* to *ekhei*.

426. Or perhaps: 'through appetition in souls'.

427. sc. conceived as a potential (cf. 263,13-24, especially 22-24).

428. For Neoplatonists from Plotinus onwards the three hypostases One, Intellect and Soul exercise causation while themselves remaining absolutely immutable. They give rise to the things that participate in them without deliberation or action on their part just by being what they are. The present phrase (*autôi tôi einai*) was probably first used to express this mode of causation by Syrianus and became a stock formula with later Neoplatonists, being a favourite with Proclus, who uses it in the second, fourth and sixteenth arguments (see 24,5; 56,2; 560,22; 561,25.26), and occurring 27 times in *Aet.*, mostly in the present chapter, where the manner in which soul initiates life and movement is at issue. (For the Plotinian background and the meaning and employment of *autôi tôi einai* see C. D'Ancona Costa, 'Plotinus and later Platonic philosophers on the causality of the First Principle' in *The Cambridge Companion to Plotinus*, ed. L.P. Gerson (Cambridge, 1996), 356-68.)

429. Changing *huph' heautês* to *hup' autês* at 245,17, as suggested by Rabe in the critical apparatus.

430. Changing *to* to *tôi* at 245,25, as suggested by Rabe in the critical apparatus.

431. Changing *kinêton* to *akinêton* at 245,26 (cf. 274,20).

432. Adding *einai* after *thaterois* at 246,12, as suggested by the reader.

433. *Phdr.* 245C-246A.

434. This proverb, which appears to mean to join like to like or to deal with matters of a similar kind, is used by Plato (*Euthyd.* 298C) and Aristotle (*Phys.* 207a17).

435. For *ouk anekhesthai* in the sense 'refuse', see Lampe s.v. B.2.

436. *EN* 1096a16-17.

437. More literally, 'for the second [sc. latter] to follow from the former', but my translation has changed the order of the two items in the previous sentence.

438. *tôi einai autês kai têi ousiâi. ousia* could equally well be translated 'being' or 'substance'. 'Being' is not available in this section because I have opted to use it to translate *einai*. The choice between 'essence' and 'substance' was more difficult. The former fits best early in the argument, where the intrinsic nature of soul is what is at issue, the latter later, where the possibility of its separate existence is being discussed. In view of the fact that essence can, if infrequently, mean a 'spiritual or immaterial entity' (*New Shorter Oxford English Dictionary* s.v. 6.), I have decided to retain 'essence' throughout.

439. *Phys.* 241b24-242a15.

440. The argument seems to require a reference to [rational] soul in general at this point, not just to the world-soul, and *tou kosmou* may be an interpolation.

441. cf. *DA* 403a3-12. Philoponus' remarks here are closely related to the exegesis of the same passage in the introduction to his commentary on *DA* (*in DA* 15,9-26) and ad loc. (*in DA* 46,18-49,14).

442. *DA* 411b18-19.

443. He probably has in mind *Enn.* 4.7.8[5], but other material in 4.7, especially in sections 8, 10, 12 and 13, may also be relevant.

444. 249,25-250,22.

445. Although I have translated it, *ton Platônos* looks like a gloss.

446. Or perhaps: 'that there is a power or activity of soul in accordance with which ...'.

447. The classification of *kinêsis* ('movement') or *metabolê* ('change') which follows is Aristotle's. In Aristotle *kinêsis* sometimes covers all four types, sometimes only the last three, when *metabolê* is used as the more general term. In English neither 'movement' nor 'change' is wholly satisfactory as the blanket term and I shall continue to translate *kinêsis* 'movement' and *metabolê* 'change'.

448. cf. 28,16-18.

449. This and the next reference are presumably, as Rabe indicates, to the part of *Physics* 8 in which Aristotle argues that rectilinear motion must be finite. (See especially 262a12-263a3).

450. On this work see the note at 134,17.

451. cf. the note at 189,21. It may not be a coincidence that the phrase *aposkeuazesthai ta enokhlounta* can mean to empty the bowels (see LSJ s.v. II.2).

452. Probably in a non-polemical work to be written after *Aet.* and the *contra Aristotelem*. Other possible references to this work occur at 9,20-26; 11,16; 117,20-21 and at *in Phys.* 430,9-10. (References from Verrycken, 'The Development of Philoponus' Thought and Its Chronology' in Sorabji (ed.), *Aristotle Transformed*, 254.) Although it has not survived in its own right, it may be the work known through an Arabic summary translated into English by Pines (S. Pines, 'An Arabic Summary of a Lost Work of John Philoponus', *Israel Oriental Studies* 2, 1972, 320-52) and, according to Wildberg, possibly also the work attacked by Simplicius at *in Phys.* 1326,38-1336,34. (See C. Wildberg, 'Simplicius: Against Philoponus on the Eternity of the World', in *Place, Void and Eternity* (London & Ithaca, NY, 1991), 100; but Wildberg also cites evidence from Arabic bibliographies which suggests that this may be yet another work on the perishability of the world.)

453. In view of *aïdiôs* at 257,7, perhaps *aïdion* ('everlasting') should be emended to *aïdiôs* ('everlastingly') here, in which case the last part of the sentence would read 'and soul does not move body everlastingly'.

454. *Phdr.* 245C-246A.

455. *Phdr.* 245C-E.

456. 252,10-256,17.

457. *autês* at 262,15 is a little odd and perhaps a case could be made for changing it to *tês* rather than adding <*tês*> after it.

458. Philoponus explains 'potentiality though capacity' in III,2.

459. 254,19-256,17.

460. More literally 'of life in capacity'.

461. sc. throughout the course of its existence, and therefore everlastingly. For the phrase, cf. 267,2 and 8.

462. This 'in the first place' (*prôton men*) seems to be answered by the 'and' (*de*) at the beginning of the next section (265,1).

463. Changing *legein* to *legei* at 264,28, as suggested by Rabe in the critical apparatus.

464. Deleting *zôiôn* at 265,12, one of several possible emendations suggested by Rabe in the critical apparatus.

465. In the myth at *Phdr.* 246 ff.

466. More literally, 'the wise [or learned] among the Hellenes'.

467. *Phys.* 192b20-2. The Neoplatonists followed Aristotle in calling the principle of change in material bodies *phusis*, or 'nature' (cf. the remarks of Siorvanes in *Proclus: Neo-Platonic Philosophy and Science* (New Haven & London, 1996), 136-7).

468. More literally 'someone who is by capacity [sc. potentially] a helmsman or charioteer'.

469. Supplying *einai* after *sôma* at 267,9. (In the critical apparatus Rabe suggests supplying *suneisagein* in the previous line, but it seems to me that 245,8, where *einai* occurs, is a more relevant parallel than the two he adduces.)

470. I would like to insert *all'* before *ou* at 267,13, but perhaps I am not construing the sentence correctly.

471. *Phdr.* 245D-E.

472. cf. 267,14-16.

473. For 'conversion by negation', see the note at 126,20.

474. Since *erastos* can mean either 'beloved' or 'lovely' and the form in the text could be either masculine or neuter, the phrase could also be rendered 'the beauty of a lovely object', and a case could certainly be made for such a rendering in a late Christian author like Philoponus. However, in other similar contexts (e.g. Sophonias *in DA* 16,29; Suda *kappa* 1640, 6) it is the effect of beauty on a lover that is in question, and Philoponus himself uses the example of the effect of a portrait on a lover at *in DA* 66,28 and *in Phys* 371,2-3 (and perhaps at *in Phys.* 355,26-7 and 875,4, although in both cases there is some doubt about the text), and so it seems likely that it is here as well.

475. 'Undergoes cessation' (more literally 'has cessation') translates *paulan ekhei*, which is, I think, merely periphrastic for *paueto*, or 'ceases'. (For such periphrastic phrases, see LSJ *ekhô* A.I.9.)

476. *Phdr.* 245C-D.

477. cf. *Phys.* 241b24-242a15.

478. cf. *Phdr.* 245C-E.

479. *Tim.* 41B.

480. 225,13-242,22.

481. 246,27-247,21.

482. Or, perhaps: 'he perverts the nature of demonstration and *all on his own* argues ...'.

483. More literally 'lays claim to [or "partakes of"] any natural and necessary conformity [or "consequentiality"]'.

484. More literally 'the wise men of the Hellenes'.

485. Supplying *ê* before *kinoumenon* at 274,17, as suggested by Rabe in the critical apparatus.

486. Punctuating with a full stop rather than a colon after *dunamei* at 275,11.

487. Removing the semicolon in 276,19 and enclosing *legô de tropon kinêseôs* in parentheses.

488. More literally 'beyond its own nature'.

489. Changing *ei oun allo ê palin* to *ê oun allo palin* at 279,26, as suggested by Rabe in the critical apparatus.

490. Assuming that the future *sunkhôrêsousin* (280,1) is either an error or another of the many instances in which Philoponus has used an indicative where one would expect a subjunctive. (For other instances, see 'indicativus pro coniunctivo' in Rabe's grammatical index, p. 698.) Another possibility, although it seems less likely, is that the subjunctive *zêtêsôsin* at 279,27 has, as a late copyist and the first modern editor seem to have assumed, replaced a future.

491. 281,13-283,8.

492. Rabe notes that this sentence needs correction but makes no suggestions. If *ê* is to be retained at 281,4, a second *ê* clause will need to be supplied.

Alternatively, *ê* might be emended to *hêmas*, or perhaps *tous*. I have opted for the switch to *hêmas*.

493. *alla de di' allou dunaton* (281,24) is awkward, and Rabe suggests correction to either *allo de di' allou* or *alla de di' allôn* ('while another can permeate another' or 'while others can permeate others') in the critical apparatus. Another possibility, which tempts me, would be to accent *alla* on the second syllable and delete *de*, which would give 'Nor is it any more the case that this body cannot permeate that but can permeate another'. I have, however, translated the text printed by Rabe.

494. In what follows 'pass through' would often be a more natural rendering of *khôrein dia*, but for the sake of the argument I have thought it best to stay with 'permeate'.

495. More literally, 'subsists in them as substrata'.

496. The next sentence in Rabe's text reads: 'For the might of the heaven (reading *ouranou* for *ouraniou*, as suggested by Rabe in the critical apparatus) can be packed into the smallest compass, or into the extent of the proverbial grain of millet'. This looks like a gloss that has found its way into the text (Rabe describes it as 'suspect') and I have excluded it from the body of the translation.

497. *Alim.* 9.106,23 (Littré).

498. Literally 'breathing together'.

499. More literally 'How, then, is it in this too?'

500. 277,14-17.

501. More literally 'What then [will be] the differences of these?'

502. *Tim.* 28B.

503. *An. Post.* 81a38-9.

504. The Greek word (*epistêmê*) could also be translated 'science' or 'scientific knowledge', and I use 'science' to render it later in this section at 286,14.

505. Literally, 'the children of the Hellenes', but the phrase is merely periphrastic for 'the Hellenes' or 'the pagans'. (For the usage, see LSJ *pais* I.3.)

506. 281,13-283,8.

507. The mention of *neura* (here translated 'channels' but actually the nerves, though not understood as such) suggests that the theory presupposed is that of Erasistratus, an eminent physiologist active in the first half of the third century BC, or one closely resembling it. For Erasistratus, inspired air, or *pneuma* (*pneuma* may be either air in motion or breath), is first refined into the vital, or life-sustaining, *pneuma* in the left ventricle of the heart and then, after travelling around the body in the arteries, in part further refined into psychic pneuma, the seat of consciousness and mental life, in the brain, whence it travels around the body by way of the nerves. (Further detail may be found in the entry on Erasistratus in the third edition of the *Oxford Classical Dictionary*.)

508. Adding *kinêsin* after *kineitai* at 288,11, as suggested by Rabe in the critical apparatus.

509. *Phdr.* 245C; previously quoted at 271,19-20.

510. Both here and in line 18 a more literal translation would be 'in regions around the earth'.

511. Changing *henoutai* to *henountai* at 289,22, as suggested by Rabe in the critical apparatus.

512. Literally 'of the children of the Hellenes', but see the note at 287,4.

513. 278,12-279,26.

514. Changing *epikheirountes hôs phasin helikoeidôs auto* to *epikheirountes helikoeidôs phasin auto* at 290,24, as suggested by Rabe in the critical apparatus.

515. *allotrios* may, in different contexts, be rendered 'belonging to another', 'foreign', 'strange', 'hostile', 'alien' (See LSJ s.v.). Here, although there is a secondary connotation of hostility, the primary connotation of the word is other-ness or separateness. I have been unable to find a single neat English equivalent and have settled for 'else' where that works (primarily in the first paragraph of the argument and in Philoponus' comments on it) and on 'other [than]' and similar phrases elsewhere.

516. cf. *Tim.* 33A.

517. As Rabe indicates, there seems to be something wrong with the text he prints at 294,8. Rabe himself, in the critical apparatus, suggests deleting *ê* at 294,7 and inserting *allotrion* after *allotriou* at 294,8, which would give 'nor would it perish into anything else, becoming other [than itself] through the agency of something else'. I would rather retain *ê* and either change *ginomenon* at 294,8 to *phtheiromenon*, or perhaps *prosballomenon* (cf. 294,1-2 and, for example, 302,15-16), or delete it altogether. In the translation I have adopted the latter alternative. (Baltes would change *ê* at 294,7 to *mê*, and, possibly, *hupo* in the next line to *apo*.)

518. cf. *Phd.* 70D-72E, especially 71A (for the two 'paths' – although Plato speaks of *geneseis*, or 'processes of generation', rather than paths), and 71E (for the need of a two-way process so that nature will not be defective).

519. In Philoponus' rather free paraphrase of this sentence at 310,7-10 the subject of the two verbs is *to atakton* ('the disorderly'), but here it seems more likely that it is *to atakton kai to tetagmenon* ('the disorderly and the ordered') and I have translated accordingly. (In his paraphrase Philoponus twice has the future *metabalei* (310,9.13) where the text of Proclus has the present *metaballei* (294,22; 295,3), and the futures would certainly be easier. However, there are similarly 'difficult' in-stances of *metaballei* at 295,7.9, and I have resisted the temptation to amend.)

520. If *ekeino* at 294,23 means, as I think it must, 'the former [change]', it is difficult to make satisfactory sense of *dioti sterêsis estin* (perhaps 'because [that which changes] is a privation'?), and, in any case, the whole clause is in contra-diction with what Proclus goes on to say at 295,16-17. When Philoponus quotes (or perhaps paraphrases) this passage at 310,11-12 he writes *dioti sterêseis eisin tines eis hexeis ametablêtoi*, of which the manuscript reading here could easily be a corruption, and I have translated that rather than the manuscript reading. (Baltes would simply add *tines* – presumably in place of *ai* – which he reports is supported by the Arabic version, or *estin hoti*, which his translation seems to presuppose.)

521. *Phd.* 70E-71B.

522. More literally, 'either the universe is not imperishable or much more ungenerated than imperishable'.

523. Changing *to* to *te* and *hômologêmenon* to *hômologêmenôn* at 295,24, as suggested by Rabe in the critical apparatus.

524. See note 1 for this rendering of *kephalaion*.

525. *Tim.* 28A.

526. *Cael.* 279b4-284b5.

527. For references on 'infinite power' arguments see the note at 235,18.

528. 297,21-300,2 = 238,3-240,9 (with minor textual variants). I have not repeated the footnotes that occur there.

529. At 239,6 the word order was slightly different and I translated 'gaining [the property of] always being'. As far as I can see, either version could be correct.

530. Changing *astheneian* to *athanasian* at 300,20. (cf. 300,9-11; 300,27-301,1).

531. 299,16-20.

532. cf. 294,2-8.

533. Adding *ôn* after *ara* at 302,19, a suggestion of Kroll which Rabe reports in the critical apparatus.

534. Changing *aiônôn* to *autou ontôn* at 302,20, as suggested by Rabe in the critical apparatus.

535. Reading *phtheiretai* for *phtheiresthai* (one of two possible corrections suggested by Rabe in the critical apparatus) at 302,25.

536. VI.28.

537. 294,9-13.

538. Adding *to* before *pan* and changing *genesthai* to *ginesthai* at 304,15, as suggested by Rabe in the critical apparatus.

539. Adding *ou* before *têi Platônos* at 304,18.

540. cf. *Tim.* 32C.

541. At line 14 above.

542. *Tim.* 32B-C.

543. There is probably, as Rabe suggests ('haec vix sana'), something wrong with the text here, but I do not think that the general sense has been affected.

544. 304,14-17.

545. 3b24-7.

546. 307,21.

547. Deleting *kai* before *hêi* at 308,12, as suggested by Rabe in the critical apparatus.

548. 70E-71C; 72A-C.

549. Changing *ek tou psukhrou to thermon* to *ek tou thermou to psukhron* at 309,21-22. (Perhaps the error is Rabe's in this case.)

550. Punctuating with a full stop rather than a comma after *kosmon* at 310,3.

551. At 294,20-295,6.

552. This first sentence is a rather loose paraphrase of what Proclus actually says.

553. *Tim.* 41B.

554. *Tim.* 41B.

555. VI.28.

556. Adding a question mark after *oun* at 311,17.

557. 308,25-26; 309,14-15.

558. 307,15-308,2.

Select Bibliography

The following is a list of the principal works cited in the notes.

Badawi, A., 'Un Proclus perdu est retrouvé en arabe', in *Mélanges L. Massignon I* (Damascus, 1956).

Baltes, M., *Die Weltentstehung des platonischen* Timaios *nach den antiken Interpreten* (Leiden, 1976).

Cornford, F.M. (tr.), *Plato's Cosmology: the* Timaeus *of Plato* (London, 1937).

D'Ancona Costa, C., 'Plotinus and later Platonic philosophers on the causality of the first principle', in L.P. Gerson (ed.), *The Cambridge Companion to Plotinus* (Cambridge, 1996).

Des Places, E. (ed.), *Atticus: fragments* (Paris, 1977).

Diels, H. (ed.), *Doxographi Graeci* (Berlin, 1879).

Diels, H. and W. Kranz (eds), *Die Fragmente der Vorsokratiker*, 6th ed. (Berlin, 1951-2).

Dillon, J., *The Middle Platonists: a Study of Platonism, 80 BC to AD 220* (London, 1977).

Dodds, E.R. (ed.), *Proclus, The Elements of Theology* (Oxford, 1963).

Edwards, M.J. (tr.), *Philoponus: On Aristotle's* Physics 3 (London & Ithaca, NY, 1994).

Erbse, H. (ed.), *Scholia Graeca in Homeri Iliadem (Scholia Vetera)* (Berlin, 1969-83).

Fortenbaugh, W.W. et al. (eds), *Theophrastus of Eresus: Sources for His Life, Writings, Thought and Influence* (Leiden, 1992).

Grimal, P., *The Dictionary of Classical Mythology* (Oxford, 1996).

Guthrie, W.K.C., *A History of Greek Philosophy*, vol. 1 (Cambridge, 1967).

Hankinson, R.J., *Cause and Explanation in Ancient Greek Thought* (Oxford, 1998).

Hussey, E. (tr.), *Aristotle's* Physics *Books II and IV* (Oxford, 1983).

Joseph, H.W.B., *Introduction to Logic* (Oxford, 1906).

Judson, L., 'God or nature? Philoponus on generability and perishability', in R.R.K. Sorabji (ed.), *Philoponus and the Rejection of Aristotelian Science* (London & Ithaca, NY, 1987), 179-96.

Kern, O. (ed.), *Orphicorum fragmenta* (Berlin, 1922).

LSJ, see Liddell, H.G.

Lampe, G.W.H. (ed.), *A Patristic Greek Lexicon* (Oxford, 1961).

Lang, H.S. and A.D. Macro (trs.), *On the Eternity of the World* (De Aeternitate Mundi), *Proclus* (Berkeley, LA & London, 2001).

Liddell, H.G. and R. Scott (comps.), *A Greek-English Lexicon*, rev. H. Jones; with a New Supplement (Oxford, 1996)

The New Oxford Annotated Bible, (eds) B.M. Metzger and R.E. Murphy (New York, 1994).

The New Shorter Oxford English Dictionary on Historical Principles, (ed.) L. Brown (Oxford, 1993).

The Oxford Classical Dictionary, 3rd ed.; (eds) S. Hornblower and A. Spawforth (Oxford 1996).

Pinès, S., 'An Arabic summary of a lost work of John Philoponus', *Israel Oriental Studies* 2 (1972), 320-52; repr. in S. Pinès, *Studies in Arabic Versions of Greek Texts and in Medieval Science*, vol. 2 (Leiden & Jerusalem, 1986), 294-326.

Rabe, H. (ed.), *Ioannes Philoponus de Aeternitate Mundi contra Proclum* (Leipzig, 1899) (repr. Hildesheim, etc., 1984).

Saffrey, H.-D. and L.G. Westerink (eds.), *Proclus, Théologie platonicienne* (Paris, 1968-94).

Share, M. (trans.), *Philoponus: Against Proclus On the Eternity of the World 1-5* (London & Ithaca, NY, 2005).

Siorvanes, L., *Proclus: Neo-Platonic Philosophy and Science* (New Haven & London, 1996).

Smith, A. (ed.), *Porphyrii Philosophi fragmenta* (Stuttgart & Leipzig, 1993).

Smith, J.A. (tr.), *On the Soul*, in J. Barnes (ed.), *The Complete Works of Aristotle: the Revised Oxford Translation* (Oxford, 1984).

Sodano, A.R. (ed.), *Porphyrii in Platonis Timaeum Commentariorum fragmenta* (Naples, 1964).

Sorabji, R.R.K. (ed.), *Aristotle Transformed: the Ancient Commentators and Their Influence* (London & Ithaca, NY, 1990).

Sorabji, R.R.K., *Matter, Space and Motion: Theories in Antiquity and Their Sequel* (London & Ithaca, NY, 1988).

Sorabji, R.R.K. (ed.), *Philoponus and the Rejection of Aristotelian Science* (London & Ithaca, NY, 1987).

Sorabji, R.R.K., *Time, Creation and the Continuum: Theories in Antiquity and the Early Middle Ages* (London & Ithaca, NY, 1983).

TLG, see *Thesaurus linguae graecae*.

Tarán, L., 'Amicus Plato sed magis amica veritas, from Plato and Aristotle to Cervantes', *Antike und Abendland* 30 (1984), 93-124.

Taylor, T. (tr.), *The Fragments That Remain of the Lost Writings of Proclus, Surnamed the Platonic Successor* (London, 1825) (repr. San Diego, 1988).

Thesaurus linguae graecae [CD ROM].

Verrycken, K., 'The development of Philoponus' thought and its chronology', in R.R.K. Sorabji (ed.), *Aristotle Transformed: the Ancient Commentators and Their Influence* (London & Ithaca, NY, 1990).

Verrycken, K., 'Philoponus' interpretation of Plato's cosmogony', *Documenti e Studi sulla Tradizione Filosofica Medievale* 8 (1997), 269-318.

Wildberg, C. (tr.), *Philoponus: Against Aristotle on the Eternity of the World* (London & Ithaca, NY, 1987).

Wildberg, C. (tr.), 'Simplicius: Against Philoponus on the Eternity of the World', in *Place, Void, and Eternity* (London & Ithaca, NY, 1991).

Willcock, M.M. (ed.), *The Iliad of Homer* (Houndmills & London, 1978-84).

Williams, C.J.F. (tr.), *Aristotle's* de Generatione et Corruptione (Oxford, 1982).

English-Greek Glossary

absurd: *atopos*
absurdity: *atopia*
accept: *homologein, sunkhôrein*
accepted premiss: *homologêma*
accident: *to sumbebêkos*
account: *logos*
accuse of: *katêgorein*
acquired: *epiktêtos*
acted upon, be: *paskhein*
active, be: *energein*
activity: *energeia*
actual: *energeiâi, kat' energeian*
actuality: *energeia*
actually: *energeiâi, kat' energeian*
ad infinitum: *eis apeiron, ep' apeiron*
add: *epagein*
advocacy: *sunêgoria*
affected, be: *paskhein*
affirm: *apophainesthai*
affirmation: *kataphasis, thesis*
affliction: *pathos*
agree: *homologein, sunkhôrein*
air: *aêr*
all at once: *athroos*
already in existence, be:
    proüphistasthai
also belong: *sunuparkhein*
also exist: *sunuparkhein*
alter (trans.): *metalambanein,
    metapherein, metatithenai*
alter (intrans.): *alloiousthai*
alteration: *alloiôsis*
always: *aei*
always coming to be: *aeigenês*
always in movement: *aeikinêtôs*
ambiguous: *homônumos*
analyse: *analuein*
analysis: *analusis*
animal: *zôion*
animate (a.): *empsukhos*
animate (v.): *psukhoun*

antecedent: *to hêgoumenon*
appear: *phainesthai*
appearance: *eidos*
apprehend: *noein*
apprehended by intellect: *noêtos*
argue: *kataskeuazein, sullogizesthai,
    sunagein*
argue unfairly: *kakourgein en tois
    logois*
argument: *kataskeuê, logos,
    sullogismos*
arrangement: *oikonomia, taxis*
ask: *skopein, zêtein*
assert: *apophainesthai, kataphanai*
assist the revolution of: *sunkuklein*
association: *suntaxis*
assume: *hupotithenai, lambanein*
at all: *holôs*
at rest, be: *êremein*
attach: *exaptein*
attach to: *exartan*
attack (v.): *prosballein*
awareness: *sunaisthêsis*
axiom: *axiôma*

bad: *kakos*
basis: *logos*
be: *huphistasthai*
become: *ginesthai*
become body: *sômatousthai*
become evil: *kakunesthai*
begetter: *ho gennêsas, ho gennôn*
beginning: *arkhê*
beginningless: *anarkhos*
being: *ousia, ousiôsis*
belief: *dogma, doxa*
believe: *pisteuein*
belong: *huparkhein*
better: *kreittôn*
bind (to, together): *sundein*
binding together: *sundesis*

birth: *genesis, genetê, genos*
bodily: *sômatikos*
body: *sôma*
body, become: *sômatousthai*
bond (n.): *desmos, sundesmos*
book: *logos, stoikheion*
brain: *nous*
bring: *paragein*
bring into existence: *huphistanai,*
　　paragein
bringing into being: *ousiôsis*
build: *oikodomein*
builder: *oikodomos*
building (sc. the process): *oikodomia*
by choice: *proairetikôs*
by itself: *kath' hauto*

call: *onomazein*
can: *endekhesthai*
capacity: *hexis*
carry around (with): *sumperiagein,*
　　sunkuklein
carry out a division: *diairein*
causal: *aitiôdês*
cause: *aitia, to aition*
cause of: *aitios*
cease: *pauesthai*
cease to exist: *phtheiresthai*
cessation: *paula*
change (n.): *kinêsis, metabolê*
change (v.): *metaballein, metatithenai*
change the meaning of:
　　metalambanein
changeable: *metablêtos*
chapter: *logos*
characteristic of: *kharaktêristikos*
characterise: *kharaktêrizein*
choice: *proairesis*
circle (n.): *kuklos*
circular: *kata kuklon, kuklikos, kuklôi*
circular movement: *kuklophoria,*
　　periphora
cite: *paratithesthai*
clear (a.): *enargês*
clearly: *enargôs*
co-everlasting: *sunaïdios*
coexist (with): *suneinai,*
　　sunuparkhein, sunuphistasthai
coexistent with, be: *sunuparkhein*
cogent: *anankaios*
cogently: *anankaiôs*
cognitive: *gnôstikos*
colour (n.): *khrôma*

combine: *suntithenai*
come into existence: *huphistasthai*
come to be: *ginesthai*
comment (n.): *exêgêsis*
comment on: *exêgeisthai*
commentary: *hupomnêmata,*
　　hupomnêmatika suntagmata
commentator: *exêgêtês,*
　　hupomnêmatistês
comments: *exêgêtika hupomnêmata*
common: *koinos*
common sense: *nous*
compel: *anankazein*
complete (a.): *teleios*
completed action: *sunteleia*
component: *stoikheion*
compose: *suntithenai*
composed: *sunthetos*
composed, be: *sunkeisthai*
composite: *sunthetos*
composition: *sunthesis*
compounded, be: *sunkeisthai*
concede: *homologein, sunkhôrein*
conception: *ennoia, hupolêpsis*
conclude: *sullogizesthai, sunagein*
conclusion: *sumperasma*
concord: *sumpnoia*
condition: *hexis*
conformity: *akolouthia*
conjunction: *sundesmos*
connect: *sunaptein*
consequence: *to hepomenon*
consider: *skopein*
consist: *sunkeisthai*
consistent (with): *akolouthos*
constitutive: *sumplêrôtikos*
construct (v.): *sunistanai, suntithenai*
constructed, be: *sunkeisthai*
construction: *sustasis*
contentious: *philoneikos*
continuance: *diamonê, paratasis*
continuity: *sunekheia*
continuous: *sunekhês*
continuous becoming: *to aeigenes,*
　　aeigenesia
contradiction: *antiphasis*
contrariety: *enantiotês*
contrary (a.): *enantios*
contrary (n.): *to enantion*
contribute to: *suntelein*
conversion by negation: *hê sun*
　　antithesei antistrophê
convertible, be: *antistrephein*

copy (n.): *eikôn*
corporeal: *sômatikos, sômatoeidês*
corporeal thing (entity, object): *sôma*
create: *dêmiourgein*
creation: *dêmiourgia, hupostasis*
creative: *dêmiourgikos*
creative activity: *dêmiourgia*
creator: *ho dêmiourgêsas, dêmiourgos*
creature: *zôion*
criticise: *apelenkhein*

darkness: *skotos*
death: *thanatos*
debasing: *katagôgos*
decay (v.): *phthinein*
decay (n.): *phthora*
declare: *apophainesthai*
deduce: *sullogizesthai*
defect (n.): *kakia*
define: *aphorizein, horizesthai*
define further: *prosdiorizesthai*
definition: *horismos, horos, logos*
demolish: *anairein*
demon: *daimôn*
demonstrate: *apodeiknunai,*
   deiknunai
demonstration: *apodeixis, kataskeuê*
denial: *anairesis*
deny: *anairein, apophanai,*
   apophaskein
deny simultaneously: *sunanairein*
deplete: *diaphorein*
deprived of, be: *stereisthai*
describe as: *onomazein*
desire: *orexis*
destroy: *phtheirein*
destruction: *phthora*
destruction, of: *phthoropoios*
destructive: *anairetikos, phthartikos,*
   phthoropoios
determine: *aphorizein*
deviation: *parektropê*
devoid of, be: *stereisthai*
dialectical: *dialektikos*
dialectician: *dialektikos*
didactic: *didaskalikos*
difference: *diaphora, heterotês*
different: *diaphoros*
diminution: *phthisis*
discordance: *ametria*
disjoin: *diazeugnunai*
disjunctive: *diazeuktikos*
disorder: *ataxia*

disorderly, the: *to atakton*
dissolution: *analusis, lusis*
dissolve: *luein*
distinct: *hôrismenos*
distinction: *diairesis*
distinguish: *aphorizein, diairein,*
   prosdiorizesthai
divide: *diairein*
divine: *theios*
divinely inspired: *theophorêtos*
divisible: *meristos*
division: *antidiairesis, diairesis*
division, of: *diairetikos*
do: *poiein*
do evil: *kakopoiein*
doctrine: *dogma, doxa*
draw a conclusion: *sullogizesthai*

earlier commentators: *hoi*
   proüpomnêmatisamenoi
earth: *gê*
eclipse (v.): *epiprosthein*
effect (n.): *pathos, to aitiaton*
efficient: *poiêtikos*
element: *stoikheion*
elemental masses: *tôn stoikheiôn*
   holotêtes
eliminate along with (also):
   sunanairein
elimination: *anairesis*
else: *allotrios*
emotive: *pathêtikos*
encompass: *sumperiekhein*
end (n.): *peras, telos*
endless: *ateleutêtos*
endlessness: *to ateleutêton*
endow with life: *zôopoiein*
endure: *diamenein, hupomenein*
enmattered: *enulos*
entailment: *akolouthia*
enumerate: *aparithmein*
environment: *to periekhon*
envy (n.): *phthonos*
equivalent, be: *isodunamein*
essence: *ousia*
essence, of the: *ousiôdês*
essential: *ousiôdês*
establish: *kataskeuazein, sunistanai*
establishment: *kataskeuê*
eternal: *aiônios*
eternally: *aiôniôs*
eternity: *aiôn*
ether: *aithêr*

etherial: *aitherios*
ever: *pote*
everlasting: *aïdios*
everlasting motion: *aeikinêsia*
everlastingly: *aïdiôs*
everlastingness: *aïdiotês*
evidence: *pistis*
evil: *kakos, ponêros*
exact knowledge: *akribologia*
excluded from, be: *stereisthai*
exhausted, be: *exasthenein*
exist: *huparkhein, huphistasthai*
exist alongside: *sumparateinesthai*
exist together: *sunuparkhein*
existence: *huparxis, hupostasis*
explain: *didaskein, exêgeisthai*
explanatory: *hupomnêmatikos*
explicitly: *epi lexeôs*
exposition: *didaskalia*

fabric: *sustasis*
fabrication: *anaplasma*
facts, the: *ta pragmata*
fall upon: *prosballein*
figure (n.): *skhêma*
final: *telikos*
finger: *daktulos*
finite: *peperasmenos*
finite, be: *perainesthai*
fire: *pur*
fit: *epitêdeios*
follow: *akolouthein*
follow from (upon): *hepesthai*
follow upon: *hepesthai*
for ever: *aei*
foreknowledge: *prognôsis*
form (n.): *eidos*
formation: *sustasis*
formative: *eidopoios*
formless: *aneideos*
fount: *pêgê*
frame (v.): *sunarmozein, sunistanai*
framing: *kataskeuê, sustasis*
free of envy: *aphthonos*
free of need: *anendeês*
freedom from want: *to aprosdees*
from everlasting: *ex aïdiou*
furnish: *khorêgein*
future (n.): *to mellon*

generally: *haplôs*
generate: *gennan*
generated: *genêtos*

generation: *genesis*
generation of the soul: *psukhogonia*
genus: *genos*
get existence: *huphistasthai*
give life to: *zôopoiein*
go on to talk about: *epagein*
goal: *skopos*
god: *theos*
God: *theos*
godlessness: *atheotês*
good (n.): *to agathon*
goodness: *agathotês*
gospel: *logos*
grow (intrans.): *auxesthai*
grow weak: *exasthenein*
growth: *auxêsis*

happy: *eudaimôn*
harmonic: *harmonikos*
harmony: *harmonia*
have (its) essence: *ousiousthai*
have a share (in): *metekhein*
have existence: *huphistasthai*
have life: *zên*
heaven: *ouranos*
heavenly: *ouranios*
hold: *hupotithenai*
hold together: *sunekhein*
holy: *theios*
house: *oikia*
human: *anthrôpeios, anthrôpos*
hypothesis: *hupothesis*
hypothesise: *hupotithenai*
hypothetical: *sunaptikos*

idea: *hupolêpsis*
ignorance: *agnoia*
ignorant, be: *agnoein*
illumination: *ellampsis*
illuminate: *katalampein, phôtizein*
image (n.): *eikôn*
imagination: *phantasia*
imagine: *anaplattein*
imbue with form: *eidopoiein*
immediately: *amesôs*
immortal: *athanatos*
immortality: *athanasia, to athanaton*
impassible: *apathês*
imperfect: *atelês*
imperishability: *aphtharsia*
imperishable: *aphthartos*
impiety: *asebeia, atheotês*
impious: *asebês*

imply also: *suneisagein*
impossible: *adunatos*
in a circle: *kuklikôs*
in a spiral: *helikoeidôs*
in a word: *haplôs*
in contact, be: *haptesthai*
in existence, be: *huphistasthai*
in existence, be already in:
    proüphistasthai
in general: *haplôs, holôs*
in (its) own right: *kath' hauto*
in need of nothing: *aprosdeês*
in thought: *di' epinoias, tôi logôi*
inalterable: *analloiôtos*
inanimate: *apsukhos*
inappropriate: *atopos*
incomposite: *asunthetos*
incorporeal: *asômatos*
increase (n.): *auxêsis*
increase (v.: intrans.): *auxesthai*
indefinite: *aoristos*
indefinitely: *ep' apeiron, ex apeirou*
indicate: *sêmainein*
indicative: *dêlôtikos*
indissoluble: *adialutos, alutos*
individual: *merikos*
indivisible: *ameristos*
induction: *epagôgê*
inescapable: *aparabatos*
infer: *sullogizesthai, sunagein*
infinite: *apeiros*
ingenious: *sophos*
ingenuity: *deinotês*
initiative: *hormê*
innate: *sumphutos*
inquire: *zêtein*
instruction: *didaskalia*
instrument: *organon*
instrumental: *organikos*
integrity: *sunekheia*
intellect: *nous*
intellectual: *noeros*
intelligible (a.): *noêtos*
intelligible (n.): *to noêton*
intention: *dianoia, nous, skopos*
intermediary: *mesotês*
interrogative: *diaporêtikos*
interval: *diastasis*
invalid: *asullogistos*
investigate: *zêtein, skopein*
investigation: *zêtêsis*
involuntarily: *aboulêtôs, aproairetôs*
irrational: *alogos*

irregular: *ataktos*

join (v.): *sunaptein*

king: *basileus*
knowledge: *epistêmê*
kind (n.): *eidos, genos*
know: *ginôskein*

lack (n.): *sterêsis*
lack of power: *adunamia*
last (v.): *diamenein, exarkein*
law: *logos*
learn: *manthanein*
learned : *sophos*
letter: *stoikheion*
licence: *exousia*
life: *bios, zôê*
light (a.): *kouphos*
light (n.): *phôs*
light up: *katalampein, phôtizein*
lightness: *kouphotês*
likeness: *homoiôsis*
limit (n.): *peras*
limit (v.): *peratoun*
limited, be: *perainesthai*
link (n.): *sundesmos*
live: *bioun, zên*
living creature: *zôion*
local: *kata topon, topikos*
luminous: *augoeidês*

magnet: *magnêtis, magnêtis lithos*
maintenance: *sôtêria*
make: *poiein*
make up: *anaplattein*
maker: *ho poiêsas, poiêtês, to poioun*
making: *poiêsis*
man (sc. human being): *anthrôpos*
manifestly: *enargôs*
manner: *tropos*
mass: *holotês*
material (a.): *hulikos*
mathematician: *mathêmatikos*
matter (n.): *hulê*
mean: *noein, sêmainein*
meaning: *dianoia, sêmasia, to*
    sêmainomenon
measure (n.): *metron*
measure out: *katametrein*
method: *tropos*
Milky Way: *galaxias kuklos*

mind (n.): *dianoia, epinoia, nous, psukhê*
mislead by fallacious arguments: *paralogizesthai*
misrepresent: *sukophantein*
mode: *tropos*
model: *paradeigma*
moon: *selênê*
mortal: *thnêtos*
motionless: *akinêtos*
mount: *epibainein*
move (intrans.): *kineisthai*
move (trans.): *kinein*
move in a circle: *kuklophoreisthai*
move (travel) in a straight line: *euthuphoreisthai*
movement: *kinêsis*
movement, be in: *kineisthai*
mutability: *to rheuston*

natural: *phusikos*
natural philosophers: *hoi phusikoi*
naturally: *kata phusin, phusei*
nature: *idiotês, phusis*
necessarily: *anankaiôs*
necessary: *anankaios*
negation: *apophasis*
non-existence: *anuparxia*
not possible: *adunatos*
notion: *epinoia, hupolêpsis, huponoia*
notionally: *di' epinoias, epinoiâi, kat' epinoian*
number (n.): *arithmos*

object of desire: *to orekton*
objection: *enstasis*
objective (n.): *skopos*
observe: *horan*
observed facts: *enargeia*
obvious: *enargês*
of any kind at all: *holôs*
of the same matter: *homoülos*
of the same nature: *homophuês*
of the same species: *homoeidês*
of the same substance: *homoousios*
on the intellectual plane: *noerôs*
opinion: *doxa*
oppose: *antidiairein, antidiastellein, antitithenai*
opposed, be: *antikeisthai*
opposite (thing): *to antikeimenon*
opposition: *antidiastolê*
order (v.): *kosmein*

order (n.): *taxis*
orderly: *eutaktos*
organ: *organon*
origin: *arkhê*
origination: *hupostasis*
other: *allotrios*
otherness: *heterotês*

paradigmatic: *paradeigmatikos*
part (n.): *meros*
partake of: *koinônein, metekhein*
particular: *merikos*
passage: *khrêsis, lexis*
passing out of existence: *phthora*
pattern (n.): *paradeigma, skhesis*
peculiar nature: *idiotês*
perceptible: *aisthêtos*
perception: *antilêpsis*
perfect (a.): *teleios*
perfection: *teleiôsis, teleiotês*
perfective: *teleiôtikos*
perform evil acts: *kakunein*
periphery, the: *perix topos*
perish: *phtheiresthai*
perish along with: *sunapollusthai*
perish together: *sumphtheiresthai*
perishable: *phthartos*
permanence: *diamonê*
permeate: *khôrein dia*
philosopher: *philosophos, ho sophos*
philosophical: *philosophos*
philosophy: *philosophia*
physical: *organikos, phusikos*
piece of sophistry: *paralogismos*
piety: *eusebeia, to eusebes*
place (n.): *topos*
plant (n.): *phuton*
point (n.): *sêmeion*
portion: *meros*
position (n.): *doxa, thesis, topos*
possession: *hexis*
possible, be: *endekhesthai*
potential: *dunamei, dunamis*
potentiality: *dunamis*
potentially: *dunamei, dunamis*
power: *dunamis*
predicate of: *katêgorein*
premiss: *arkhê, to hêgoumenon, lêmma*
present, be: *huparkhein, pareinai*
present in, be: *enuparkhein*
preservation: *to sôizesthai*
preservative: *sôstikos*

preserve: *sôizein*
prevent: *kôluein*
privation: *sterêsis*
problem: *problêma*
produce (v.): *apotelein, poiein*
production: *paragôgê*
production of form: *eidopoiia*
pre-exist: *proüparkhein*
proof: *apodeixis, epikheirêma,*
   epikheirêsis
proposition: *protasis*
prove: *apodeiknunai, sullogizesthai*
providence: *pronoia*
psychic: *psukhikos*
pupil: *mathêtês*
put out of tune: *dialuein*
put together: *harmozein,*
   sunarmozein, sunistanai,
   suntithenai
puzzle (n.): *aporia*
puzzle over: *aporein*

qualification: *prosdiorismos*
quality: *to poion, poiotês*
question (n.): *problêma, zêtêsis*

race (n.): *genos*
raise a puzzle: *aporein*
rational: *logikos*
ray: *aktis, augê*
reason (n.): *aitia, logos*
reasoning: *epikheirêsis*
rebuttal: *antilogia*
receive: *lambanein*
receptive: *dektikos*
rectilinear movement: *euthuphoria*
refer to: *sêmainein*
refutation: *anaskeuê, elenkhos, lusis*
refute: *apelenkhein, elenkhein, luein*
refute along with: *sunapelenkhein*
region: *topos*
relation: *skhesis*
relative terms: *ta pros ti*
relatives: *ta pros ti*
religious thinker: *theologos*
remain: *diamenein, menein*
remain intact: *sôizesthai*
remove: *aphairein*
renew: *episkeuazein*
repair: *anuphainein*
replace: *metapherein*
represent: *kataskeuazein*
responsible for: *aitios*

rest (n.): *êremia, stasis*
restore: *episkeuazein*
restored: *episkeuastos*
reveal: *deiknunai*
revolve: *ekperierkhesthai, periagesthai*
ridicule (n.): *gelôs*
ridiculous: *geloios*
rigour: *akribeia*
rotate: *kuklophoreisthai,*
   peripheresthai
rotation: *kuklophoria, peridinêsis*
rule out: *aphairein*

sagacity: *ankhinoia*
salvation: *sôtêria*
say of: *katêgorein*
science: *mathêma*
scripture: *logion*
scriptures: *grammata*
section: *logos*
see: *horan*
seek (out): *zêtein*
seem: *phainesthai*
seen, be: *phainesthai*
self-evidence: *enargeia*
self-evident fact: *enargeia*
self-moved: *autokinêtos*
self-movement: *autokinêsia, to*
   autokinêton
self-sufficiency: *autarkeia*
self-sufficient: *autarkês*
sensation: *aisthêsis*
sense: *aisthêsis*
sense (sc. meaning): *dianoia, khrêsis,*
   nous, to sêmainomenon, tropos
sensible: *aisthêtos*
separate (a.): *kekhôrismenos,*
   khôristos
separate (v.): *khôrizein*
shape (n.): *morphê, skhêma*
shapelessness: *to askhêmatiston*
share (in): *koinônein, metekhein*
show: *deiknunai*
sight (n.): *opsis*
sign: *sêmeion*
signify: *sêmainein*
simple: *haplous*
simply: *haplôs*
sometimes: *pote*
sophistical: *sophistikos*
soul: *psukhê*
soul, of the: *psukhikos*
sound (a.): *hugiês*

soundly: *hugiôs*
source: *arkhê*
source of illumination: *to phôtizon*
speciousness: *to pithanon*
sphere: *sphaira*
spherical: *sphairikos, sphairoeidês*
spiral (n.): *helikoeidês, helix,*
    kokhlioeidês
spirally: *helikoeidôs*
spirit: *daimôn*
stability: *diamonê*
state as a philosophical principle:
    philosophein
statement: *apophansis, lexis, logos*
stronger: *kreittôn*
structure: *diakosmêsis*
student, be a: *mathêteuein*
subject: *skopos, to hupokeimenon*
subject to, be: *paskhein*
substance: *ousia*
substitute (v.): *metalambanein*
substitution: *metalêpsis, metathesis*
substratum: *to hupokeimenon*
successor: *diadokhos*
suffer: *paskhein, hupomenein*
sun: *hêlios*
sun's: *hêliakos*
superior: *kreittôn*
supernaturally: *huper phusin*
supertemporal: *huperkhronos*
suppose: *hupotithenai*
surface: *peras, periphereia*
survival: *sôtêria*
synthesis: *sunthesis*

take: *lambanein*
take as equivalent: *metalambanein*
teach: *didaskein*
teacher: *didaskalos*
teaching: *didaskalia*
temporal: *khronikos*
temporally: *khronikôs*
tense: *khronos*
text: *lexis*
theologian: *theologos*
theory: *theôrêma*
thing: *pragma*
think about (of): *noein*
thought: *dianoia, ennoia, epinoia,*
    noêma, noêsis, nous
three-dimensional: *trikhêi diastatos*
time: *khronos*
time, at some: *pote*

to quote his exact words: *epi lexeôs*
toe: *daktulos*
touch (v.): *haptesthai*
transcend: *huperanabainein,*
    huperekpiptein
transcribe: *metagraphein*
transparent: *diaphanês*
travel around: *ekperierkhesthai,*
    ekperipolein
travel in a circle: *kuklophoreisthai*
treatise: *logos, pragmateia*
true: *alêthês*
true at the same time (at once), be:
    sunalêtheuein
truth: *alêtheia*
tune (v.): *harmozein*
tuning: *harmonia*

unable to change: *ametablêtos*
unable to coexist: *asunuparktos*
unbind: *luein*
unbinding: *lusis*
unchanging: *ametablêtos*
uncombined: *haplous*
unconscious: *aproairetos*
undergo: *paskhein, hupomenein*
undermine: *anaskeuazein*
undertaking: *hormê*
undo: *dialuein, luein*
ungenerated: *agenêtos*
unholy: *asebês*
universal: *holikos*
universe: *to pan*
unlimited power: *to apeirodunamon*
unmoving: *akinêtos*
unordered: *ataktos*
unrefuted: *anelenktos*
unrelated to: *askhetos*
untune: *dialuein, luein*
usage: *khrêsis*
use (n.): *khrêsis*
use of: *katêgorein*

valid: *anankaios*
various: *diaphoros*
vice: *kakia*
view (n.): *doxa*
visibility: *to horaton*
visible: *horatos*
visible, be: *phainesthai*
vision: *opsis*
visual image: *opsis*
vital: *zôtikos*

waste: *phthisis*
waste away: *phthinein*
way: *tropos*
weak: *asthenês*
weakness: *astheneia*
whole (a.): *holos*
whole (n.): *to holon*
will (n.): *boulêsis*
will (v.): *ethelein*
wish (v.): *boulesthai, ethelein*

wit: *nous*
with a spiral movement: *helikoeidôs*
without any relation: *askhetôs*
without beginning: *anarkhos*
without qualification: *adioristôs*
without relation: *askhetos*
word: *lexis, onoma, prosrhêma*
work: *logos*
world: *kosmos*
world-creating: *kosmourgos*

Greek-English Index

This index lists a selection of more important words from the Greek text together with my translations of them. I have not attempted to distinguish between Philoponus' own words and those of Proclus and other authors he quotes. The rubric 'other tr[anslation(s)]' covers cases where a word has been translated in such a way that there is no one-to-one correspondence between the Greek and the English. The page and line references are to Rabe's Greek text and the occurrence of 'etc.' at the end of a listing of such references means that it is incomplete.

abakion, board, 208,17
aboulêtôs, involuntarily, 260,18; 269,17
adêlos, non-evident, 273,11; unclear, 154,12
adiakopos, uninterrupted, 288,3.21
adialutos, indissoluble, 129,12; 144,14; 227,24; 230,18; 272,23; *[to] adialuton*, indissolubility, 241,24
adiaphoria, lack of discrimination, 170,11
adioristôs, without qualification, 171,16
adunamia, lack of power, 240,6; 299,21
adunatein, cannot, 282,19; to be unable, 132,18.19; 282,1; to not be able, 131,23;
adunatos, impossible, 120,4.5, etc.; not possible, 119,22; 122,10; 123,5, etc.; **adunatos [einai]**, cannot be, 217,12.13; *[to] adunaton*, impossibility, 178,1, etc.; **adunatôs ekhein**, cannot, 302,1
aei, always, 123,7, etc.; for ever, 238,19.24, etc.; **eis (es) aei**, everlasting, 312,24; for ever, 213,2; 234,5; 235,18; 303,19; 312,22
aeigenês, always coming to be, 123,23; 193,10.12.16.17; *[to] aeigenes*, continuous becoming, 193,22

aeigenesia, continuous becoming, 240,16
aeikinêsia, everlasting motion, 240,16
aeikinêtôs, always in movement, 271,18
aêr, air, 202,6-16; 231,11; 232,4; 269,26; 280,20; 287,27; 289,2; 306,23; 309,6
agathos, good, 119,22, etc.; *[to] agathon*, good thing, 179,21
agathotês, goodness, 121,4; 130,25; 131,7.9; 133,13; 134,2.9; 172,14; 224,25
agein, to bring, 132,12; to throw, 267,20; other tr., 164,16; 178,25; 270,1
agenêtos, ungenerated, 120,12, etc.
agnoein, to be ignorant, 183,8; to not know, 131,11; 132,19; 133,20; **agnoeisthai**, to be unknown, 131,10; 273,6
agnoia, ignorance, 180,14; 255,7.8; 309,5
agnômôn, 197,18, inept
aïdios, everlasting, 120,13, etc.; *ex aïdiou*, from everlasting, 143,14, etc.; **aïdiôs**, everlastingly, 169,1, etc.
aïdiotês, everlastingness, 125,15; 167,9; 248,10; 249,9; 258,25
aiôn, eternity, 141,5, etc.

aiônios, eternal, 138,23, etc.;
   aiôniôs, eternally, 169,8
aisthanesthai, to be sentient,
   210,15; 263,18; to employ [one's
   senses], 258,4; to have senses,
   265,14; to observe, 280,18
aisthêsis, observation, 166,17; 202,4;
   sensation,137,7.16; 139,23; 168,6;
   169,18; 178,5; 258,1; 263,25;
   264,6.8; 265,7; 266,12; 285,28;
   286,1.13.14.15; sense, 166,21;
   194,10; 258,2.4.5; 270,4;
   285,19.23.24; 286,7; *[to]*
   aisthêseôs metekhon, sentient,
   270,26
aisthêtikê antilêpsis,
   sense-perception, 194,19
aisthêtos, perceived, 137,14; 138,1.2,
   etc.; perceptible, 124,8, etc.;
   sensible, 130,2; *[to] aisthêton*,
   perceptibility, 201,23; sensual
   thing, 131,14
aithêr, ether, 241,4; 276,9
aitherios, etherial, 278,24
aitia, cause, 121,3, etc.; reason,
   187,2-191,6; 203,18; 215,25;
   232,14.16; *kat' aitian*, with
   respect to causation,
   122,22-123,14; 148,7; 149,20;
   167,27; 171,22-173,19;
   176,24-178,15
aitiasthai, to hold responsible, 184,9
[to] aitiaton, effect, 197,25; 252,2.3
aitiôdês, causal, 160,19; causally,
   159,2
aitios, cause 130,9, etc.; responsible
   for, 189,19; 262,5; 266,2; 267,2;
   [to] aition, cause, 122,12, etc.
akhôristos, not separate, 251,28;
   252,8.9
akinêtos, free of movement, 274,20;
   motionless, 194,17, etc.; unmoving,
   275,26; *akinêtôs*, without any
   movement, 140,25
akoê, act of hearing, 270,7; hearing,
   236,4; 270,3.24.27
akolouthein, to follow, 150,20;
   204,24; 268,19; 296,17; 311,25
akolouthia, conformity, 273,26;
   entailment, 268,12; other tr.,
   200,22
akolouthos, consistent (with), 134,7;
   226,12.18; appropriate, 168,25;

akolouthon einai, to follow,
   126,19; 127,16; 183,20; 189,16;
   260,19; *kata to akolouthon*, as a
   consequence, 311,9; consistently,
   182,9; 293,1; *akolouthôs*,
   consistently, 124,21; 204,17.18; in
   due order, 139,13; other tr., 216,12
akoustikos, afforded by hearing,
   286,2
akribeia, rigour, 181,6
akribologia, exact knowledge, 142,3
aktis, ray, 266,15; 282,16
akurologia, misuse of words, 157,9
akuros, incorrect, 161,23
alêtheia, truth, 120,20, etc.; *kat'
   alêtheian*, really, 125,24; *pros
   alêtheian*, real, 219,10; *meta tês
   alêtheias*, correctly, 297,4
alêthês, genuine, 217,2; 220,8; true,
   120,11, etc.; real, 221,18; the
   truth, 301,5; *alêthôs*, really, truly,
   219,17.28; 221,6; other tr., 165,17;
   190,19
alloiôsis, alteration, 137,19, etc.
alloiousthai, to alter (intrans.),
   257,22.27
allotrios, else, 294,2-305,27; foreign,
   256,14; other, 294,5-307,4
alogos, irrational, 137,7, etc.
alutos, indissoluble, 119,15, etc.;
   unresolved, 163,6; *[to] aluton*,
   indissolubility, 226,6
ameibein, to change, 259,20; to
   replace, 202,20; to exchange,
   290,18
amêkhanos, immeasurable, 163,4;
   inconceivable, 119,21; 128,5.18;
   130,21; other tr., 162,13
ameristos, indivisible, 196,26
amesôs, directly, 281,4; immediately,
   262,23; 266,3.8.12; 280,2.4
ametablêtos, unable to change,
   295,1; 310,11; unchanging,
   205,6-211,3; 219,13; *[to]
   ametablêton*, that which is
   unchanging, 210,28
ametria, discordance, 303,15
ametrôs, overmuch, 233,9
ampelos, grapevine, 307,23
amphiballein, to express doubt,
   176,28
amphibolia, doubt, 176,18
amphibolos, ambiguous, 174,12;

etc.; *[to] antikeimenon*, opposite, 174,2, etc.

antilambanesthai, to grasp, 151,23

antilegein, to argue against, 167,4; other tr., 296,24

antilêpsis, perception, 194,19; 285,24; 286,7

antilogia, rebuttal, 151,6

antimetaballein, to revert, 311,23.27; to turn into, 296,14.19

antiphasis, contradiction, 151,4; 227,18; 291,13; 302,10

antiphatikos, into contradictories, 182,11

antistrephein, to be convertible, 206,7; 207,15

[hê sun antithesei] antistrophê, conversion by negation, 126,20; 150,14; 204,12; 225,18; 268,20

antithesis, antithesis, 181,22; for other occurrences see *antistrophê*

antitithenai, to oppose, 173,24; 181,19.23; 192,3; 193,17; to set in opposition, 180,5.6; 182,4.10

anuparxia, non-existence, 142,2; 182,5; 268,21.22

anuphainein, to repair, 138,7.13; 235,28; 236,25

aoristos, indefinite, 160,15

apagein, to bring, 150,21; to reduce, 161,28

aparabatos, inescapable, 184,11

aparallaktos, exactly alike, 188,18

aparithmein, to enumerate,160,9; 193,25; 257,5; 263,27

apathês, impassible, 236,25; 237,1; other tr., 237,3; *[to] apathes*, impassibility, 241,21

apeirodunamon, [to], unlimited power, 312,19

apeiros, infinite, 132,11; 167,17; 213,8; 233,1; 235,6.8; 238,10-240,17; 258,16.17; 281,17; 289,23; 25; 297,15; 298,1-300,6; *eis apeiron, ad infinitum*, 239,25; 299,13; *ep' apeiron, ad infinitum*, 167,20; 206,22; 280,1; indefinitely, 258,7; *ex apeirou*, indefinitely, 176,2

apelenkhein, to criticise, 191,21; to expose, 126,28; to refute, 135,2; 166,24; to vindicate, 127,7; other tr., 153,16; 171,20

aphairein, to remove, 146,18; 151,12; to rule out, 209,17.18

aphanês, hidden, 203,17

aphistanai (intrans. forms), to move away, 276,14

aphorizein, to define, 156,14; 192,2; to determine, 135,25; 288,26; to distinguish, 185,11; to indicate, 156,5.24

aphtharsia, imperishability, 216,3.6; 240,8.22; 304,6; 312,20

aphthartos, imperishable, 120,5-14; 126,22-128,13; 189,7-9; 212,6, etc.

aphthonos, free of envy, 225,5

[hê] aplanês [sphaira], sphere of the fixed stars, 198,9.15.19.25; 292,2; *[ta] aplanê*, the fixed stars, 147,4; 198,28

apodeiknunai, to demonstrate, 154,11, etc.; prove, 259,14; 263,28; 282,11; reveal, 194,15, show, 127,20; 130,11; other tr., 282,23

apodeixis, demonstration 154,13, etc.; (deductive) proof, 135,7, etc.

apodekhesthai, to endorse, 167,2.10

apodidonai, to assign, 169,26; to give, 183,9; to return, 294,17

apodosis, interpretation, 193,8

apôleia, destruction, 268,2

apophainesthai, to affirm, 135,19, etc.; assert, 135,12; declare 124,22; say, 223,21, etc.; state, 142,11, etc.; other tr., 200,16

apophanai, to deny, 193,23; 209,12

apophansis, statement, 248,13; 268,11

apophasis, negation, 192,22.24; 227,7

apophaskein, to deny, 124,14; 205,23; 209,15

aporein, to introduce as a puzzle, puzzle over, raise a puzzle, other tr., 162,24; 163,6.13.14.17; 166,20; 172,15; 176,16.28; 279,28; 284,22.23

aporêtikôs, in aporetic vein, 162,7

aporia, puzzle, 134,18; 143,20; 192,11.17; 259,4

[ta] aporrhêta, secret matters, 279,2; secrets, 194,13

aposkeuazein, to deal with, 259,5

apotelein, to produce, 165,9; to perform, 210,11

aproairetos, unconscious, 260,12;
   aproairetôs, involuntarily,
   244,18-271,3
aprosdeês, in need of nothing,
   230,24; 231,13.21; *[to] aprosdees*,
   freedom from want, 235,25
apsukhos, inanimate, 266,21.27
Arês, Ares (sc. the planet Mars),
   199,17.21
aretê, excellence, 175,19; virtue,
   255,9
aristeros, left (opp. right), 197,8;
   198,20.21.24
arithmos, number, 141,10, etc.; *kat'*
   arithmon, numerically,
   202,11-203,22
arkhê, beginning, 146,5, etc., (esp.
   ch. 6); origin, 178,21, etc.; premiss,
   296,23; source, 243,10, etc., (esp.
   ch. 7)
artêria, artery, 288,7
asebeia, impiety, 182,20; 191,1
asebês, impious, 191,7; unholy,
   133,12
[to] askhêmatiston, shapelessness,
   308,24
askhetos, unrelated to, 252,12.17.23;
   without relation, 196,5; *askhetôs*,
   without any relation, 195,27
askhistos, unsplit, 197,10
asômatos, incorporeal, 253,5
astheneia, weakness, 300,5.20;
   301,3; 303,1.8.12
asthenês, weak, 300,6
astrapê, flash of lightning, 149,2
astron, star, 141,9; 281,27
astronomikos, astronomer, 135,28
asullogistos, invalid, 154,18; 161,19;
   163,21; 264,26; *asullogistôs*,
   invalidly, 204,26
asumbatos, incompatible, 235,22
asunêthês, unfamiliar, 156,2.8;
   unusual, 122,3
asunkritos, incomparable, 255,19;
   asunkritôs, beyond comparison,
   255,16
asunthetos, incomposite, 155,23;
   156,20; 157,5.7.13.15; 159,20.23;
   164,6; 206,19.20; 207,13
asunuparktos, unable to coexist,
   182,11
ataktos, irregular, 201,13;
   unordered, 217,11.12; *[to]*

atakton, the disorderly,
   294,19-313,3; *ataktôs*, disorderly,
   164,17
ataxia, disorder, 188,18, etc;
   disordered confusion, 220,3;
   221,14; disordered heap, 219,29
atelês, imperfect, 121,9; 132,8.9.25;
   225,8
ateleutêtos, endless, 257,9.20; *[to]*
   ateleutêton, endlessness, 144,8
athanasia, immortality, 124,24, etc.
athanatos, immortal, 124,23, etc.;
   [to] athanaton, immortality,
   230,6; 272,25
atheotês, godlessness, 176,19;
   impiety, 134,15
athroos, all at once, 167,16
atopia, absurdity, 129,21; 133,2;
   161,23; 178,24; 193,9; 218,13
atopos, absurd, 121,1, etc.;
   inappropriate, 239,25; 299,16;
   300,22
augê, ray, 282,10
augoeidês, luminous, 245,23; 288,18
autarkeia, self-sufficiency, 235,26
autarkês, self-sufficient, 175,2;
   179,17; 230,23; 231,15.20; 236,12;
   autarkôs, independently, 129,2
authis, again, 223,7; 267,25; 268,4;
   back, 258,19; once more, 309,16;
   subsequently, 309,21.25
autokinêsia, self-movement,
   254,3.7.9
autokinêtos, self-moved,
   243,10-273,1; *[to] autokinêton*,
   self-movement, 243,12-271,15
automatos, independent, 174,16; of
   its own accord, 228,15
autonomia, licence, 155,8
autonomos, self-willed, 170,13
auxesthai, to grow (intrans.),
   263,19; to increase (intrans.), 258,7
auxêsis, growth, 236,20; 256,21;
   264,6.8; increase, 258,6.9
axiôma, axiom, 154,27
axiopistia, reputation, 144,26
axiopistos, credible, 211,20
axios, deserving of, 151,6; worthy of,
   161,23; *axion (esti)*, it is
   appropriate, 135,8; proper, 249,8;
   worth, 134,6, etc; other tr., 186,6
axôn, axis, 198,15